Seriality

PSYCHOANALYTIC HORIZONS

Psychoanalysis is unique in being at once a theory and a therapy, a method of critical thinking and a form of clinical practice. Now in its second century, this fusion of science and humanism derived from Freud has outlived all predictions of its demise. **Psychoanalytic Horizons** evokes the idea of a convergence between realms as well as the outer limits of a vision. Books in the series test disciplinary boundaries and will appeal to scholars and therapists who are passionate not only about the theory of literature, culture, media, and philosophy but also, above all, about the real life of ideas in the world.

A list of volumes in the series appears at the end of this book.

Seriality

Media and the Psychic Form of Everyday Life

Ryan Engley

BLOOMSBURY ACADEMIC
NEW YORK • LONDON • OXFORD • NEW DELHI • SYDNEY

BLOOMSBURY ACADEMIC
Bloomsbury Publishing Inc, 1359 Broadway, New York, NY 10018, USA
Bloomsbury Publishing Plc, 50 Bedford Square, London, WC1B 3DP, UK
Bloomsbury Publishing Ireland, 29 Earlsfort Terrace, Dublin 2, D02 AY28, Ireland

BLOOMSBURY, BLOOMSBURY ACADEMIC and the Diana logo
are trademarks of Bloomsbury Publishing Plc

First published in the United States of America, 2026

Cover design by Daniel Benneworth-Gray
Cover image © StockSnap / pixabay

Library of Congress Cataloguing-in-Publication Data

ISBN: HB: 979-8-216-19779-9
PB: 979-8-216-19778-2
ePDF: 979-8-216-19781-2
eBook: 979-8-216-19780-5

Series: Psychoanalytic Horizons

Typeset by Integra Software Services Pvt. Ltd.
Printed and bound in the United States of America

For product safety related questions contact productsafety@bloomsbury.com.

To find out more about our authors and books visit www.bloomsbury.com
and sign up for our newsletters.

To John Colón, who will never read this,
and to Dorothy and Ramona, who cannot yet read

CONTENTS

ACKNOWLEDGMENTS

Writing a book requires direct and indirect support of so many kinds. Since this is my first book there is much thanks to go around.

Early research for this book was generously supported by the Graves Award in the Humanities. I would like to thank Henni Alftan for generously granting permission to reprint her artwork, *Non-stop (In-between)*, in this book's introduction.

Some of my ideas on seriality were first explored in "Psychoanalytic Seriality as Media Theory: From Freud's Couch to Yours," *Continental Thought & Theory* 3, no. 2 (December 2021). Portions of chapter 6 were first published in "The Social Sinthome," *CLCWeb: Comparative Literature and Culture* 24.4 (2022). A version of chapter 4 appeared as "The Limitation of the Bottle Episode: Hegel in Community" in *New Review of Film and Television Studies* 21, no. 4 (2023).

Endeavoring to write an approachable book that advanced an original theory of media and the psyche's intrinsic relation would not have been thinkable without the pathbreaking work of Mari Ruti. Her influence on these pages is everywhere implied.

Joan Copjec indelibly marked this project, as an advisor, scholar, and friend. I cannot thank her enough for pushing me to theorize and teaching me how to write.

Much thanks go to my dissertation committee at the University of Rhode Island, including Naomi Mandel, Carolyn Betensky, Scott Kushner, Christine Mok, Kyle Kusz, and David Faflik, for helping to shape my initial ideas.

To Danny Cho, for convincing me that this book's central argument was worth serial revision.

To Anna Kornbluh and Alfie Bown, for their generous commentaries and insights.

To Major Jackson, for teaching me the weight of caesura through poetry.

To Todd McGowan and Hilary Neroni, for making me feel like literal and theoretical family.

To Jennifer Friedlander and Henry Krips, for great dinners and better conversations.

To my Pomona College colleagues who have helped me think this idea through, especially Kevin Wynter, Susan McWilliams-Barndt and Will Barndt, Jonathan Lethem, Prageeta Sharma, and Paul Cahill.

To Tim Doherty, Rebecca Doris, Chris Lindstrom, Matt Messer, Caragh Poh, Kaileen Powers, Elena Colón, Dan Stone, Taylor Sacco, Joanna Oh, Rosalía Romero and Bill Sharman, Seth Alt and Ally Hermé, Molly and Micah Hall, and Jake Witcher, for all their love and encouragement and for making two different coasts across two and a half decades always feel like home.

I owe such gratitude to the wonderful students at the Claremont Colleges, the University of Rhode Island, Clark University, and University of Vermont who engaged the ideas contained in these pages at different stages of their complexity and coherence over the last thirteen years. I'd like to thank especially the following students who engaged most directly with seriality and its vicissitudes: Hayley Manges, Melina Durre, Luna Lopez, Lily Wellington, Mouminatou Skye-Thiaw, Lucy Thompson, Sebastian Fish Mathurin, Lucy Shephard, Eliza Levy, Lele Murer, Eleanor Henderson, Harper Denniston, Manu Dominguez, William La, Nina-Jean Saligman, Frankie Maestas, Taylor Wanke, and Darya Blyednova. Likewise, James Wallace, Menah Khalil, Jay Still, Jenna O'Connell, Jordan Costa, Fabian Coronado, Jose Alvarado, Shiloh Clerjuste, Jude Amoako, and Joe Magee, for making me feel like a real teacher when I was a graduate student. Lastly, a special and most heartfelt thanks goes to Coco Percival (Chickasaw), who taught me how to stop harmful repetitions and start joyous ones.

To all the *Why Theory* listeners but especially to frequent correspondents-turned-friends Jack Murphy, Sean King, Sarah Gagnon, Airhead Sam, Fabricio Moreira, Gretchen Krueger, and Joe Aisenberg. Thank you all for taking my words seriously even (and especially) when I didn't know how.

To my parents, Chuck and Linda, and my sister, Lauren, and my brother-in-law, Mike St. Read, and my uncle Dave Engley, you are the first people I want to talk to about every film and TV series

I see. You taught me how to communicate through pop culture and showed me how unbreakable bonds can be made through superficial art.

To Nonna and Nonno, my aunts Ro, Anna, and Patty, my uncles Tony and Frank, and my cousins Christopher, Victoria, Anthony, Alexa, Luca, Leo, Paul, Pia, and Isla, I just want to say: *Questo è per tutti noi.*

To Signa, Dale, Jillian, Patrick, Dorothy, and Ramona, thank you for being the most encouraging and supportive family-in-law I could possibly ask for.

Finally, to Kara—my sharpest reader, my fiercest advocate, my most stubborn critic, and the most principled person I have ever met—without you there is nothing worth saying.

Introduction: Mind the Gap

Seriality is the shape of material and psychic life. Seen most evidently through the scheduled and segmented release of ongoing narrative and non-narrative content (e.g., television episodes, podcasts, professional sports matches, iPhone updates), seriality seems to be everywhere. Viewed as capaciously as possible, everything starts to seem serial. Making morning tea is serial, going to work is serial, going on dates (or not) is serial, and seeing friends (or not) is serial. If everything is serial, then perhaps seriality is too diffuse to act as a standalone concept or is only fit to serve as the name for a point of confluence that links together disparate things. Indeed, the immanence of the serial is precisely what makes it seem unremarkable. Most inquiry into seriality occurs in the adjectival sense: serial *narrative*, serial *fiction*, serial *film*, serial *television*, even serial *killers*. In all cases, the object of study is the second term, not the first. Seriality, however, is not a stage upon which something else is performed. It is not perfunctory background, an arbitrary element that, through repetition, is necessary for *something else* to happen. In this book, I uncover what is inherent to seriality, not constituted after the fact of material or psychical recurrence. Seriality is a disturbance of causality always lying in wait for repetition. Seriality is drawn toward its own deadlock, the impasse and imbrication of expansion and end, disclosure and closure.

From the moment of its inception within nineteenth-century print culture, seriality was both material and psychosocial. The psyche, as psychoanalysis understands, has always been gapped, its contours becoming traceable through slips of the tongue, mishearings, misreadings, and misrememberings. The serial is defined by installments and gaps, a dialectical relation between holes and wholes. Toward the end of the nineteenth century, Sigmund Freud uncovers the serial workings of the psyche.

It is no coincidence that Freud's intervention is made *after* the serial's material invention. Seriality is an *a priori* homology of the gapped psyche and the successive cultural production that defines a material series. The psyche has always been serial. The proliferation of material series has thrown the shape of the psyche into the world. Arguing that seriality is a psychic phenomenon is the throughline that knots together this book's various other aims and ambitions. The social and political consequences of this move will by developed in a supplemental fashion as the central argument unfolds. Seriality is a theory of mediation urgently needed. Seriality, as I theorize it, enables us to see how we occupy a place in sustaining that which does us injury at personal, social, and political levels.

Seriality is a saturating logic first graspable in material things. That logic needs to be seen in all manner of phenomena, material or not. Psychoanalysis, as Freud once remarked, concerns itself with the dregs of world phenomena.[1] Accordingly, I will examine objects of popular culture to demonstrate how seriality works and what the exigency and efficacy of thinking this way is. The way we will demonstrate this logic is through tracing a homology between the way the psyche works and the way pop cultural objects, ideas, and phenomena proliferate serially. Acknowledging the complexity of homology enables us to likewise see the psychical, political, and social ramifications of seriality.

Homology, as the French psychoanalyst Jacques Lacan once remarked, does not mean analogy or metaphor. It does not mean that something is *like* or *akin to* something else. Rather, it means that the stakes of two seemingly unalike things are exactly the same.[2] What is at stake materially with the series is the same as what is at stake in the psyche. Technological advancements in nineteenth-century printing made the widespread material existence of the serial possible for the first time. Serial publications, especially novels, newspapers, magazines, and political journals, flourished. Clare Pettitt's exhaustive historical and sociopolitical engagement with seriality in *Serial Forms: The Unfinished Project of Modernity* explains, "Seriality developed into the dominant cultural form of the nineteenth century: an ever more insistent and dynamic syncopated rhythm of repetition and development which begins to format print, literature, history, politics, and concepts of citizenship."[3] Seriality was not simply a novel kind of material production. Rather, seriality names the form of a social, existential, and political imbrication—a tie knotted through what we would today call popular or mass culture that, prior to the 1830s, did not exist. It should not surprise us that psychoanalysis would develop toward the end of the nineteenth century as a way of understanding the syncopated and gapped rhythm of the psyche—a rhythm that was forming and informing the very material of the still nascent serial world. Seriality is an inherent and primary structure of relation. It is not constituted after the fact.

Etymologically speaking, seriality is initially defined by the biological. Earliest uses of the word "serial" come from biology and refer to parts of an organism arranged in some form of ordered succession (e.g., "serial teeth").[4] This usage of the word "serial" was coined in 1823, a little over a decade before the print serial explosion. The popularity of successively released installments of an ongoing publication, particularly literary publications would become the world's hallmark association starting around 1835.[5] This definition is closest to how we think of the serial most often today.[6] Not unlike Leibniz and Newton simultaneously developing calculus independent of each other during the seventeenth century, 1836 would see Charles Dickens publish *The Pickwick Papers* and Honoré de Balzac *The Old Maid* (*La vielle ille*), both serially. These were not just the first serial novels for each writer but the first attempt made by anyone at writing something in successive installments *alongside* its release. Previously, already finished publications, such as *Robinson Crusoe*, had been published in volumes after the novel's completion. The change that Dickens and Balzac were at the forefront of was writing novels in installments according to a regular release schedule *without* the text having been finished prior to its release. This opened up what previously had been a closed relationship between author, a complete work, and the audience. This cut in the serial—both the gap between installments and the gap within it as an unfolding incomplete work—made the text permeable to the demands and passions of the public.

Any series is by necessity punctuated by gaps. Thinking the serial gap as temporal opening or a gap in time has attracted considerable scholarly interest. Recently, narrative scholars such as Sean O'Sullivan, Jason Mittell, and Frank Kelleter have regarded the temporal opening between installments of a fictional series as a site where both the author(s) of a fictional series itself and audiences reflect and interpret.[7] It is true that, whether we are discussing gaps between television episodes or NFL games, we live more in these gaps than we live those discrete instances of content. After all, to continue the example, an episode of a narrative television series is typically a half an hour or an hour, an NFL game is usually four hours. The time before *the next* installment—the temporal opening in which you can ruminate, relish, or stew about the most recent installment—is typically a week and this temporal opening enables meaning to be generated by fans (e.g., through microblogging about your favorite series; calling in to an FM radio sports talk show to voice your displeasure about your team's star player, coach, or general manager; engaging in fan communities either online or in person). While this approach to serial media, particularly the narrative variety, has its advantages and virtues, there is a problem of consequence. By privileging a notion of the serial gap as interstitial time made remarkable through some other kind of activity—such as individual reflection or the accumulation of audience engagement—the gap itself becomes insubstantial. In other words, the serial gap becomes blank space simply waiting to be filled.

I will look to avoid repeating the common gesture whereby seriality is discussed only as an adjectival form of some other kind of activity.[8] To theorize seriality *in itself*—as in, its internal operation regardless of content and context—and *for itself*—as in, without reducing it to the operation of some other kind of media, social formation, or reoccurring phenomenon—means distilling it down to two almost banal yet immanent properties: the gap and repetition. Every attempt to discuss or understand the serial has included reference to one of these two terms. However, these discussions often act as synecdoche for the wider undertheorization of seriality itself where the qualities of the gap and repetition are assumed.[9]

The idea of a constitutive gap and the role of repetition are generally accepted as immanent features of seriality across different attempts to proliferate an understanding of the concept. Anything we might conceivably consider serial has this dialectical dynamic between gap and repetition, holes and wholes. Seriality is unlike a social media platform such as Facebook, X (formerly Twitter), Reddit, or TikTok, where the form of these platforms is shaped entirely by audience activity. These websites do not make or produce anything on their own. These platforms aggregate user-generated content and even rely on users to curate the content that appears on their platforms. Despite how much agency we give to the entities called Facebook, X, Reddit, or TikTok to determine what they are, these companies and their algorithms are utterly dependent on user activity for their platforms to mean anything at all. Concretizing seriality as a theoretical notion in a way that does not rely on reference to the specific shape of a given serial manifestation (e.g., serial novels, television, a videogame series, breaking news) nor to the amalgamation of audience activity means paying close attention to that which remains stubbornly the same across various and varied iterations of serial appearance. This is how I define form. Remaining stubbornly the same across various and varied iterations of serial appearance is the gap. Seriality is a gapped form.

The topic of form has received a number of thorough treatments in recent years. C. Namwali Serpell's *Seven Modes of Uncertainty*, for example, explores how unique affordances are generated through limitation and textual constraint. Caroline Levine engages the always already political status of form in *Forms: Whole, Rhythm, Hierarchy, Network*. Anna Kornbluh, in *The Order of Forms: Realism, Formalism, and Social Space*, traces the ontological coextension of the material and the social. I interrogate the serial as an at-once material and psychical form, paying attention to the presence and torsion of absence. Seriality is not a linear form but a retroactive one where we work *backward* from the gaps in content to understand the content. Ultimately, we work retroactively from the shape of different material appearances to understand seriality as an immanent psychical and existential form irreducible to the contingency of content.

Toward Psychic Form

Through a novel fusion of Freudian and Lacanian psychoanalysis, the dialectical method of G. W. F. Hegel, and Jean-Paul Sartre's existentialism, I will argue that the fundamental trauma of modern life is that it is radically connected. It is not fragmented and disconnected as Jean-François Lyotard's influential notion of the "postmodern condition" argued. A deep cross-study of media will help to highlight the radical connectivity central to my overarching claims that to theorize seriality means reckoning with this kind of radical connectivity—especially when it is easier to see disconnection, fragmentation, and isolation. We need to see this connection out in the world through media objects to be able to properly see it in ourselves. As mentioned above, we demonstrate a psychical attachment to media through our engagement with it and through the way society is ordered around and through that serial organizing. What is more, understanding the structure of seriality means acknowledging not just a gap between things but a gap within them and in ourselves.

For an example of a popular obverse logic, we can look to the current grip of conspiracy thinking (e.g., Flat Earthers, QAnon, PizzaGate). There are no gaps in a conspiracy theory which offers an underlying comfort of preordained order. All gaps are accounted for by the conspiracy itself. Any information that might point away from a conspiracy is either discounted (e.g., you can't trust "official" stories) or folded into efforts to prove the conspiracy (e.g., this evidence is planted, doctored, manufactured, distorted, and this is just what they want you to think anyway). There are no split subjects in a conspiracy, nor is there any notion of the unconscious. Missing is any idea that the conspiracy theorists themselves might be contributing to covering up the urgently banal seriousness of oppression under capitalism occurring everywhere in plain sight. In short, the conspiracy theorist is never part of the conspiracy. Rather than analyzing and critiquing structural violence or corruption, conspiracies point to a more ordered universe where the other of the other—the true puppet master—operates behind the scenes, controlling minute daily relations at a level only a Greek god would attend to. What's worse, the conspiracy is often so vast, so undefeatable that there is no hope to alter its course. The conspiracy theorist has simultaneously found a way to be scandalized by the world and absolve themselves for not attempting to change it. By contrast, seriality, as I understand it, is a confrontation not a comfort.

Excavating a largely uncommented on concern with seriality in the formative bedrock of both Freud's and Lacan's thought, I will articulate a way of seeing the serial as a primary and prior form of the psyche. Freud first begins to theorize the serial workings of mental life by trying to understand the structure of trauma. As Freud uncovers in the *Project for a Scientific*

Psychology, trauma is serial. In the *Project*, a text written in 1895 but unpublished until 1950, he outlines how trauma operates *as series* and can only be apprehended retroactively. This is no mere statement that trauma can only be understood after the fact. Freud posits that the aetiology of trauma—its cognizable trajectory—is such that the retroactive recognition of some prior traumatic event seems to *cause it*. Effectively, the initial event happens *again* but as though it is the first time for the subject's consciousness. "We invariably find," Freud writes, "that a memory is repressed which has only become a trauma by *deferred action*."[10] Indeed, twenty-five years later, in Freud's *Beyond the Pleasure Principle*, Freud will see this traumatic serial structure operating in a more everyday fashion with his notion of repetition compulsion. As he writes, "we come now to a new and remarkable fact, namely that the compulsion to repeat also recalls from the past experiences which include no possibility of pleasure, and which can never, even long ago, have brought satisfaction even to instinctual impulses which have since been repressed."[11] This experience of "unpleasure" is "repeated," as Freud writes, "under pressure of a compulsion."[12] What is repeated matters a lot less to Freud than the fact and act of repetition itself. Repetition is not something that happens *after* something has been released. Repetition preexists the release of any individual piece of serial material. Repetition is the refinding of an object *again*. Chapter 1 will pursue this argument at length but for now it will suffice to note the importance of retroactivity and repetition in the serial for Freud.

For Lacan, in his second seminar of public lectures, the logic of the series underpins his burgeoning notion of the symbolic order, the web of undergirding social structures we are confronted by every day that we step outside (or, for the purposes of the present moment, when we interact with people online). In "Seminar on the Purloined Letter," Lacan uses Edgar Allan Poe's famous short story to sketch how meaning arises through symbolic relations (e.g., between people in the social sphere). Lacan's position courted no shortage of detractors. Jacques Derrida, Gilles Deleuze, and Jean-Paul Sartre each attempt to bypass the symbolic order that Lacan establishes. Chapter 2 deals most centrally with this topic.

The Hegelian dialectic—understood as constitutive contradiction—is needed to help explicate the potential radicality in the series. The Hegelian dialectic demonstrates the necessity of seeing opposite as apposite, a hardening of conflict until an impasse that knots together opposition is found. This way of seeing the dialectic will be put in contradistinction to Jean-Paul Sartre. Historically speaking, Hegel's dialectic has tended to be represented without recourse to contradiction. Instead, it is rendered as a position of dispassionate synthesis or, as Sartre puts it, a "monism."[13] Sartre, then, is a conflictual figure. He rejects both the psyche of the unconscious and the dialectic understood as constitutive contradiction. Further he names seriality as an oppressive force ordering the world externally through capitalism. As he writes in *Critique of Dialectical Reason*, "*a series is a mode of being for individuals both in relation to one another and in relation to their common being* and this mode of being transforms all their structures."[14] Sartre's most well-known example of this kind of seriality is the "plurality of isolations," that is, a line of people queueing up to get on a bus.[15] For Sartre, capitalism arranges each person in a "series," a superficial grouping that radically separates each person from each other.

To put it bluntly, Sartre's writing on seriality positions him firmly against the theoretical method I employ throughout these pages. As Alfred Hitchcock might very well have said, an academic book is only as strong as its villain. It would be easy to read Jean-Paul Sartre as this book's villain. In some senses he very much is, as he vigorously condemns seriality as a concept across two major philosophical works. Sartre's idiosyncratic but fecund objections to psychoanalytic and dialectical thinking buttress his total refusal to admit seriality into a politics of transformation. However, it is through his absolute disgust with the series as an idea that he sees its immanence and importance. Where most if not all theorists of seriality propose it as a *kind* of media phenomena or *type* of pop-cultural engagement, Sartre treats it as the primary form of postindustrial existence—an idea that orders material and psychic life. It is this gesture in his work that I would like to preserve. Despite his absolute rejection of seriality, I am closer to Sartre theoretically than I am to others who embrace seriality in less capacious or more anodyne configurations. In many ways, he is the first to posit that seriality is the psychic form of everyday life, making him closer to the book's hero than its villain. Even Sartre's rejection of psychoanalysis and Hegel put him at odds with the trajectory of this book's argument but, again, in the negation of his negation we can see what is at stake in psychoanalysis and Hegel more clearly. In other words, this book will perform its understanding of dialectics—the contradiction that knots opposite as apposite—in the way it reads Sartre, who will serve as figure necessary for elucidating critical ideas both in psychoanalytic theory and in Hegelian thought.

Sartre sees in seriality an isolation where the connection between us is rendered superficial.[16] As he writes, "isolation becomes, for and through everyone, for him and for others, the real, social product of cities" and "the reciprocity of isolations in a society which creates *masses*" and that this "massification" makes every person utter flattened and interchangeable.[17] With *Critique of Dialectical Reason*, Sartre works to marry the existentialist project he developed in *Being and Nothingness* with Marxism. The idea that the material takes up residence in consciousness and exerts a force on mental life is at the forefront of Karl Marx's philosophical intervention. Marx states in *The German Ideology*, "If in all ideology men and their relations appear upside-down as in a *camera obscura*, this phenomenon arises just as much from their historical life-process as the inversion of objects on the retina does from their physical life-process."[18] The reference to media technology by Marx (the *camera obscura*) is no simple metaphor. He sees this as the precise way that material relations influence conscious thought and the mental processes of everyday people. Marx deserves immense credit for seeing nascent visual media technology as a way to understand the conscious mind. In fact, it is the ordering function that Marx locates in the material production of the ruling classes and, I would argue, its link to media technology that influences Sartre into identifying the form of serial production as a totalizing oppressive force.

For different reasons, both Marx and Sartre see only parts of the serial picture. Sartre sees seriality as a ceaseless succession. There may be gaps between people at the bus stop, but they are superficial to the point of being meaningless. Seriality, for him, is flattening and gapless. Marx sees multiple gaps: the gaps between commodities, and the gap between the commodity (as it is in its raw materiality) and the surplus value of the commodity for the capitalist. However, due to the flattening function he sees characteristic of the ruling class, he cannot see the subject as gapped in any way other than as a deficit. Neither Marx's nor Sartre's approach can allow that the psyche is gapped in a prior and primary way. The gaps between material and within material coinciding with the gaps in the subject's psyche are not graspable through either a pure Marxist project nor the Marxist and existentialist project that Sartre proffers. Each thinker's approach to the serial logic of industrial capitalism makes manifest an intrinsic and oftentimes illuminating conflict besetting modern life. There is conflict here, yes, but not existential contradiction; the expression of a prior paradoxical relation between us and the material, the material and us, us and the social, the social in us.

Contra Sartre's Marx-informed position, I find that seriality instantiates an isolation necessary for the formation of both collective and individual subjectivity. We need to be able to see the gap within to be able to make this move. Highlighting the gap within the material and the individual—substance and subject—is our only inoculation against seeing the serial strictly as an overwhelming external force proliferated largely by capital. Capitalism is serial. Not just in its base-level necessity of producing a succession of goods worth accumulating but in its promise of a constant stream of "nows" that will be more satisfying than the last one.[19] It wants us only to pay attention to the gap between products *not* the gap within (e.g., how were they constructed, how did they get here, through what suffering was this MacBook I am currently writing on even produced?). Crucially, and this is where we need the unconscious, *we want to ignore the gap within as well.* It is much easier for us to live everyday under capitalism ignoring the same things capital wants us to ignore. It is much easier to live everyday ignoring the ways that we are contradictory.

To pursue a line of argumentation that digs out what I am calling the psychical and existential contradiction besetting everyday life requires a notion of the unconscious and a notion, as Freud discovers in *Beyond the Pleasure Principle*, that people could desire something that does them injury. These two ideas are crucial to understanding ideology or the theoretical principle that attempts to explain why deleterious, self-defeating, and masochistic behavior persists even when individuals and society know that there is a better or more just way. Being predicated on consciousness, rather than the unconscious, Marx's system cannot and does not account for why people actively desire and do things to their own detriment. In our contemporary era, the primary masochism of the psyche that Freud terms death drive is perhaps best expressed by the phrase "people voting against their interests." Rising to explain the shocking result of the 2016 US Presidential Election (and its zombie-like return in 2024), this phrase fails to understand that those voting against their interests are, in fact, showing precisely what their interests (desire) are.[20] In other words, there is a gap between what we consciously want and what we unconsciously desire. Reading Marx to the letter, he could only have attributed the undermining behavior Freud identifies with the death drive to a deficit in knowledge (which, perhaps coincidentally, is the exact same thing liberal commentators do when writing about the plight of so-called low information voters). As Marx writes, "The class which has the means of material production at its disposal, *consequently also controls the means of mental production*, so that the ideas of those who lack the means of mental production are on the whole subject to it."[21] Marx is arguing that the ruling class extend their dominion over material life to mental life by structuring the world in such a way that it is difficult, if not impossible, for "those who lack the means of mental production" to imagine any alternative to it. This program of occlusion is achieved by the ruling class mystifying the innerworkings of capitalism—a process of mystification that likewise occludes the minds of the working class. Marx sees a gap in class that produces and reproduces a gap in knowledge. It thereby sustains the gap in class. Developing a notion of the psyche as understood by Freud and Lacan, however, enables us to imagine a way out of the deadlock that Marx posits and points us in the direction of theorizing the gap itself.

My theory of seriality comes not from the gaps in between material production. Nor does it arise from the temporal gap in a release schedule. It comes from the subject apprehending serial media—the gapped subject encountering gapped material. We are all serial subjects. All material is serial. We are all gapped. All material is gapped. The serial is not an epiphenomenon. It is not an inevitability of economics. It works because it is form at once so intimate and so disavowed. At first glance, it seems as though the gaps between something make it serial. My claim is that it is the gap within the apprehending subject *and* within the material. Capitalism succeeds because it mirrors the way our conscious mind tries to dismiss the fissures of the unconscious. It smooths over the gaps as it evinces them. In other words, we deny the gaps in our psyche everyday through actions both mundane and significant. Capitalism succeeds not because it clouds minds but because we desire clouded minds. In enjoying the commodity, we get to disavow our own gaps just as we disavow the gaps in the commodity. This is how capitalism succeeds. It wants us to focus on the gaps between and not the gap within—neither the gap in the commodity nor the gap within ourselves.

The Gap Within

The materiality of the serial has been enthusiastically written about and this examination has permeated many popular and academic fields of inquiry. The psychosocial aspect of seriality—specifically the psychical part—has received much less treatment. Opening up the way we think about seriality in this way, however, means articulating a theory of radical causality and connection. Restricting a definition of the serial to the material or even giving the material priority means imagining that only the physical can be concrete, not the social or the psychical. As Chapter 4 explores, it also means privileging the immediacy of the particular over the mediation of the universal. Redressing this balance in favor of universality is politically urgent. Privileging the particular over the universal has been capital's greatest strength. As every labor organizer knows, individuating employees against each other is the best way for management to keep salaries and benefits low. As every fan of a team sport knows, a collection of talented individuals does not necessarily a team make. The collective is always stronger than an amalgam of particulars, no matter how individually enticing any one of those specific particulars may be.

My contention is that seriality is no mere metaphor from which we can organize material production and social formations. It is the very structure of our psyches made physical that we actively shape and are shaped by. Seriality as form is made graspable through the collision of the material and the psychical. We are invested in ourselves being self-identical and gapless—apart, perhaps, from one or two quirks that we have grown comfortable discussing with others—and capitalism wants us to be likewise comfortable with a commodity being identical to itself.

The historical development of the serial sees a material form collide with the shape of our psyches. Seriality is glue. It is binding and bonding. Paradoxically, it is also by necessity gapped, fragmented. The gaps in the serial mirror the gaps in our psyche. One's stream of consciousness follows an internal logic jumping from one topic to the next seemingly seamlessly. What smooths over the seams is the gap from one topic to the next. Like *Monty Python*, our psyche connects unalike things periodically according to the logic of "And now for something completely different." Psychologists call this "mental wandering" or "task-unrelated thinking," and this can be the hallmark of a "creative mind," while "too much" can lead to any number of diagnoses for mental disorders.[22] Phenomenologically speaking, however, it is imperative to recognize that our mind wanders, and this wandering is in itself connective. This wandering may interrupt us from continuing to do a single task either for work or for pleasure, but the key insight of viewing seriality as a psychic structure is regarding the interruption itself as the link between one thought and the next. Take, for example, Paris-based painter Henni Alftan's diptych titled *Non-stop (In-between)* (oil-on-canvas).

At first glance we are struck by the centrality of a blank space between the two paintings indicating that something is missing. Due to the information on either side of the blankness, however, we can complete the picture. Mentally we are meant to complete the image of a neon sign that reads "Non Stop" or "Non-stop," as the title suggests. Rather than looking at these paintings and concluding that something has been taken away or removed from us, to think seriality in the way I am proposing and the way Alftan's diptych demands, we need to see that the absence completes the image. This diptych is not structurally incomplete; the incompleteness at the heart of it is what completes it.[23] There is a hole in the whole that constitutes this not as a single painting but as a series. We need

FIGURE 0.1 *Non-stop (In-between)*, 2022, oil on linen, 38¼ × 157½ inches. © Henni Alftan & ADAGP.

to understand that this hole is not a blank, not a nothing, but rather is a site of negation that instantiates it serially, completing its meaning through absence. Similar to how Scott McCloud has emphasized that the action in comic books and graphic novels occurs between the two frames rather than within any one frame, the hole in the whole—the constitutive negativity of the gap—is active as a caesura.[24] The nothing is not produced by the diptych; rather, the diptych relies on the nothing that is lying there already active. For this reason, we should perhaps be moved to think of this series of paintings as a triptych, emphasizing the importance of the gap even further.

Again, at first glance we might be tempted to say that the presence of the two paintings either side of the absence is what confers meaning onto it. This would be a mistake. It is the absence—the gap in the series—that makes the presence mean anything at all. A "complete" painting on a single canvas that simply reads "Non-stop" is not worthy of formal investigation. The gap makes it a diptych (or triptych)—makes it a series. What is more, the materiality of the gap taps into the gapped way that our psyche's function. We are predisposed to understanding meaning making absences as this is the way our psyche works. We can grasp this logic all around us by adjusting the way we engage with mundane and ordinary phenomena and objects. Imagine a chain link fence. Rather than seeing the metal as that which forms the link between one chain and the next, think of the gaps between them—literally the "nothing" that knots across a chain link fence that is only visible because the fence is there in the first place (otherwise it is simply formless space, uninteresting air)—as fulfilling this necessary function. Whether we are conscious of this gap or not, the gap is there cohering the look of the fence itself.

Seriality against the Particular

With the material serial moving to a place of prominence in all manner of media through an explosion of film series, streaming series, podcasts, tweet storms, TikTok trends and the like, it should not surprise us that interest in theorizing seriality is here again. Invoking the work of Gérard Wajcman, a French psychoanalyst,

Alenka Zupančič has recently written on the topic of the series. As she writes: "the series-form or format is not just an esthetic or artistic phenomenon. Rather, the series-form is the language of the world such as it is: a world in crisis. Series is a form of crisis."[25]

This idea of the series matches very closely to my own but there is an important distinction. In this book, the words series, serial, and seriality are not synonyms for material, psychical, social, or environmental repetitions. Seriality needs to be understood as a process of dialectical recognition. If a series of repetitions is mired and sustained by a non-recognition or misrecognition of its component parts, we do not have seriality. In other words, a set of isolated particulars having only a perfunctory association to each other—the classic example of a group of talented individual athletes not amounting to a winning team—does not give us seriality. Throughout, I will try to use the words serial to refer either to a certain kind of literary and culture production (e.g., the Victorian serial, film serials, serial television). I will use the word series to refer to a repetition in kind (e.g., an ordered succession of television episodes, intrinsically related climate disasters, the shape of psychical processes). Seriality, in my theorizing, names a dialectical relation between parts where we can encounter the self as other, substance as subject.

I do not mean this as a mere semantic disagreement with Zupančič and Wacjman, who both rightly see the serial form as primary in the world and implicitly note the connection between the serial and the existential which Sartre brings together. What I mean to articulate is that understanding seriality as a dialectical relation offers a solution to the problem of the series. Not every series of shots in a film is an example of Eisenstein's concept of *montage* which, in English, is often unhelpfully often translated as "editing." *Montage*, as in Eisenstein's own famous "Odessa Steps" sequence in *Battleship Potemkin*, puts every cut in dialectical relation producing a political recognition that is not possible to achieve looking at single shots disconnected from each other. Nor is it bare shot-reverse shot capturing a casual coffee shop conversation but a way of arranging film parts to produce an emotional, political, ideological, or psychical change in the viewer. Seriality, as I develop and theorize it, attempts to bring an understanding of cultural objects we take for granted (e.g., montage) to personal, psychical, social, and political phenomena we have a harder time seeing as serial. Or, worse, we *do* see it as serial but conclude there is nothing left to be done to address it, the moment gone. This at once avows and disavows seriality, distancing us from a recognition that would disturb and shake us.

This is one of the reasons why we should insist on seriality being on the side of radical retroactivity and cut. It is quite easy to avoid serializing whatever it is we don't want to see collocated and wherever it is we don't want to see ourselves implicated. We need to see how we occupy space in a dynamic that we otherwise would prefer to distance ourselves from. To put it plainly, are no points to be gained from sitting in the cheap seats and critiquing everyone going to the theater as though you're not there yourself? Chapter 6 will play the following dynamic out regarding social media, but for now it will suffice to say that I will argue that seriality needs meaningfully to be understand and articulated as being on the side of universality at odds and in conflict with the tyranny of the particular. It is the only way for the idea to be urgent enough to understand and interrupt all the series without seriality that plague the current moment. The particular is the crisis form of the current moment—not the serial or the series. The particular extracts itself from a whole and wants to be reducible to nothing. It operates in a way that makes connection structurally untenable. Social media as discrete form of media that inheres a logic unto itself, as we saw in the previous chapter, privileges the particular. Indeed, it requires the particular—the logic of the infinitely separable—to sustain itself. The universal changes irrevocably the way a series of particulars relate such that the undergirding logic is overthrown. The universal forces us beyond seeing isolated instances and moves us toward seeing seriality.

The logic of the particular, however, wants to see events as true "one-offs" and wants all phenomena to be irreducible to wider structures. Despite knowing this, it's hard to remain committed to reconciling oneself to the seriality of everyday life where it is more comforting to see the exception—even a series of exceptions. Even when we are aware of systemic or structural issues, it is all too easy to be sucked in by the particular. Consider the naming conventions we routinely use to refer to tragic occurrences from mass shootings, to school shootings, racist police murders, to climate devastation. The Last Vegas Shooter. Sandy Hook. The George Floyd Protests. The Paradise Fire. Each of these takes a systemic problem and affixes it to a town, city, person, or geographic location. The event in each instance becomes exceptional, wrestled from its web of connection to like events. We know that, for example, climate change is an ongoing and constantly unfolding existential crisis. Yet, climate change tends only to make the front pages of newspapers or monopolize time on news broadcasts either when climate scientists further prove the doom we are dawdling into or when there has been a new disaster. When discussed in these terms, climate change becomes implicitly a staccato phenomenon visible only in extremes. Speaking of peculiar climate *events*, say atmospheric rivers, floods, or freezing temperatures in parts of countries and continents not used to such temperatures, rips us from seeing the seriality of climate change and enforces a notion that climate disasters are an unpredictable series of self-contained episodes rather than a very predictable new norm.

Consider Uvalde, Texas, site of the most recent highest profile school shooting in the United States, at the time of this sentence being written. Most reacting to the breaking news about a shooting and standoff at Robb Elementary School in Uvalde, Texas, will have thought the same thing: not again. Reading that nineteen children and two teachers were killed along with seventeen wounded will have reminded American onlookers of Columbine, Sandy Hook, or Parkland (a hardly exhaustive list of US school shootings since 1999). In the hours, days, and weeks after the shooting details emerged that shocked and horrified. The shooter killed his grandmother before going to the elementary school, where he was previously a student, to carry out a mass shooting. Police were on the scene for over an hour and did not engage the shooter. They stood in the school's hallways and outside the building as they could hear gun shots in classrooms. An off-duty Border Patrol officer is the person who entered the school to kill the shooter and he drove to do so only because his child went to the school. Parents were arrested and restrained by police as they tried to enter the school to save their children. The police chief treated the shooting as a "barricaded subject" situation and not an "active shooter" event. The town of Uvalde briefly backed the embattled police chief and refused to let reports, surveillance video, and other information come out about the event. Texas Governor Greg Abbot made statements supporting the police based on "inaccurate" information. Eventually we learned that the police chief encouraged children to "distract" the shooter before police were prepared to go in. Arnulfo Reyes, a teacher who was shot three times trying to protect his students, called the police cowards. Texas politician Beto O'Rourke confronted the governor live during a city hall meeting on the shooting, demanding that he stop protecting police and the gun industry.

I want to stop us here on this information trajectory. Where we started was a general description of a heinous act of violence that is all too common in American society. It is numbing and shocking at the same time, but the problem is that where we started was a better place than where we ended up. I want to recall Freud's maxim that knowledge about the unconscious does not cure the symptom. Approaching the repetitive injunction of the symptom—or the grotesque symptom of systemic issues like gun violence—as though they are the result of a deficit of information does little to halt them from happening. At the beginning of the previous paragraph, with little specific information, the shooting in Uvalde resembled every other numbing and shocking school shooting in the United States. It resembled Columbine, Sandy Hook, and Parkland. Where we ended up, though, was with a cowardly police chief who actively prevented the rescue of trapped children. We had a governor offering unblinking support for police and then retracting his support after the release of politically uncomfortable details. We have an off-duty border patrol officer ending the active shooter situation. We have more extreme measures taken by police to prevent parents from rescuing their children than there were measures taken to address the shooter. The more information we have, the more Uvalde does *not* look like Columbine, Sandy Hook, or Parkland. The more it only resembles itself.

Here we've "learned more" as we've gone along but we've lost the connection between like events. The particular has completely overwhelmed us. The "exceptional status" of the event stands above its seriality. The more we lean into the particular or a logic of "case by case basis" we acquire more information at the expense of getting dumber overall. The more particular knowledge we gain, the more we lose sight of the structure of seriality. We lose the glue and the connection between the most recent tragic event and the web of congruity it shares with others.

Seriality is a form of radical connectivity. When understood in this way, we can grasp the homology between the material serial (such as a Victorian novel or television series) and the existential serial (climate change or systemic violence). Accordingly, this book is ordered by three moments of serial culture convergence: the first centering on print culture in the nineteenth century, the second engaging television's place as unquestioned center of gravity for serial media production beginning in the mid-twentieth century, and the last covering the 2000s with social media and the advent of streaming. The histories of these periods have already been written (or are currently ongoing) but the theory knotting the media together across these moments has not been fully made. Chapter 1 discusses Freud's encounter with serial fiction and his initial grappling with the seriality he found in the psyche and in the practice of analysis. This opening chapter also creates a dialogue between Freud and Marx, proposing a way to think the materiality of the psyche. Chapters 2 and 3 discuss Lacan's theorizing of serial operations and the rift this opened up between he and French contemporaries Jacques Derrida, Gilles Deleuze, and Jean-Paul Sartre. Chapter 4 uses the historically derided television format known as "the bottle episode" to stage the dialectical division between Sartre and Hegel. Chapter 5 discusses the serial gap in the context of a form of media that alleges gapless entertainment: the Netflix binge serial. Chapter 6 discusses social media. Social media offers commentary on every social problem except for the problem of the social as such. As a set of discourses, social media is a discourse that does not include itself. The idea of masses and the public is a concern throughout the book and Chapter 4 discusses the co-opting of any notion of public through the privacy and privacy concerns of social media platforms. With recourse to Pixar films and Japanese Role Playing Games, the final chapter explores the idea of a so-called "bad series" in relation to Hegel's notion of the "bad infinite" while moving to trace how cynicism sustains ideology. Ideology is here understood as the unconscious engagements that work to uphold status quo and smooth over contradictions in the symbolic order. Seriality is needed to pierce the prevalence of the cynical position, as it exchanges self-satisfaction for a disavowal of one's role in buttressing to which the cynic claims to be diametrically opposed.

In theorizing seriality, I trace a logic of gapped repetition, of interruption. The trajectory of argumentation I employ aims to help us identify a series—a procession of related parts—and move us toward thinking in terms of seriality—a dialectical repetition.

Being able to articulate seriality within media, pop culture more generally, and, most importantly, in ourselves, is perhaps the book's most important claim. Just because there is a series does not make it seriality. A series of unfortunate events does not seriality make. Just because something repeats or continues does not make it seriality.

The book's chapters are designed to push the reader from being able to recognize and theorize seriality through literature and visual media examples with prominent gaps (e.g., the temporal gaps in the release of Victorian novels and television series) toward being able to see the presence of the serial gap where it is not so structurally evident (e.g., cynicism). The practice of vocal compiling in popular music—selecting the best bits of dozens of recorded vocals of one song—presents that which is serial or gapped as a singular totality.[26] What vocal compiling entails is making the "take" we hear in the finished product something which did not exist as a single performance. It was sung by the performer over the course of many takes but, as a singularly continuous set of consecutive vocal intonations, it was never sung by the performer. The commonplace slander that "no one is really a good singer anymore" because of this level of technological manipulation is a cynical take that misses the formal point. The point is that out of the serial emerges something impossible. From the gaps between the takes, a throughline emerges. We hear it as a singular piece, but it is serial. Beginning with increasingly more complicated studio technology in the 1960s and onward, popular music has frequently pushed its sensibilities forward by soliciting the impossible continuity of the serial. "Strawberry Fields Forever" by The Beatles is a perfect example of such an impossibility. The final recorded version issued in 1967 is comprised of several takes of the song split into two dominant takes played at different speeds from their original recording laid on top of each other to give the appearance of a unity.[27] Within that appearance the attuned ear can hear the different takes, the tension, the aural contradiction. The unaware ear, however, hears only a unity. We have to train ourselves to hear, see, and feel seriality—especially where a unity, exception, or one-off is more immediately apprehensible. This is how we will show that seriality is a psychical form—a way of thinking and existing in relation to ourselves and/as other.

1

Psyche Is Extended: Dickens, Marx, Freud, and Seriality's Theoretical Beginnings

Seriality was in the air in the early part of the nineteenth century, with serial fiction taking root simultaneously in England and France through Dickens and Balzac and then later in Germany, Russia, North America, and China. As much as seriality shook up and reformatted modern life, it also acted as its glue. As Jennifer Hayward writes in *Consuming Pleasures: Active Audiences and Serial Fictions from Dickens to Soap Opera*, serial literature functioned "for nineteenth-century society as social cement."[1] The publication of serials from writers such as Dickens, George Eliot, and Wilkie Collins in England; Honoré de Balzac, Gustave Flaubert, Alexandre Dumas, and Eugene Sue in France; Fyodor Dostoevsky and Leo Tolstoy in Russia; and Mark Twain, Harriet Beecher Stowe, and Henry James in the United States snapped into relation a notion of the public that had not theretofore existed. *Uncle Tom's Cabin*, serially published from June 5, 1851, to April 1, 1852, in the *National Era*, rather underlines Hayward's claim, as it became so popular that the only book to outsell its bound volume publication for the rest of the nineteenth century was the Bible.[2] The kind of social reconfiguration that seriality inspired can be seen here in synecdoche: a movement from Sunday Mass to masses.

The modern psychosocial tie begins with the development of the serial. Tied together by holding the same position toward a text, of waiting to read the next installment, the segmented release of a serial story helped foster the idea of a larger public (or social). While an older form of fiction, such as the epic poem in the oral tradition, may have been serially told across generations, the print serial beginning with the likes of Charles Dickens unfolded as they were being written. In other words, for the author, text, and audience a dialectical relation unfolded. There is a living alongsideness to print and contemporary media serials that did not exist prior to seriality's material invention. Simply put, we grow as people as the stories themselves grow and proliferate. The seeming aliveness and mutability (and cancelation) of the serial brings it closer to our own more intimate form of existence.

Pushing Hayward's metaphor of seriality as social cement, I claim that seriality is *psychic cement*. While cement appears solid and whole, it is permeable and eventually becomes riddled with cracks and holes—literally the gaps beneath our feet. "Water cooler" narratives, binge-worthy television and film series, repeated social practices, distressingly regular crises are our common pop cultural ground. It is these holes that cohere the whole. The gaps in seriality paradoxically introduce break as that which binds a material series and the subject. Riddled with gaps, breaks, and slips, our subjectivity is serial. Moving from seeing this cultural material as that which grounds the superficial social tie and also serves as the basis from which we can apprehend a serially gapped psyche is the work of thinking seriality as psychic cement. Moving toward seeing seriality as psychic cement—as an immanent psychical form—does not mean we by necessity leave the realm of the material behind. Far from it. Theorizing seriality requires us to think the material and the social as coextensive with the psyche and the subject. In fact, I want to suggest that this is how Freud himself came to an intuitive understanding of many of the major tenets of psychoanalysis that he would develop later in life. I argue that it is through Freud's repeated encounter with the form of the serial itself—with its insistence on retroactive meaning making—that the form of psychoanalysis begins to foment for him.

A Method of Refinding

The roots of psychoanalysis lie in the serial form itself. Sigmund Freud, born 1856, came of age after the initial boom of serial production. His personal and professional writing are marked by the serial structure present in everyday life. In 1895's *Studies on Hysteria*, Freud makes a meaningful reference to the practice of reading daily serials in newspapers. He considers serials a way to think through the consequences of the most basic problem of the clinic—the clock. A session has to end not with some revelation on the part of the patient but because of a predetermined end time.

Studies on Hysteria, cowritten with Josef Breuer, is the text that announced the psychoanalytic method to the world. In that publication's fourth section, "The Psychotherapy of Hysteria," written by Freud alone, he notes that analysis has a serial problem. While the talking cure requires the analysand's narrative to form free of interruption, the analytic session itself has to end at some point. It is these "interruptions ... imperatively prescribed by incidental circumstances in the treatment, such as the lateness of the hour," which occur "at the most inconvenient points, just as one may be approaching a decision or just as a new topic emerges," Freud writes.[3] In short, the purely practical endpoint to a session means that an analyst and analysand cannot talk about everything in a single session. The interruption, the end of the session, confronts the analysand with an ending that occurs before the analysand is really ready to leave. Freud is compelled to liken this to the experience of reading serial fiction:

> Every newspaper reader suffers from the same drawback in reading the daily installment of his serial story, when immediately after the heroine's decisive speech or after the shot has rung out, he comes upon the words: "To be continued." In our own case the topic that has been raised but not dealt with, the symptom that has become temporarily intensified and has not yet been explained, persists in the patient's mind and may perhaps be more troublesome to him than it has otherwise been... since by themselves they cannot take any steps towards getting rid of it, they suffer more, to begin with, than they did before the treatment.[4]

The phrase "To be continued" interrupts the narrative in a serial story. It announces that continuation is *not* forthcoming at the moment and this is what makes the serial interruption so fascinating: it imposes an ending *while announcing itself as a link to the next installment*. The interruption *cuts* the narrative. "To be continued" makes the reader aware of the structure of the story, breaking the continuous fictive world while simultaneously binding it to the next installment.

It is worth pausing again on the *weight* that interruptions give to that which precedes them. Freud writes, "the topic that has been raised but not dealt with … persists in the patient's mind and may perhaps be more troublesome to him than it has otherwise been."[5] The acknowledgment here is what *form* does to *content*. Whatever "topic" the patient brought up may have been innocuous but because that discussion could not end of its own volition (through a formal interruption), the specter of it "persists" and becomes more "troublesome" than it would be otherwise.

Freud draws a corollary between the patient who "suffers more" as a result of the psychoanalytic session ending abruptly and the newspaper reader who is confronted by "To Be Continued." Freud here is describing the effect of a cliffhanger. Debatably invented by Thomas Hardy, the cliffhanger is one of serial storytelling's trademark narrative tools. Hardy leaves Henry Knight, one of the protagonists of *A Pair of Blue Eyes*, hanging off a cliff between two installments. While hanging between installments—between life or death—Henry contemplates the implacable rock in front of him, its permanence, its evidence of the geological history of the earth, as his own impermanence seems about to be confirmed.

In the next installment, Knight is rescued by Elfride Swancourt, a woman he has been courting, who ingeniously fashions a rope out of her clothes (including, scandalously, her undergarments) to hoist him up to firm terrain. Whether Hardy genuinely invents the cliffhanger here or not is the subject of scholarly debate, and is less important to my purpose here. The idea of the cliffhanger is suggested by the serial form itself, something Hardy simply (though profoundly) demonstrated an openness to. The cliffhanger names precisely a dynamic in the structure of the serial, a dynamic that becomes important to Freud as he draws the connection between psychoanalysis and seriality. A cliffhanger interrupts a narrative scene before its resolution, holding the reader/viewer/listener in suspense, causing them to "suffer more" than if the tense situation had simply reached its conclusion. What both serial narrative and analytic experiences share, as Freud shows here, is a gap that breaks continuity at the same moment that it binds it. Just as we feel we are on the verge of some knowledge—knowing who the killer is in a serial story or reconciling with why we acted with unexpected hostility to a family member the week before in analysis—the time is up. The narrative suspended. We have to get off the couch and wait a week to take up the same topic again.

As Freud writes in *Three Essays on the Theory of Sexuality*, "the finding of an object is in fact a refinding of it."[6] The roots of Freud thinking through the everyday existential consequences of serial structure can be seen in private letters Freud wrote to his wife, Martha, when they were beginning their romantic courtship. This correspondence predates *Studies on Hysteria* by twelve years. Freud wrote frequently to Martha about literature, with the work of Charles Dickens occupying a special place in those letters. Freud admired Dickens so much that the first gift he ever gave her was a copy of *David Copperfield*. Such was Freud's love of Dickens that he wrote brief critiques, such as the following "review" of Dickens's *Bleak House* dated October 5, 1883: Freud tells Martha it "ranks far below [*David Copperfield*]," calling *Copperfield*, "that incomparable work."[7] He thought *Bleak House* "tendentious and hard," like most of Dickens's later writings but, he adds, "I don't want to spoil it for you; its beauties are obvious, while its faults have to be sought for."[8] (I write only half-kiddingly that this may have been the first "spoiler alert" in the history of written communication.) Such was the influence Dickens's work had on Freud, he goes on to write in this letter that he felt so captivated with Dickens's characters and narrative world that he found it hard to write to his wife in German rather than "Dickens's English."[9]

Where it might be tempting to brand the *Studies on Hysteria* reference to seriality as a one-off, looking at his private letters tells us we shouldn't be so quick to make this judgment. To the extent that we can take these brief statements from Freud's personal correspondence as representative for things he was thinking through in his everyday mental life, we can see that the contemplation of serial fiction exerted a hold over him, influencing not just his taste in popular culture but even altering his language (lest we also forget that letter writing is itself a serial endeavor). Taking Freud's personal investment in the serial form into proper account, it would be a mistake to regard Freud's connection between psychoanalysis and seriality as simply a metaphorical one. Freud makes clear that the situation of the serial reader and the patient undergoing analysis is exactly the same. Where he could have distinguished the seriousness of analysis from the everydayness of reading newspaper serials, he instead makes an exact parallel between the "To be continued" of the newspaper serial to the end of the analytic session by writing, "In our own case, the topic that has been raised but not dealt with ... persists in the patient's mind." We are in the territory of homology here, not metaphor. In tracing an argument of homology, the obligation is to show where the stakes are the same in two ideas or to show how the two are intrinsically, intimately tied. The task of the rest of this chapter will be to deepen the connection between seriality and psychoanalysis with a view toward justifying the claim that there is a homology between the two that begins with Freud's reading and later knots together his most important ideas. To further this inquiry requires recourse to underlining the materiality of the psyche and for that we will turn to Marx.

A Broken Form

Freud's apprehension yet attraction to the serial structure, of the "To be continued," has theoretical support from an unlikely source. The French edition of the first volume of Marx's *Capital* appeared in installments between 1872 and 1875. Marx was convinced to publish the translation serially, as opposed to the full-volume treatments it received in its initial publication and later English translation, as "In this form the book will be more accessible to the working class, which to me outweighs everything else."[10] When Marx writes that it "outweighs everything else," he is referring to one of seriality's central obstacles and impetuses: the deferral of meaning. As Marx writes, "[due to serialization] it is to be feared that the French public, always impatient to come to a conclusion, eager to know the connection between general principles and the immediate questions that have aroused their passions, may be disheartened because they will be unable to move on at once."[11] Marx realizes that, while a serialized version of *Capital* will increase its readership, it will also cut off its readers from the conclusions he is painstakingly building toward. The passions of French readers and the desire to get to the end (something the fiction of Balzac and Eugene Sue inspired to great effect) are things Marx would prefer not to arouse. Marx wants the serial—in his case, widespread accessibility—*without* the serial—the complication of desire and the deferral of the end.

Marx is very much responding to the serial moment of his time but also to a conflict that the serial has occasioned throughout time. During the nineteenth century, serials became hotter and hotter commodities and, as such, came to be attended by ethical and political problems. The introduction and success of ad revenue allowed for newspapers to reduce their price per copy and enjoy wider distribution to an eager public. As has so often been the case throughout the history of mass media from which the serial has always been at the center, the rapid and expansive production of serial media appears, as Elizabeth Carolyn Miller writes in *Slow Print*, "a synecdoche for reproducing the logic of mass production" itself.[12] We can see this in early Soap Operas, ongoing narrative radio plays designed to foreground specific consumer products (such as Ivory soap). We can also see this issue appear in an analogous way with WEBZ Chicago's *Serial*, which told a true crime story supported in part by ads for the web service Mail Chimp, something many listeners found problematic (e.g., should *any* corporate entity make money from a grisly true crime story?).[13] Marx's preface to the French edition of *Capital* brings together a number of issues constitutive of seriality: accessibility, temporality, the deferral of meaning, the necessity but insufficiency of the installment, and seriality's formal relationship to the logic of capital.

However, we must not reduce seriality to merely its commercial complicity at the exclusion of considering its aesthetic and formal invention that is often sharply and meaningfully at odds with its production. Chapter 3 will pursue this argument in greater depth, but we can already see the efficacy—and anti-capitalist potential—of the serial in Marx's decision to publish *Capital* in a more working-class-friendly format for French readers. While Marx had qualms with *Capital* being published according to a serial structure in France, he need not have had them; the literariness to the way Marx writes helped his work be both novelistic and philosophical. It is arguable that this is enough to declare Marx the first serial narrative theorist. Marx uses the dialectical form—a form of argumentation that observes the interdependence of things on their own internal opposition—to tell a compelling narrative of the life of the commodity in *Capital*. (It is for this reason that Anna Kornbluh has argued that *Capital* is a novel.) Marx concerns himself with form and content in the way the Russian formalists would pick up decades later. Marx begs us to pay attention to structure—particularly the play between episodic and serial meaning.

Episodic meaning in seriality is, of course, possible, but it is the lingering questions and the lack of *totality* of meaning that stoke interest in serials, as Freud hints at with his reference to the "To be continued." Serials are premised on saying too much and not enough, producing a gap in meaning. It is this tension between the demand of episodic totality and the necessity of retroactive serial meaning that propels seriality. In a very meaningful sense, something like the cliffhanger radically refuses totality. It seems to be a blaring signal that *there is more to the story*. And yet, a sufficient amount of storytelling *must* be accomplished for a cliffhanger to have any meaning at all. With a serial television show, novel, or podcast, it is the impossibility of communicating *all* possible meaning in a single episode that drives the interest in the episodes themselves. It is this lack, or gap, in the individual units of meaning that propels the audience to take an interest in the series.

Freud, by focusing on the felt dimension of the cliffhanger that Marx alludes to, shows that a cliffhanger—experienced as a reader of fiction or a patient in analysis—cuts the psyche. The kind of interruptions Freud is writing about are "incidental" to the treatment. It is precisely this incidental interruption that causes the psychic suffering Freud details. Whereas a perhaps strictly narratological understanding of the cliffhanger might look at how a text signals the coming cliffhanger and the sense of urgency it built up to that point, Freud observes that the cut *itself* provides this urgency. The inability to continue the session (or continue reading the story or watching the television episode) is what engenders a quality of urgency—the sense of the "To be continued." The cliffhanger is a refusal of closure that, nonetheless, acts as closure. It matters not whether this urgent feeling is narratively earned or not; the mere presence of the interruptive closure of the cliffhanger—not "interruption *of* closure" but *interruptive closure*—is what generates urgency and distress.

Paying close attention to the function of the cliffhanger in both narrative storytelling and psychoanalysis enables us to see a potentially universal dimension of seriality: action occurring within a gap. A cliffhanger does not just pause a narrative, suspending its action. The cliffhanger cuts a whole into pieces. The gaps—the holes in the whole—have action in them. While, yes, an overarching narrative is paused, action continues to be generated by these serial gaps. Importantly, this is not just a temporal gap but a psychic gap. What Freud emphasizes is how the gap itself—the mere presence of this cut—causes tension and distress, as though this psychic torsion is just lying in wait for the subject. It is always acting on us regardless of our participation in it. Interruptions give weight to whatever it is that precede them. When Freud writes, "the topic that has been raised but not dealt with … persists in the patient's mind and may perhaps be more troublesome to him that it has otherwise been," he acknowledges what serial interruptions do to the psyche.[14] Whatever "topic" the patient brought up may have been innocuous, but because that discussion could not end of its own volition (through a formal interruption), the specter of it "persists" and becomes more "troublesome" than it would be otherwise.

A Theory in Deferral

By taking seriously the structure of the serial and granting it the dignity of standing co-equal with the analytic situation, Freud notes the interruptive and retroactive continuity of analysis. Starting with the beginning, as in, *Studies in Hysteria*, we can see seriality is ingrained into the analytical structure through the "To be continued" of the session itself. The connection is deeper, however. The canonical story told of Freud's development in understanding trauma post-1919 is that the experience of treating soldiers after the First World War changed Freud's understanding of neurosis.[15] Perhaps those experiences in the clinic unlocked his own "deferred" understanding of seriality as an analytic structure. I say this because the next step in our look at psychoanalytic theory's encounter with seriality is to see that serial fiction has the structure of trauma as understood by Freud. Deferred information in a serial always makes sense of a prior question, to the point where it seems the later revelation caused the initial event. This is what Freud comes to understand with greater clarity after the First World War and, to my mind, it is not an observation that grows out of Freud encountering an entirely new situation (e.g., analyzing postwar patients) but one where the new situation makes sense of Freud's prior thinking on seriality.

On this point, we turn our attention to retroactivity and the etiology of trauma. James Strachey, the most prominent of the canonical translators of Freud into English, translates *nachträglich*, which is an adverb, as "deferred action." The word "retroactively" might be closer to Freud's meaning and it is this sense of the term that I will use most often. There is, however, something about the phrase "deferred action" that speaks to the argument I am constructing about Freud and the serial. It is only through the deferred action of his professional writing on psychoanalysis that the threads of seriality become visible in Freud's thought. While the "To be continued" of *Studies on Hysteria* announces itself to readers as being serially inflected, other concepts have to be harder won and fought for.

In *Project for a Scientific Psychology*, written in 1897 but unpublished until 1950, Freud outlines how trauma is—in a meaningful way—serial. Through the course of psychoanalytic treatment, "We invariably find," Freud writes, "that a memory is repressed which has only become a trauma by *deferred action* [*Nachträglichkeit*]."[16] Freud concludes this only after recounting the story of a patient, Emma, who is "subject at the present time to a compulsion of not being able to go into shops *alone*."[17] Emma attempts to explain her behavior by reference to an incident which occurred at a shop when she was twelve. As Freud recounts, "[Emma] went into a shop to buy something, saw the two shop-assistants ... laughing together, and ran away in some kind of *affect of fright*."[18] The patient explains her symptom—not being able to enter shops alone—by reference to this singular event.

Freud, however, is unconvinced of this singular explanation for the symptom. Referring to the initial event as "Scene 1," analysis unearths *another* "Scene," an even earlier one, which better explains the symptom but only by thinking the two Scenes together. Through analysis, Emma recollects that, when, she was just eight years old, she was sexually assaulted by a shopkeeper who laughed as he grabbed at her through her clothes.[19] What Freud understands is that Emma's symptom cannot be the result of a one-off occurrence, "We can now understand Scene I (shop-assistants) if we take Scene II (with the shopkeeper) along with it. We need an associative link between the two. She herself pointed out that it was provided by the *laughing*: the laughing of the shop-assistants had reminded her of the grin with which the shopkeeper had accompanied his assault."[20] This trauma can only be understood *as a series* and the series can only be apprehended retroactively.

The series does not require a procession of many minimally different events to be a series. There is no numbered requirement of parts to make something a series. What's more important than the number of parts in a given series is recognizing when something—some moment, some episode, some event—snaps into relation a new way of understanding what preceded it. Through retroactivity a series emerges. The series is not a chronological continuum where new things just add on to the last. We tend to experience most popular series (e.g., *Star Wars*, *Harry Potter*) and even series in our own lives (e.g., relationships) as though there is a *progression* of meaning. The shopkeeper example dramatizes how the next "part" alters fundamentally the last similar seeming event and, though it is only two key events that are drawn out in Emma's analysis, Freud helps us to see that it is not the forward or teleological momentum that determines a series but rather this backwards looking and redefining gaze. The series requires seeing that a new "part" modifies irrevocably the last.

What Freud engages with here as analyst is a search for coherence in a discontinuous and gapped narrative. Coherence is not on the side of continuity, however, as the analysand's narrative is an interruptive one that can only be made sensible retroactively with careful attention paid precisely to its gapped structure. These two scenes were four years apart. The first scene, being laughed at by shop-assistants, is determined by the analysand as the genesis of her present compulsion to not go into shops alone. To have such an extreme reaction to this laughter suggests to Freud that there must be something else imbuing the laughter with its powerful content. This unearths another memory, again at a shop, but this one far more serious—a sexual assault. What Freud realizes is that the sexual assault suffered by Emma at age eight was not registered *as a sexual assault* until her visit to a shop at age twelve. The laughter of the shop-assistants at her clothes felt assaulting in nature and brought to light "an affect which ... did not arouse as an experience" initially.[21] Put another way, it was the laughter of the shop-assistants in the near present that retroactively called forth the trauma of the assault from Emma's past which did not—could not—register *as* an experience until the later event.

Trauma, for Freud, relies on this precise understanding of retroactivity: a seemingly innocuous incident calling forth the trauma of a previous event. This is the way for a prior event to even register as a trauma in the first place. What Freud begins to understand here is that trauma does not occur continuous with the subject's linear experience of time. Freud is able to show this through the two scenes of Emma's recollection—a series which shows backward causality.[22] Seriality as form shares exactly this same structure: it appears continuous and linear but our understanding of it relies, crucially, on *Nachträglichkeit,* or retroactivity.

To think according to the logic of *Nachträglichkeit* enables us to see that meaning emerges not linearly from cause to effect but retroactively from effects that posit their own causality. While trauma studies, particularly the work of Cathy Caruth, has been influential at emphasizing the inarticulability of trauma, a close understanding of Freud's meaning here obliges us to note that he thinks trauma *is* representable *but* only through the necessity of *Nachträglichkeit*. It isn't that the first event is inaccessible; it is that access to trauma is opened up retroactively. Trauma is an impossible hole in our symbolic experience. It cannot be recalled like an innocuous memory. Rather, trauma confronts us. The series makes trauma apprehensible and *Nackträglichkeit* is Freud's way of understanding this. The registration of trauma is retroactive. It does not occur continuous with the subject's experience of linear time. This makes trauma a series. We might recall Marx's famous correction of Hegel that history repeats itself, first as tragedy then as farce. We might imagine a Hegelian riposte: that one needs the farce to be able to fully register the tragedy.

Contrasted with what Freud discusses in *Studies on Hysteria*, this is a far more serious example of trauma than the quotidian horror of the "To be continued." However, focusing on the gulf in severity between the two examples obscures their intrinsic connection. Where the assault Emma recounts pushes Freud to see the retroactive aetiology of trauma, we might be moved to consider the "To be continued" a trauma of the everyday. This is precisely what Freud discovers: it is the quotidian everyday event that registers as traumatic. Here he sees the same (serial) structure at work in analysis itself.

There is even compelling reason to see how Freud's future notion of repetition compulsion could have fomented from his serialized conception of analysis as practice. For example, when we are talking about serial stories we are already talking about repetition, just as we are talking about repetition in the very act of going to analysis. So, when Freud discovers the repetition compulsion of the death drive in *Beyond the Pleasure Principle*, we should not fail to note the resonance it has with encountering serial narrative, "*It seems, then, that an instinct is an urge inherent in organic life to restore an earlier state of things* which the living entity has been obliged to abandon under the pressure of external disturbing forces."[23] James Strachey translates both the German words "*Instinkt*" (biological instinct) and "*Trieb*" (drive in excess of biological necessity) as the English word "instinct." Nevertheless, what Freud is getting at here is the drive—"an urge in organic life to restore an earlier state of things." The Freud who stayed up late to finish reading *Daniel Deronda* is here, endeavoring to "return to an earlier state of things"—a state where Freud was *not* possessed by the tension of needing serial closure. To help us with the above statement, we need to look at the Lacanian reading of this passage from *Beyond the Pleasure Principle*. This "earlier state of things" is a prior state of loss or lack. Like characters in a sitcom, we agitate to return to the very state of lacking the object that troubles us (breaking up with a partner with whom we long lusted after ... before actually getting to know them; leaving the job we thought we always wanted ... until we actually did it). Freud is stuck in the middle and wishes to return to the Freud who was not troubled by the encounter with the serial. The drive *delights* in this middle space—this failure to obtain closure. The death drive enjoys failing to obtain its object rather than obtaining it. It doesn't desire the end but to remain stuck in the middle. In fact, we might even see that the Freud who wanted rid of *Daniel Deronda* is a Freud attempting to rid himself from the drive. It would not be until 1920—thirty-eight years after he sent the above letter to Martha—that he discovers the drive and ever after it remained a concept that challenged Freud's entire thought process. As he writes in *Civilization and its Discontents*, his last major work, "To begin with it was only tentatively that I put forward the views I have developed here [that of death drive], but in the course of time they have gained such a hold upon me that I can no longer think in any other way."[24] We see though that Freud does not first encounter the drive in *Beyond the Pleasure Principle*, but that the radicality of the drive first foments in Freud's thought through his encounter with serial fiction. It was a preoccupying notion, for Freud, one that would later be taken up and explored by Jacques Lacan.[25]

Toward a New Vulnerability: The Death Drive and Dickens

Despite understanding that the serial structure offers something new, perhaps even provocative, what Freud and Marx regard as the problem of the serial—this frustrating gap—is fundamental to its very appeal. Seriality causes us to suffer more and because we suffer more, we love it more. It would not be until Freud discovers the death drive that this suffering dynamic would occupy a primary place in his thought but, as with his thoughts on the structure of analysis itself and the etiology of trauma, there is a serial resonance to the concept, one we can see by further playing out the consequences of Freud's encounter with the work of Charles Dickens.

Literary scholars have frequently used Freudian ideas to enrich understandings of Dickens' work.[26] The reason this connection is so potent, as I've suggested from the start, is that the form of Dickens influenced Freud's thinking at an intimate level. One of the most common characteristics of Charles Dickens's fiction—especially in *David Copperfield* and *Bleak House*, two novels Freud wrote extensively about to his wife—is the idea of being born too soon. As is well-known, Dickens's characters are often orphans, abandoned and thrown into an indifferent world. Often with the help of unlikely benefactors and friends, these characters find their way through the world. These are not simply feel-good stories of overcoming obstacles, however. What Dickens foregrounds in his fiction is the existential deadlock of being always already vulnerable. Many of Dickens's major characters, such as the aforementioned David Copperfield, Esther Summerson from *Bleak House*, and someone such as Oliver Twist, are born into the world more fragile than more fortunate peers. It's only through encountering a later vulnerability—one that tears old wounds—that these characters are able to come to some truth, some understanding of themselves or the shape of the world. Dickens's characters always have a complex relationship to the primary negativity that begins the story of their lives.

Freud's death drive is often understood in terms of raw negativity. Freud himself does describe it as a "primary masochism."[27] It is my contention, however, that the death drive needs to be understood as a dialectical and not dualistic concept.[28] The chief task in highlighting the dialectics of the drive is to show how the negativity of something like a primary masochism could be beneficial, say an uplifting antagonism. We see this repeatedly in Dickens. His characters are not simply born too soon or born too vulnerable; they continue to be thrust—and thrust themselves—into situations that they are not ready for. Esther Summerson is not ready to have a relationship with her mother when she meets her and not long after the recognition that her mother lives must she reckon with her mother's death. David Copperfield, when he is born, has to reckon not just with his father's death but in viewing his father David's tombstone, must also reckon with his own finitude, his own space in life between two deaths. The point in Dickens is not a cynical truism such as "life sucks and then you die." Dickens shows that the only way to live is to re-inflict a primary wound into oneself again and again. Esther, for example, keeps pushing herself toward her mother, Lady Dedlock, even though it is wrenching for her. When Lady Dedlock apologizes to Esther, she cries at Esther's feet for abandoning her. Esther narrates her discomfort at having to effectively console a sobbing child. Esther here is thrust into a mothering role while attempting to emotionally reconcile *with* her mother. As Carolyn Dever notes, Esther loses her mother three times throughout the novel and that this repeated loss structures Esther's narrative trajectory/narration in *Bleak House*.[29] This, in a prior narrative form found in Dickens, is the dialectical shape of Freud's death drive.

Undermining oneself into a new vulnerability is the productive masochism of the death drive.[30] A constant re-infliction of a primary wound. The drive is a prior masochism, as in prior to any experience. The compulsion to repeat loss is as consistent a thread in Dickens as it is in Freud. The idea that the finding of an object is always the refinding of it likewise occupies a similar place for both. The drive relentlessly thrusts us into ever newer vulnerabilities. It is through mobilizing this masochism that we are thrust and thrown continually into situations we are not ready for. In a banal way, the drive throws us into jobs we are not ready for, relationships we are not equipped for, thoughts we are not ready to fully explain either to ourselves or to another person. If this is the negativity of life, that Freud associates with the death drive, we cannot fail to note that this kind of dying again and again is the very thing that makes us live. We are always undermining ourselves. Sometimes we undermine ourselves forward. This is a series that plays out through our entire lives.

Completely Incomplete

Filmmaker and film theorist Sergei Eisenstein believed that, with *Bleak House*, Dickens invented cross cutting. He is variously credited (or blamed) with having calcified—if not outright invented—many Christmastime traditions. His literary work is responsible for seizing a moment of material production that led to the formation of a new kind of public. I am also at least halfway suggesting that he may have invented psychoanalysis for Freud to uncover in his fiction. Perhaps this is all too much to credit solely to one person. If I was saying he did these things on purpose and intentionally, then yes, but there is a mixture of Dickens being both incidental and integral to all these discoveries and advancements. His influence and importance surely exceed his intention. It doesn't matter whether we can say for which thing he definitively shepherded into being and for which thing he was merely a famous passenger.

Mass culture begins with seriality, and it begins with the ravenous attention serial novels received—of which Dickens was no small part. The public that calcified around serial fiction did so around ongoing pieces of secular culture, a departure from religious gatherings or the spectacle of things such as the Roman Coliseum. The idea of an audience that followed a work as it was written and published was a new thing. Of course, Shakespeare had a public and an audience at his plays. He even had a public and devoted followers who saved his plays for the rest of us. Dickens and other Victorian Era writers did not invent the idea of an audience. What was invented with the material serial novel was the border breaking down between author, audience, and text in such a way that the trajectory of a text could be altered. Dickens's *The Pickwick Papers* as originally schemed did not devote so much attention on Cockney bootblack Sam Weller. But as so often happens in serially published stories, the effect of the audience overwhelmed the plans of the creator. Audiences loved Sam Weller, and as a result Dickens made him a more important figure to *The Pickwick Papers* than he would otherwise have been.[31] The always already incomplete state of the serial novel opens gaps where previously the novel was a closed shop.

Where the idea of "masses" inevitably conjures either the text emblazoned on the Statue of Liberty or Marxist proletariat-focused political critique, the kind of masses formed by serial texts are different in that they include high, middle, and lower classes and cut across age demographics. There is a diagonal cut across classes when we discuss the mass audiences for Victorian Era literature and for something such as ABC's *Lost*, HBO's *The Sopranos*, NBC's *The Office*, CBS and Paramount's *Yellowstone*, and the like. Obviously, a base level of technological access is required to be an audience member for one of these television shows today; however, the point is that the audiences of Victorian serials and the audiences of television series contain within them the economic contradictions of the moment. If we understand "the masses" as the proletariat, the 99 percent, those groups do not contain as in-members the bourgeoisie, the oppressors. The serial audience—the mass culture audience—does.

This is one way that seriality, as an encompassing existential logic, is meaningfully different from being simply a narrative synecdoche for the production of capitalism. While, as we saw earlier, Marx directly references serial printing in the Preface to the French edition of *Capital Volume 1*, Marx's most significant contribution to a theory of seriality may appear in *Capital Volume 3*. It is there where Marx explains that capitalism requires crisis. There is no "crisis capitalism"; rather, the need for crisis is intrinsic to capitalism as such. Capitalism is not vulnerable to crisis but rather requires it. Popular seriality emerges in response to Marx's dictum: through aesthetic seriality we try to arrest an understanding of the invisible and the intrinsic, the systemic and the structural. Popular seriality is an aesthetic response to existential crisis. As the crises besetting our world proliferate, it is unsurprising that popular seriality has trended toward seeming gaplessness as Chapter 4 will discuss and comment on.

Marx does have an interest in gaps, in the seriality of the commodity. The gaps he's interested in occur in the dashes between *M—C—M'*, which he describes as "A sum of value is cast into circulation in order to extract a greater sum. The process that creates this greater sum of value is capitalist production; the process that realizes it is in the circulation of capital."[32] Surplus value transforms the commodity. Surplus value, for Marx, is not generated by the capitalist selling a commodity for a higher raw number expressed in a dollar value over its material cost, labor cost, and labor time. The capitalist mode of production makes this relationship *appear as though* it is a fact of materiality that surplus value is produced when it is actually produced by the capitalist extracting more in labor than is paid out to the worker(s). There is, however, a psychical relation of disavowal that supports the thesis of surplus value that Marx himself advances. He is aware that, again, surplus value is not created simply by a capitalist buying for a dollar and selling for two; rather, the value is attained by exploiting the labor that led to the labor cost of a dollar. But how can this relation be sustained? Fetishistic disavowal. The Freudian answer is a necessary to buttress to Marx's own theorizing. With fetishistic disavowal, we implicitly adhere to the following logic: "I know very well that X, but even still I don't believe it."[33] We know very well that we are not paid enough for our own labor, that we work too much and too long for too little, but even still, when we buy any product anywhere at any price, we do not believe these immanent and intimate truths about the production and sale of goods and services. Put more simply, there is a gap in every product that should be too volatile to ignore but which, in banal fact, is too horrible to accept. The benefit of accepting it, however, is immediate. Simply put, we get to have the good product at a nice price.

Marx perfectly understands that capitalism succeeds not because the capitalist leverages material cost against labor cost to find a commodity price point that allows for the reproduction of that very same commodity but because capitalism is, fundamentally, a system of social relations whereby the commodity has a relationship between people and the commodity—again, through people—has a relationship with and between other commodities. It's for this reason that the dashes of *M—C—M'* should be thought of as marking social links and not economic transactional movement. The process of mystification that Marx turns to again and again in *Capital vol. 3* occurs between the production and exchange of the commodity and the generation of surplus value. It is through this seemingly secondary exchange that surplus value is extracted. In looking for reasons for why and how this relationship is sustained, Marx finds external answers (e.g., the constant crises of market capitalism). I am arguing the answer is in the commodity itself and its relationship to the psyche of the everyday consumer. The surplus value that underwrites capitalist production produces a gap in every product. This gap is on the surface of our everyday economic interactions. It is too horrible for either the capitalist, say, Tim Cook, to reflect on how cobalt is mined to make iPhones, and too horrible for us on the other end as consumers. (The workers mining cobalt, in this relationship, are much like the workers in many of Marx's examples whose only relationship to the commodities they produce is that they produce them. They do not, crucially, possess them.) Capitalism creates this primary gap that indicts us. The benefit for this indictment? Any number of creature comforts. Marx believed the unsustainability of profit and its need to create and rely upon the proletariat would be its ultimate undoing. The gap between the wealthiest 0.1 percent and the rest of the world increases every day. It is not an exaggeration to say that each new day breaks the previous unofficial membership record for the proletariat. And yet, despite this gulf, it appears as though the grip of the capitalist is stronger than ever. The grip of the mystification of the capitalist is perhaps stronger than ever, as Marx tried to dispel, but this serial relationship, the bad infinite of capital, cannot be interrupted nor will it dissipate until we pay closer attention to the corresponding gap within us and within the commodity. As individuals we disavow the gap and as a collective, we smooth it over, aiding the mystification process required by capital.

The incompleteness in the commodity completes it, stabilizes it. Our own incompleteness is not, crucially, *causal* for capitalism but it does help to make its abuses make intimate sense. This is my point. It is harder to see the seriality of something than it is to engage in and sustain a series. We do this all the time. To interrupt an unthought series requires disturbing ourselves into a new vulnerability, as Dickens shows in his fiction and as Freud shows with the dialectics of the drive.

"Make them laugh, make them cry, make them wait"

As much as Dickens's characters and worlds occupied Freud's thoughts, it is the serial form, its constraints, and its dialectic of closure and disclosure that affected the development of Freud's professional thinking. Most importantly it is the problem of the gap that captured Freud. Variously attributed to Charles Dickens, Wilkie Collins, or Charles Reade, the phrase "Make them laugh, make them cry, make them wait" neatly summarizes the serial writing ethos. The gap is represented here as an active feature of the writing and content itself. It is not simply an absence which readers or viewers fill with paratext engagement, nor is it the incidental design of a publishing schedule. It is alive in the text and it is not reducible to the "live" experience of a serial.[34] The serial writing ethos urges *making* readers wait. The serial publishing schedule forces readers to wait by design but that delay means nothing if the content is not itself gapped in some way.

As we saw in Freud's letters to Martha, it is the gap that he responded to as a reader. As we saw in *Studies on Hysteria*, it is the gap that troubled him as an analyst. Freud understood the virtue of "make them wait" as a reader, as evidenced by his hurry to get to the end of *Daniel Deronda*. He also understood the imposition of the gap for analysis. Understanding the formal necessity and the psychical cut of the serial gap is the connective tissue for many of Freud's most important insights and discoveries (as discussed above). The gap is the decisive element in seriality. It is the condition of possibility for repetition and iteration, which narrative seriality is premised upon. Gaps, as we saw in the example of Freud's patient named Emma, allow for the retroactive articulation of meaning. Gaps haul us back, force us to repeat or rehearse. They undermine us forward.

Repetition, central to the serial form, has been a constant source of inquiry for Freud. Indeed, psychoanalysis—from the very beginning—has been deeply invested in thinking through the consequences of seriality, as we have seen through references to both personal and professional writings of Freud's. Through positing a serial starting point for his thinking of the psychoanalytic project, we can see how understanding such core psychoanalytic notions as *Nachträglichkeit*, the unconscious, repetition, and death drive require a theoretical consideration of seriality as a gapped logic.

Psychoanalysis, at bottom, is a retroactive investigation of the psyche. What psychoanalysis effects, with its discrete sessions, is the exact form of a serial, in this respect. On the one hand these sessions are discrete and self-contained but on the other they are connected via the gap that both separates and binds them. This is both the problem of the structure of analysis that Freud considers in *Studies on Hysteria* and a problem in the content of sessions themselves. As Freud notes in *Beyond the Pleasure Principle*, "Patients repeat ... unwanted situations and painful emotions in the transference and revive them with the greatest ingenuity. They seek to bring about the interruption of the treatment while it is still incomplete."[35] In 1895's *Studies on Hysteria*, Freud notes that sessions end too soon, always in the middle of the analysand recalling or thinking through something. This creates a gap in the session itself, a gap of unresolved content. This lack of resolution causes the analysand to suffer more as they cannot rid themselves of what has been left unsaid. In 1920's *Beyond the Pleasure Principle*, Freud is moved to observe that this meta-structure to the scheduling of psychoanalysis is active in the individual sessions themselves, where patients "seek to bring about the interruption of the treatment while it is still incomplete."[36] This self-sabotaging action is, as Freud understands, the work of the drive and its compulsion to undermine and repeat. The drive, being the motor of the unconscious as Freud discovers, ingrains repetition into our psychic functioning. The unconscious is structured on a repetition that does not progress—like the patients Freud observes in *Beyond the Pleasure Principle*—but nonetheless moves forward, recalling the Library of Congress's definition of seriality—a publication expected to continue indefinitely. Theorizing the serial gap, and its influence on psychoanalysis, is to fully consider the mind as understood by psychoanalysis. While not every psychoanalytic concept can be understood with recourse to seriality, the core of how psychoanalysis understands the subject and the function of analysis itself is deeply rooted in the logic of seriality.

Theorizing the serial gap entails nothing less than understanding the gapped nature of the psyche itself. The closer we examine seriality, the more we find it in psychoanalysis. The development of psychoanalysis is often discussed alongside the development of film, as both emerge in 1895. It is arguable that the serial form of media deserves similar pride of place. Freud is born twenty years after the birth of the literary serial's invention in 1836, when Charles Dickens publishes *The Pickwick Papers*. It is in this period of serial media's movement from the literary to the filmic that the serial appears in Freud's thought, both in the *Project for a Scientific Psychology* and in *Studies on Hysteria*. On the latter text, Lacan called *Studies on Hysteria* "... one long account of the discovery of the analytic technique."[37] As I have argued in this chapter, an overlooked but crucial aspect to this account is Freud's recourse to seriality as a way of explaining analysis. Freud's analytic technique evinces an understanding of seriality—an understanding that emphasizes the confrontational effect interruptive closure has on the psyche. Freud's work then begins to establish what I call psychoanalytic seriality. Where it is easier to see continuity in a series, we need to emphasize the radicality of the traumatic gap. In fact, seeing absence where it is easier to see presence would perhaps be the most radical thing of all.

Toward the end of his life, Freud writes, "Space may be the projection of the extension of the psychical apparatus. No other derivation is probable. Instead of Kant's *a priori* determinants of our psychical apparatus. Psyche is extended; knows nothing about it."[38] This beguiling note, left teasingly undeveloped but collected for posterity in a section of *The Standard Edition* just called "Shorter Writings," helps bring us back to the beginning of our enquiry. Freud seems to be observing that psychical space is prior to our apprehension of it. What is more, it is no mere blank form but one marked, punctuated. This is the psychic cement of the everyday. A series of gaps extended out from us. We may think we are walking on new ground but are instead treading on the extended psyche already in front of us. The finding of an object is, of course, always the refinding of it.

2

Lacan, Relation, and the Serial Symbolic

It should not surprise us that seriality first became theorized as a notion knotting together the social and the subject by thinkers such as Freud and Marx. After the widespread popularity of the serial novel took hold of the nineteenth century, seeing the subject and the social as concretized in the materiality of the serial was evident. Moving from the Victorian Era to the early twentieth century, the influence of the serial novel form waned and thus its participation in shaping a public also changed. Writers such as James Joyce, Virginia Woolf, and William Faulkner pioneered changes in the novel that made it more experimental, more demanding, and—crucially—left the gapped serial form behind.

However, the serial form itself would linger in pulp comics and radio and film serials. Where the novel form would remain something that evolved chiefly in print, the serial form would spread across technological innovations in visual and aural media. A later chapter will take an extended look at early film serials and how their popularity paved the way for the current fascination with something like the Marvel Cinematic Universe today. For now, it will suffice to say that while the serial form was present through a variety of emerging mass media technologies, it would not be considered a driving feature *of* any technology until the emergence of television. While film serials were quite popular with early film audiences, the feature film would gradually become the center of film media—especially after the development of synchronous sound. Likewise, while serial radio dramas such as *The Shadow* and *The Lone Ranger* were popular from the 1930s into the 1950s, the radio also offered news, music, and self-contained radio dramas such as Orson Welles's famous retelling of *The War of the Worlds*. With the advent of and wide availability of the television after the Second World War, seriality again took hold of an emerging mass technology.

In the 1950s and 1960s seriality was again "in the air," fomenting a new mass public domain through the television. Soap operas and serial melodramas migrated from the radio to dominate television—this new mass serial object. Like radio, television was and is an intimate technology. Like a fireplace, radios and televisions took the literal center of living spaces. While the trajectory of radio was to become smaller—to the point now where it is an effectively invisible supplemental feature of smartphones—televisions commanded attention both as object and as content. Both in terms of raw numbers and its location as nexus point of discourse, we can see television occupying the same space that the print serial did in the Victorian era. By 1960, 90 percent of American households had at least one television.[1] Further enhancing television's gravity, as Lynn Spigel puts it, "magazines, advertisements, newspapers, radio, film, and television itself spoke in seemingly endless ways about television's status as domestic entertainment."[2]

This period of material change for the serial would once again occasion the advancement of new approaches to understanding seriality as a tension between and within the social and the subject. Through a shared interest in understanding what I call the seriality of everyday life, Jacques Lacan, Jean-Paul Sartre, Jacques Derrida, and Gilles Deleuze each offered a way to understand the serial as a psychical, social, or material phenomenon. Each theoretical intervention into seriality for each of these thinkers is, in some significant way, in conflict with each other. Rather than trying to wrangle a so-called common ground—which would require subordinating one thinker's thought to another at points of impasse—this chapter will insist on this conflict as an inflection point. Why? The conflict in these differing ways of understanding seriality helps to clarify what is at stake for each thinker, both in works that grapple with trying to understand the series as a wide category of repetition and/or in works that have little to do with any notion of seriality.

Chiefly, what this chapter will do is engage Jacques Lacan as a way of staging this theoretical conversation. As opposed to Sartre,

Derrida, and Deleuze, Lacan's approach to seriality includes both the social and the psyche and it offers the possibility for radical action. Like Freud, Lacan does not explicitly develop a theory of seriality. However, also like Freud, Lacan leaves crumbs and sprinkles. What's more, across his writings and the series of lectures he gave as seminars, Lacan creates an understanding of seriality even when he is discussing something else (e.g., ego psychology, psychosis, or Edgar Allan Poe). In this way he reverses the dynamic whereby inquiry into seriality typically ends up developing an understanding of something else. In this reading of Lacan, his talking about "something else" develops an understanding of seriality. To return to the above metaphor, this chapter will work with and against the theories of Sartre, Derrida, and Deleuze to turn Lacan's crumbs and sprinkles into a donut (preserving the hole in the whole). The following chapter will take the framework we can excavate from Lacan's thought and proffer a new argument for the "quilting point," a concept Lacan mentions briefly in his seminar on *The Psychoses* and then scarcely mentions again for the rest of his career.

At times, Lacan, Sartre, Derrida, and Deleuze will use the terms serial, series, and seriality in ways that make them seem like interchangeable terms. In some cases, each term can act as the big umbrella term for either of the other two. Simply put, tracing how others have theorized seriality can produce a seeming equivocation in terminology. To attempt to stay some of this potential confusion, I write here, plainly, what it is that I mean by these terms and what I am trying to argue and support:

> Seriality is an internal order that emerges against conscious intention in a series.
> Not every series has seriality.
> Seriality is a logic opposed to a series of infinite particularity, the shampoo aisle of small differences.
> Seriality is on the side of universality, the radical transformation of the existing order.
> The universal is the element in a series that changes irrevocably the relation between parts.
> We have agency in seriality. We are not mere observers of series we perpetuate and participate in but ultimately have no purchase on.

This chapter will lay crucial groundwork for these arguments that will develop more gradually as the book unfolds.

The Real Structure of Chance

Freud introduces two ideas that are foundational for how I theorize seriality: (1) The idea that trauma is intrinsic to a series and (2) that interruptive closure causes suffering. In the 1950s, the French psychoanalyst Jacques Lacan furthers Freud's insights by putting the logic of the traumatic serial at the center of his own notion of the symbolic order. By integrating Freud's understanding of trauma into his conception of the symbolic order, Lacan brings together two seemingly disparate appearances of seriality in Freud's thought. Lacan offers us an opportunity to see how order and meaning emerge in a series. In *Seminar II*, Lacan shows how order emerges even in a series of chance relations. In *Seminar III*, with his idea of the quilting point, he shows how meaning emerges to structure our understanding of a given series. These ideas will return again in the book and help to ground our inquiry moving forward.

Reckoning with the structural function of punctuated absence is necessary to understand the serial life of the gap. To theorize seriality means we must recognize the holes that sustain the seeming whole. Lacan helps us see how seriality is operative in the foundation of the function of the signifier. It is embedded in the structure of how meaning arises in language. Seriality creates the confrontation with contradiction in signification, rather than hiding it.

Whereas Freud implicitly draws from his ardent love of serial fiction to think through foundational elements to psychoanalysis, Jacques Lacan begins his own implicit intervention into seriality through the work of an author who hated the literary serial. In fact, the first line of Poe's 1846 essay "The Philosophy of Composition" name checks and lightly castigates Charles Dickens.[3] In that essay, Poe argues that the form of serial storytelling, of which even by 1846 Dickens was the major proponent of, has two major problems: it is not brief, and it is not complete. Indeed, in lacking both brevity and totality, Poe believed that—from a structural standpoint—serial storytelling was a lacking form when compared to the short story. Poe believed all successful literary works must be able to be read in one sitting. Why? Because even a second sitting means the spell of the fiction is broken and "the affairs of the world intervene" (as a contemporary idea, this perhaps makes sense of the appeal of binge-watching longform television).[4] Poe is also radically against the idea of the "To Be Continued," the cliffhanger (a term not yet invented when Poe is writing). He believes that any installment of a fictional work should be whole and complete. To leave a story in a suspended state is to hurt the hold of the fictive world over the reader. For that reason, successful fiction must be brief and must contain everything in it that a reader needs to know. Poe's formula is perhaps most useful for understanding the construction of self-contained episodic fiction, as he is radically against seriality.

For Lacan's purposes, though he does not make this connection, Poe stands out as a theorist of punctuation and how punctuation affects and effects the subject. Broadly speaking, *Seminar II* continues the critique of Ego Psychology that Lacan began in *Seminar I* and lays out Lacan's developing notion of the symbolic order and how signification has a determinative effect on the ways in which subjects act and on what they can or cannot do. To explain his idea, Lacan turns to the fiction of Poe. In "The Purloined Letter" Detective Auguste Dupin is tasked with recovering a sensitive private correspondence between the Queen and a figure of whom her relations she wishes to remain hidden from both her husband and the wider public. Minister D—, an unscrupulous political figure, has taken possession of the letter and is discreetly blackmailing her. The Queen asked the police for their discreet help in recovering the letter. The police, however, are (indiscreetly) stumped. They have turned D—'s house upside down and not been able to procure the purloined letter. Dupin manages to find the letter seemingly without trouble and explains his method to the police, who are baffled at what he has been able to accomplish. The short version is that Dupin realized that D— would know the police would search his home so he hid the letter in plain sight. The long version of how Dupin knew this involves Dupin recounting how an eight-year-old boy made a fortune predicting results in a game of "Odds and Evens." For Lacan, this is the key to understanding the symbolic. Dupin, Lacan argues, knows how to read his opponent—the corrupt Minister—just like how the eight-year-old boy knew whether his opponent would put an odd or even number of fingers behind his back in the children's game. The symbolic is not formed through a series of intersubjective exchanges. It does not emerge through a collision of intersubjective situations. It is an alien order formed before we enter into it and develops further as we are a part of it. How does this occur? Lacan answers through exploring the internal logic and rules that emerge through a series of coin tosses.

While the result of each individual toss of the coin is itself arbitrary, if we *group* coin tosses together, certain groupings become impossible. Lacan stages his intervention in the realm of chance to push back on the core Saussurean idea that the relation between signifier and signified itself is arbitrary. If we can observe a signifying and structuring order even in the realm of chance, Lacan wagers, then we can start to "see" the symbolic, which otherwise is akin to trying to "see" the air. Lacan is saying that while the factor of chance does not on its own eliminate symbolic necessity because it is serially structured, the symbolic order takes up chance events and inscribes them in a system of necessity. This necessity enables us to see the way in which the symbolic does not just determine what is possible but also enables points of impossibilities—the real—to emerge.

In Lacan's example, + and – stand in for heads and tails. Through this he generates a rudimentary "language" and "chain of signifiers." Paying attention to Lacan's method explicated in the "Odd or even" lecture, Bruce Fink's *The Lacanian Subject* offers the following instructive chain:

1 2 3 4 5 6 7 8 9 Toss Numbers
+ + – – + – – – + Heads/Tails Chain

There is, obviously, a 50/50 chance that an unloaded coin will flip either heads or tails on each and every toss. Lacan's point is that, when subjected to signification and serial sequence, what seems to be arbitrary and random is ordered by rules that emerge from the gaps in the serial sequence itself. Such an order can be seen when grouping the tosses. For example, grouping tosses in pair combinations gives us four possible pairs: ++, – –, + –, and – +. Fink designates pair + + as 1, "the first level of coding we are going to introduce, and it marks the origin of the symbolic system we are creating."[5] The two alternating combinations of + – and – + are given the number 2 and the tails-tails (– –) pair is given the designation 3. These numeric designations form a signification matrix that changes random coin tosses into a system with memory and order. As Fink shows:

+ + – – + – – – + Heads/ Tails Chain
1 2 3 2 2 3 3 2 Numeric Matrix Category

Reading this random set of coin tosses in terms of pairs already produces the kinds of memory and order that Lacan's notion of the serial is premised on. A category 1 series (++) cannot be followed by a category 3 (– –), it can only be followed by a category 2 series of + –. As Fink explains, "We have thus already come up with *a way of grouping tosses* (a 'symbolic matrix') *which prohibits certain combinations* … We have generated *an impossibility in our signifying chain*, even though we have not determined the outcome of any particular toss."[6] There is no exception to the rule that this string of chance relations demonstrates. Playing the string out with more tosses shows that "the chain prohibits the appearance of a second 1 until an even number of 2s has turned up."[7] This prohibition is Lacan's justification for his claim that the signifying chain "remembers or keeps track of its previous components."[8]

Fink is helpful for understanding how Lacan thinks through chance relations in his symbolic system; however, I want to push an aspect of Lacan that does not appear in Fink's account: the real. Perhaps it is for reasons of clarity and pedagogy that Fink's working through of "Odd or even" appears as a theory of continuity and on this we cannot fault Fink. But understanding seriality as a material phenomenon coextensive with the psyche's experience of the world requires attention paid to the traumatic gap. Emphasizing the structural function of the real in Lacan's understanding of how series form shows us that, in seriality, there is always a gap: a publication gap between serial installments, a temporal gap between analytic sessions. The rules that order the chance relation between coin flips emerge in the gaps between them. The presence of a gap is immanent and inerasable in the serial and, for Lacan, the serial gap is a site to observe the inextricable relation between the symbolic and the real.

While the above is sourced from early Lacan seminars, it cannot be overstated how central seriality and its relation to the symbolic are to Lacan's entire theoretical system throughout his public lectures. Lacan will never focus on the serial the way he does in *Seminar II*, yet he never completely abandons this way of thinking. Six years later, in "The Subversion of the Subject and the Dialectic of Desire in the Freudian Unconscious," Lacan writes,

> what is omitted in the platitude of modern information theory is the fact that one cannot even speak of a code without it already being the Other's code; something quite different is at stake in the message, since the subject constitutes himself on the basis of the message, such that he receives from the Other even the message he himself sends.[9]

Again, Lacan is clarifying that what is at stake in psychoanalysis is something that looks beyond the bare fact of an intersubjective exchange where one might "read" the code(s) exchanged between themselves and another person. Neither the analyst nor the psychoanalytic theorist can occupy the position of the boy who guesses correctly the game of Odds or Evens. What is at stake is a message (a letter, let's say) exchanged where the meaning is determined by the punctuation of who receives it. Just like how the actually stolen letter in "The Purloined Letter" means something different to each person who has it—to the Queen it is a love letter, to the unscrupulous minister it is blackmail, to the police it is an index of their failure, to Dupin it doubles as certification of his expertise as a detective to both the minister *and* the police, despite the content of the letter itself never once being revealed nor being directly relevant to any party other than the Queen—the signifier is always already other, social, and serial. What is not at stake in "The Purloined Letter" is properly understanding the content of the letter itself. The content is irrelevant. What matters is the form the letter takes, and that form takes shape in negotiation with the other.

Twelve years later, Lacan explicitly links his overarching theoretical project to the serial in *Seminar XX*. In the "To Jakobson" lecture, Lacan reminds his audience that structural linguistics took root around the idea that the relationship between signifier and signified was arbitrary. Lacan rejects the arbitrariness of the signifier saying that if the meaning effected by signifier and signified "seem[s] to bear no relation to what causes them, that is because we expect what causes them to bear a certain relation to the real. I'm talking about the serious real. The serious—one must of course make an effort to notice it, one must have come to my seminars now and then—can only be the serial."[10] Again, the relation between signifier and signified is not arbitrary, as the signifier "smoke" is to actual smoke. Nor is it indexical, as "smoke" is to fire, but as smoke is to a *smoker*. The first two examples have nothing to do with a series. This is the important point. Just as trauma arises in a series so too does signification. To use Lacan's terms, "smoke" to actual smoke and "smoke" to fire do not form a series and, thus, are not "serious." What is serious is our third example: smoke to smoker. This is not an arbitrary relation between signs and objects in the world; nor is it an existential relation, which implies continuity and contact; rather it introduces a more radical alterity and an interruption.[11] In the examples of smoke and fire, there is continuity but there can be no "smoker." In smoke and smoker, we see the *discontinuity* that the serial privileges. The only way the smoke and smoker are related as signifier and signified is through a repetition that creates a new rule for signification, forging a serial symbolic relation through the gap.

Crucially this rule can only be registered retroactively. Reading back from *Seminar XX* to "Odd or even?" in *Seminar II*, we see the role of the real in the serial relation clarified. The real allows for the emergence of the new. It is an impasse of formalization that curves the symbolic around it. To bring into conversation the early Lacan of *Seminar II* and the late Lacan of *Seminar XX* is to see fully how his theory of seriality is central to his thinking in general. We can further explain Lacan's idea by way of a pop culture example: between books three and four of George R. R. Martin's *A Song of Ice and Fire* book series (popularly translated to television by HBO as *Game of Thrones*), Martin wanted to advance the plot by four or five years to age some of his characters. Martin quickly realized that this was not something he could do. He had set far too much in narrative motion to claim that certain key characters and storylines would remain in relative stasis for multiple years. The end of book five required Martin to put several characters in the same place, a port town named Meereen. The problem of getting all these different characters from all different corners of Martin's vast fictional world to *all* be in the same place at same time came to be called by Martin "The Meereenese Knot."[12] This knot would take Martin years to untangle and require him to write three separate versions of events to see which was the right answer. While this may, on first glance, appear to be a teleology—a succession of the signifier—it is only possible to apprehend this relation retroactively. As Lacan says in "Odd or even?," "It's not what happens afterwards which is modified but everything which went before. We have a retroactive effect—*nachträglich*, as Freud calls it—specific to the structure of symbolic memory, in other words to the function of remembering."[13] With the "Meereenese Knot" Martin experienced a traumatic confrontation with seriality, an encounter with the symbolic order.

In the Martin example, there is a collision between the actual process of writing a literary serial and what I am developing as a theory of seriality. Just because one writes a series of books does not mean that series of books has seriality in it. When Martin was confronted by the limits and constraints of rules that emerged against his conscious intention, he arrived at the cliffs of seriality. Reaching the end of a path he believed written of his own design, Martin butted up against how the signifying chain "knew" what he did not. Martin here is demonstrably not the subject-supposed-to-know. The point here is instructive of a psychoanalytically informed notion of seriality: the process of segmenting a long-form story (i.e., writing serially) creates rules that one must abide by as though serial storytelling itself is creating rules, not the author. In this specific example, limit emerges to other the subject and determines what it can or cannot do. Just as a category 3 coin toss cannot follow a category 1, one does not author the relation that emerges through the chain of symbolic signification. The curve of the real in a series does this. As Dr. Yakov Smirnoff might say, in seriality, *book writes you!*

Derridean Frames on a Lacanian Picture

Lacan enables us to see how seriality—a logic of impossible connection and causality—forms out of a bare series. To fully understand the significance of this idea, it helps to pit Lacan's position against engaged interlocutors who would disagree with him. Building a notion of seriality on the side of the traumatic gap, of the real, as Lacan's work points us toward, is hardly a dominant theoretical position. The more popular approach has been to see in seriality an oppression of succession, an unrelenting continuity. It is from this position that Derrida and Sartre proffer notions of seriality and solutions to the oppressive logic it inheres. John P. Muller and William J. Richardson, in setting up Lacan's "Purloined Letter" seminar in *The Purloined Poe*, read his argument with a distinctly Derridean inflection. In summarizing Lacan's "Odd or evens?" lecture, they write, "the thrust of the argument remains ... that the symbolic order determines the subject according to laws that govern a finite number of possibilities, even for what appear to be matters of 'chance.'"[14] What Muller and Richardson have done is invert Lacan's argument: where Lacan shows the impossible irruption of order in chance relations, Muller and Richardson see the impossibility of rupture—that Lacan has structurally eliminated the possibility of chance or a way out of the "domination" of signification. This understanding of Lacan's symbolic as a system of "domination," while incorrect, is at the heart of Derrida's response to the notion of seriality we can extract from Lacan's work. (The idea of seriality as a being a part of a system of domination appears in Sartre as well.)

Derrida, in "The Purveyor of Truth," takes aim at Lacan's reading of "The Purloined Letter" and psychoanalysis in general. Specifically, Derrida finds issue with Lacan's famous conclusion that "a letter always reaches its destination."[15] At the root of Derrida's critique is that Lacan at no point troubles the position of the narrator in "The Purloined Letter," despite speaking at length on the positions of the Queen, D—, and Dupin.[16] He also accuses Lacan of turning signifier—the letter—into signified—"the recounted object of the short story."[17] Derrida's point of departure is that Lacan "treats ... only the content of this story ... Not the narration itself."[18] Nor the short story's form. Derrida also argues that Lacan finds nothing more profound or complicated than what Marie Bonaparte did in her 1933 psychobiographical reading of "The Purloined Letter."[19] Indeed, this becomes Derrida's critique of psychoanalysis *as such*: it is a form that only finds itself. It is only in a structure or philosophical framework such as this that anyone could say, "The letter always reaches its destination."

Derrida is correct to say that Lacan does not undergo a formal analysis of "The Purloined Letter." This is because, as we saw above, the "Odds or even?" lecture does the formal heavy lifting for Lacan. In the effort of fairness, it is unclear if Derrida was familiar with the *Seminar II* version of "The Purloined Letter" lecture. As Muller and Richardson recount, Derrida familiarized himself with the *Ecrits* version of the lecture, which does not include the material covered above from "Odd or even?"[20] Still, in the post-script to the Seminar as collected in the *Ecrits*, Lacan works through some of the coin flip logic, though more obtusely. (Tellingly, Derrida references nothing from the post-script in "The Purveyor of Truth.") Regardless, Derrida's point is that the frame of psychoanalysis finds only itself. For Derrida, the analytic session is an unjustified and untheorized box that only labors to find its own previously agreed-upon conclusions. In the same way that Lacan does not trouble the narration of "The Purloined Letter," Derrida claims, so too does psychoanalysis not trouble its own formation.

Derrida does not comment on Lacan's discussion of chance relations, but it is easy to see what his objection would be. Derrida would argue that Lacan says he's looking at pure chance but chooses as his example something with an internal order to then find internal order. In other words, a coin is already internally ordered by having two sides. The accusation would follow, then, that finding an order of coin flips afterwards is not that big of a deal. Of course, there will be an order—there can only be two possibilities of a coin flip.

The problem with this Derrida-style objection is that it ignores that to even comment on this problem we are using language—which has an order to it. So, for Derrida to argue that language is inherently incomplete (as he does throughout his career), he needs language to signify for his purposes. In other words, to say that language can never reach full symbolization we need full *enough* symbolization to make the claim. Further, this ignores Lacan's discovery. Lacan's point is not that he has found a way to arrest true randomness by the way he talks about coin tosses but that true randomness does not exist. "The letter always arrives at its address" does not mean language or the symbolic order is predetermined but rather that an order is established coextensive with our existence in the signifying chain. We can't know the order of the flips ahead of time. Even still we know beyond doubt that an internal order unique to the coin flips will emerge. Despite not knowing ahead of time what the flips will be an order will still emerge that groups them. It is because this order has to do with the unconscious, which is relational rather than logical dimension that Derrida would rather dismiss (or disavow).

Attempting to Escape the Serial Symbolic

Had Derrida read "Odd or even?" or interrogated the postscript to "The Seminar on *The Purloined Letter*," would he be entitled to claim that, again, Lacan has limited the frame of his inquiry (e.g., to a binary flip of heads or tails) which *again* determines what he finds? Yes. He'd likely see in coin flips an arbitrary limit that leads to Lacan's eventual conclusion, forcing "design into destiny" as he summarizes Lacan's method at the end of "The Purveyor of Truth." Clearly, Derrida would see a *telos* in Lacan's argument, just as he wrote in *Dissemination*.[21] But it's here that the radicality of Lacan's serial thinking emerges. His entire point is that radical break can burst through any structure and that the shape of that break is relative to the terms of the frame—any frame. What Derrida introduces is a gesture of infinite difference toward signification. If Lacan is guilty of finding what his frame predetermines then, according to the shape of Derrida's argument in "The Purveyor of Truth," Derrida is guilty of the same. For Derrida there is no frame for signification. It slides. There can be no reliable fixed points that determine meaning, only variable positions one can take up relative to a kind of meaning that is variable and differential.

Accordingly, "The Purveyor of Truth" ends with a syntactic sleight of hand: a final paragraph bracketed by quotation marks, seeming to be a quotation with quotations within it, with no clear sign of who or what is being quoted.[22] Derrida wants us to wonder who the speaker is. Just as Derrida claims there are "invisible quotation marks" that frame Poe's story, Derrida puts literal quotation marks over the voices of Poe, Lacan, and, presumably, himself. So, who is speaking? Derrida wants to make this an open question, even though it is simply him organizing the entire paragraph and thus becoming the coordinating point of meaning for Poe, Lacan, and himself. Again, if Lacan can be found guilty of finding only what his frame designates, then Derrida is guilty of the findings of *no frame*.

No frame, however, is still a frame—a structuring metaphor—which allows Derrida to think the multiple, the infinitely possible. What Lacan enables through theorizing seriality is thinking the impossible way that the symbolic takes shape. Possibly still thinking of "The Purloined Letter" in *Seminar III*, Lacan says, "The signifier doesn't just provide an envelope, a receptacle for meaning. It polarizes it, structures it, and brings it into existence."[23] One *specific meaning* is never "full" and predestined to arrive for Lacan. Despite this, meaning will *always* arrive. This is something Derrida completely misses about Lacan. "Full speech" is not a point where meaning becomes absolute and immanent as positive categories—in other words, where the "fullness" of meaning accumulates through a succession of speech acts that increase as water from a faucet fills up a jug. Full speech is a concept of lack, lacunae. It is a moment where we see not how we speak but how we are spoken, how we are subjects of the unconscious in that we are subjected *to it*.

Observing a series of coin tosses allows for groups, order, and rules to emerge as though they constitute natural laws (noting the corollary to how he describes the symbolic, imaginary, and real emerging at once as an apparent whole). "It isn't a game for the subtlest," Lacan says; "it isn't a psychological game, it is a dialectical game."[24] For Lacan, dialectical meaning arises through a gap—an impossible hole in the symbolic that curves signification around it. All of this is achieved and only thinkable through Lacan's "limiting" frame of coin tosses which we see in "Odd or even?" Lacan is adamant that form arises through the signifying chain itself, as form is an internally manifesting object. Where Derrida sees pure difference, Lacan sees the emergence of form. Through a series of coin tosses Lacan demonstrates not just possible results but impossible results.

As Lacan shows, a series forms with its own memory and internal order seemingly out of nothing. Contra Derrida, the memory and internal order of a series will be precisely what Gilles Deleuze takes seriously and attempts to designate an escape from in the pages of *The Logic of Sense*. Rather than fighting to unsettle the notion's foundations as Derrida does, it is fair to say that Deleuze accepts the premise of Lacan's symbolic order. However, Deleuze accepts Lacan's premise only to a point. Instead of being the name for a web of impossible congruity undergirding everyday exchanges and relations as it is for Lacan, for Deleuze the symbolic is a trap to be escaped. Taking the symbolic order seriously, however, was a consistent concern throughout Deleuze's writings. (Speaking euphemistically, we might say Deleuze agreed to a mail a letter from Lacan's house but would not agree with him on the letter's final destination.)

Understood this way, we can see that several of the defining ideas of Deleuze's career are attempts to escape how the symbolic arises as a series. Indeed, in several of his most enduring texts, we can see a throughline that attempts to exceed the rules governing the symbolic as a serially constitutive order: the novelty injected into the repetitive series in *Logic of Sense*, the pure difference that Deleuze articulates arising through and against repetition in *Difference and Repetition*, the body without organs that escapes the internal order of its own anatomy in *Anti-Oedipus*, the anyplace-wherever of *Cinema*. Deleuze's project of seriality, expressed in *Logic of Sense*, is purposed with finding a way to inject novelty into the series or find novelty within it as a means of resisting staid and stuck signification. Deleuze is intriguing here because, similar to Lacan, he sees the series as generative of that which transcends. For Lacan, however, that which exceeds the series—its impossibility—is also its condition of possibility. Contra Lacan, Deleuze is looking for a space that disturbs a series of signification without falling into signification itself.[25]

Possibly anticipating the "anyplace-wherever" of Deleuze's *Cinema* books, Deleuze writes of a paradoxical entity that is split, "Its excess always refers to its own lack, and conversely, its lack always refers to its excess ... For that which is in excess in one case is nothing but an extremely mobile *empty place*; and that which is lack in another case is a rapidly moving object, an *occupant without a place* always supernumerary and displaced."[26] Like a baker rolling, flattening, and fanning out dough, Deleuze is interested in stretching the terrain of signification to find spaces the signifying chain itself cannot account for. Again, this neatly splits the difference between Derrida and Lacan: it is similar to Derrida in that it endeavors toward a plurality of fleetingly stable significations, but it is rooted in how Lacan understands the signifier. As Lacan concludes the "Odd or even?" lecture of *Seminar II*, "signification as such is never where one thinks it must be."[27] What Lacan means is that the subject cannot and does not have a one-to-one relationship with the signifier. With the signifier, Lacan expresses a view of subjectivity as a chained relation. What's signified through this chained relation is *something else*—not a sum of its relational parts.

While for Lacan the signifying chain produces what cannot be held within it—due to the gaps between parts, the unconscious spilling across a metonymic relation—for Deleuze, the signifying chain produces an order that must be subverted. For Lacan, the signifying chain is its own subversion. For Deleuze, it is imperative to remove this kind of apparent agency from the side of the signifier. In short, Deleuze wants to signify; he does not want to be signified. For example, Deleuze refers to Samuel Beckett's novel *Watt* as "the great serial novel."[28] Now, Deleuze is aware that Beckett did not publish *Watt* in parts over a yearlong period as Dickens and other nineteenth-century novelists did with their novels. In calling *Watt* "the great serial novel," he is refusing to adhere to the commonplace standard by which serial novels are identified. Deleuze is uninterested in how something was published. That doesn't make something serial to Deleuze. That word—serial—is too meaningful and should not be used to refer to the segmented release schedule of how a fictional work came to be. Rather *Watt*, in its narrative form, presents an "exhaustive" and "exhausting" series of tumbling associations and movement.[29] It is serial in the sense that Beckett generates constant resistance to predictability and stability. Deleuze's concept of seriality is premised on generating this precise kind of constant novelty—a simultaneously excessive and lacking paradoxical entity that disturbs signification. For Deleuze, to nail down an example of pure novelty in a series would undermine the entire idea. Rather, he works to designate a process by which novelty escapes predictive signification (which is what is at stake in the *Watt* reference).

However, while Deleuze's seriality of shambling novelty may be intended with resisting the idea of the quilting point, it does not escape what Lacan discovers. A Lacanian argument contra Deleuze's position would hold that even in a series of pure novelty or across examples of pure novelty within disparate series, there would still be patterns, unexpected continuity, and repetition. As every child who grows up in a cold weather climate learns, no two snowflakes are exactly alike. For Deleuze's purposes, it would be entirely legitimate at first glance to refer to this as a series of pure novelty. We avoid the Derridean objection to Lacan's coin tosses (e.g., it's an unnatural series with built-in order) and observe something that occurs outside of human intervention and the signification of the symbolic order. And yet, even in this purely random naturally occurring series, there are still repeating patterns from which the difference between snowflakes arises. What's more, snowflakes are effectively "geo-tagged" in that one can tell where a snowflake fell due to the minerals and particulate matter internal to it. The same is true of clouds. Further, snowflakes are a perfect example of how pure difference becomes everyday and banal. Put plainly, everybody knows every snowflake is unique and no one really cares. The shock of the new can get very old.

The Sartrean Series

Even though his account of seriality appears in the relatively unexamined *Critique of Dialectical Reason*, Sartre articulates what has become common sense: seriality is just an aggregate of particulars and thus complicit in capitalist ideology. As opposed to Deleuze's more idiosyncratic terminology, for Sartre, seriality can only be a superficial grouping. Sartre believes seriality is only embedded in capitalist logic and, thereby, has little connection to the constitution of the self as subject. Testifying to the staying power of Sartre's argument, Alain Badiou writes in his recent *The Immanence of Truths*, "Serial existence [...] is the subjectivated process of repetition in the field of dominant capitalism."[30] It is my insistence that understanding "serial existence," as Badiou phrases it, requires a theory of seriality untethered to capitalism for external support. Seriality is a category more encompassing than a consideration of relations in and under capitalism. It is intrinsic to being as such. Lacan's work points us in the direction to understand this as he breaks fundamentally with Sartre on this point. Through the very aspect that Sartre criticizes—the gap between the parts—we can grasp in Lacan's work a way of understanding seriality as a curvature around something. Operating in a manner similar to his own notion of the real, Lacan finds that the series is never predetermined before it occurs. The only thing that we *can* know in advance of the formation of a series is that an order *will* emerge in any given series. Any series of chance or random relations produces an order, possibilities, impossibilities, and structure.

This is where Sartre and Lacan can be brought to bear on theory of seriality that is bound to psychoanalysis and bound to the psyche as form. Because seriality includes in it a necessary structural interruption—the gap constitutive of its own construction—a theory of seriality lays bare the relationship between the ideological social order and the point of the real (where ideological order loses its hegemony). The break is not arbitrary or coerced but structurally necessary. Seriality reveals that an order of chance operations or connected narrative installments must include within itself points of its own suspension, precisely the points that psychoanalysis makes its central concern.

For Lacan, as I have said, the serial is aligned with real, the impossible hole in the symbolic. Seriality makes graphic and thinkable the point of nonarticulation in the symbolic. Since rules emerge to form a series, as Lacan explains in his seminar on "The Purloined Letter," we can see the effect of the real in the way the signifying chain curves to accommodate the rules that the series introduces. Seriality, then, has no preexisting character. Seriality constitutes itself as the series forms.

Sartre, by contrast, articulates his theory of seriality as that which separates people politically into artificially arranged groups. It is the name of the thing that keeps people from organizing as a collective. Sartre's seriality needs to be thought of as a "series" of *individuals* grouped by capital and given superficial reasons to relate to each other. Sartre's most famous example of seriality—people in a queue waiting for a bus—shows "the intensity of isolation, as a relation of exteriority between the members of a temporary and contingent gathering, express[ing] *the degree of massification* of the social ensemble, in so far as it is produced on the basis of given conditions."[31] Rather than becoming a collective—or "group-in-fusion," to use Sartre's terminology—seriality is what keeps people a series of individuals. In other words, the demands of modern life and capital produce groups of individuals who, passively engaging in the same activity (waiting for a bus), are alienated from each other. This alienation is key for Sartre and it is the element that can turn a series into a "group-in-fusion," a politically motivated collective. The group-in-fusion is predicated on the awareness that "everyone is the same as the Others in so far as he is Other than himself."[32] (There is overlap with Lacan here about the necessity of alienation in subjectivity.). This is what Sartre means when he says that "members of the group are third parties."[33] The group-in-fusion must remain alienated from their circumstances, as "the most lively and united group is always in danger of relapsing into the series from which it came."[34]

Where Lacan links the symbolic appearance of the serial to the radicality of the real, Sartre sees seriality as a structure to be escaped. For Sartre, seriality is the name for how people are ordered by capitalism into inert, disaffected, and disconnected alienated individuality. Seriality, for Sartre, names an oppressive structure, a problem to be solved. The only way out of seriality is the "group-in-fusion," a politically active collective that is needed to throw off the shackles of seriality. Philosophically speaking, the group-in-fusion overcomes the "anti-dialectic" of seriality. As Sartre writes, "This anti-dialectic, or dialectic against the dialectic (dialectic of *passivity*), must reveal *series* to us as a type of human gathering and alienation as a mediated relation to the other and to the objects of labour in the element of seriality and as a serial mode of co-existence."[35] Rather than a dialectic which is driven by the recognition of interdependence of things on their own internal contradiction, as Hegel would have it, this anti-dialectic is premised on inertia and passivity that obscures all contradiction. It turns the way the world works (currency exchanges, let us say) into a kind of magic. Viewed this way, we can see that Sartre's theory of seriality constitutes, for him, a theory of ideological formation. If ideology is that which eliminates contradiction in the world (as Marx and Althusser have formulated in various ways), seriality, for Sartre, is the prime mover, so to speak, in that formula. Seriality is all about eliminating the appearance of contradiction. It is about grouping people superficially in a way bereft of political potential. It is, in other words, pure continuity. Gapless.

While Sartre sees seriality as a structure that eliminates contradiction and must be done away with, Lacan's seriality is *all about* bringing recognition of impossible contradiction in to the symbolic (i.e., how can order and memory emerge *ex nihilo*—from the gap, the real—when a series forms?). We can link this position to Sartre's disavowal of the unconscious found in *Being and Nothingness*. In proposing his own notion of "existential psychoanalysis," Sartre lays bare the difference between his presuppositions and what he offers as the orthodox psychoanalytic view: "Empirical psychoanalysis in fact is based on the hypothesis of the existence of an unconscious psyche, which on principle escapes the intuition of the subject. Existential psychoanalysis rejects the hypothesis of the unconscious; it makes the psychic act co-extensive with consciousness."[36] Lacan's seriality, explained above, absolutely "escapes the intuition of the subject." It is only something one can register retroactively. This does mark a stark difference between Sartre and Lacan where it is perhaps unfair to criticize Sartre. For Lacan, seriality is in the foundation of the function of the signifier. It is embedded in the structure of how meaning arises in language. Seriality does not travel along similar terrain for Sartre.

While this is firmly the point where psychoanalytic seriality departs from what Sartre may have to offer, it is interesting to push forward along Sartrean lines a little further to show how accepted the idea of seriality as ideological continuity is. If we follow Sartre's ideas to the letter and push them to their conclusion, we are obliged to *reject* seriality wholesale and favor something else in its place (the group-in-fusion is Sartre's answer). Following Sartre, we would have to acknowledge the insidiousness of seriality and its close ties to the logic of capitalism, perhaps drawing conclusions similar to James H. Wittebols, who makes seriality and capitalist expansion the cornerstone of his analysis in *The Soap Opera Paradigm*. As Wittebols argues, "[serial] storytelling has increasingly overtaken other forms of storytelling on television over the last few decades, and that this storytelling form serves well the priorities of media conglomerates."[37] Taking the cliffhanger as our example, the cynical approach to serial storytelling across media would hold that interruptive closure binds people to a text almost against their will. This kind of analysis leads always to its own prior conclusion: we need to get out of seriality. Or, as Wittebols later argues, it is "the emphasis on profit to the diminution of social and aesthetic values has had an effect on the creative process behind television programming and has resulted in a sameness to all television programs regardless of the particular genre."[38] The point is not that Sartre and Wittebols are wrong, the point is that neither of their approaches to seriality can generate a position other than rejection. as neither approach seriality dialectically as Lacan does.

We could say the same of Jonathan Crary's *24/7*, a study of sleep and capitalism, which turns to Sartre's *Critique of Dialectical Reason* in the book's final pages. Sartre looks at the role of media, specifically radio, in producing "indirect gatherings" of people in modern life (his example is a disconnected group of people all listening to the same radio program but separated—alienated—from each other). Relevant for this discussion is how Crary marries a suspicion of television with Sartre's notion of seriality. He maybe has reruns in mind when he writes, "Seriality is the numbing and ceaseless production of the same."[39] Further, Crary writes that "it is regrettable that [Sartre's] plan for a study of television in Volume 2 of the *Critique* was never fulfilled."[40] This interests Crary, who has serious misgivings about television and, by extension, seriality. Citing a widely criticized and discredited 2006 Cornell University study on a preposterous link between television viewing and autism, Crary lauds the researchers for "bypass[ing] the notion that television is something one *watches* in some attentive manner, and instead ... [treats] it as a source of light and sound to which one is *exposed*."[41] Rather than emphasize how Crary's claim undermines itself, I want to underline instead that Crary, Wittebols, and Sartre crystallize an important attitude for us: *seriality is dangerous*. In fact, it is so volatile that we must censor ourselves from it and protect our children from it. We should not overexpose ourselves to something like Netflix, even though we want to immerse ourselves in it. This is a naïve approach to media, particularly serial media forms, but it is important to note the kind of suspicion the serial form has received.

Whatever merits there are in Sartre's notion of seriality as a theory of political formation, it leaves us very little room to continue an investigation of seriality itself as a theoretical form. Seriality, in the view of this short survey of thought from Sartre to Crary, is capitalism made oppressive media form and needs swift rejection. The only conclusion to fully accepting a Sartrean view of seriality is to overthrow seriality, expose the evils of the "Soap Opera Paradigm," and urge for the group-in-fusion to forge a "possible route out of the nightmare of serialization and isolation."[42] It is possible that, though their sense of the insidiousness of seriality differs greatly from mine, Sartre, Wittebols, and Crary see the reality of seriality in the symbolic. Seriality is not a neutral or neutered form in these accounts; it is *a priori* filled with manipulative and damaging content. It is a confrontation, as Sartre, Wittebols, and Crary rightly see. However, it is a confrontation worth grappling with rather than a dangerous element in need of rejection. Put another way, where the Sartrean account sees the serial as coercive and limiting—as ceaseless sameness—Lacan shows how serial discontinuity and repetition are the precondition for the new.

3

Theorizing the Cut of Seriality: Why the Quilting Point Arrests and the Master Signifier Obscures

For Derrida, Lacan's symbolic order amounts to a sleight of hand. For Deleuze, the staid order of the symbolic Lacan identifies operates as the name for our modern confinement. The serial is his name for the way out. For Sartre, the staid order of seriality is the name of our modern confinement. The group-in-fusion is his way out. All three attempt to designate a path to break from what each sees as the oppressive order of the modern world. If one imagines the serial to be a notion of the symbolic order *without* the curvature of the real, then it is the totalizing mass each of Derrida, Deleuze, and Sartre imagine it to be. By dint of imagining the serial not as gap-filled but gap *erasing* in its construction, then it is oppressive and alienating as a matter of course. However, by foregrounding the gap—the real at the heart of seriality—Lacan allows us to work with and theorize the radicality in seriality's symbolic appearance.

The separation between Derrida, Deleuze, Sartre, and Lacan can be meaningfully distilled to a single Lacanian concept: quilting point. If "Odd or even?" highlighted how the symbolic order emerges through serial relations for Lacan, the quilting point highlights how meaning arises in a given series and becomes arrested within the symbolic. As we have said, the quilting point is Lacan's idea for punctuated meaning. Establishing the radicality of punctuation (i.e., "the cut" and retroactivity) is Lacan's most important contribution to understanding seriality as a social and existential concept. In *Seminar III: The Psychoses*, Lacan states, "The schema of the quilting point is essential in human experience."[1] Even though the idea of quilting point drops out of Lacan's public lectures, the idea of punctuation is crucial to his thought. It is the mechanism that causes his notion of seriality to differ from his contemporaries. This chapter will look to explain and expand Lacan's notion of the quilting point, first by exploring the conceptual drawbacks to equivocating the quilting point with an end or ending. I will then demonstrate why the quilting point must be placed in contradistinction to the master signifier, another notion of Lacan's that often appears to cover similar theoretical terrain to the quilting point. Uncoupling the quilting point from its association with the master signifier and complicating its relationship to a theory of end will bring new theoretical attention to the quilting point. Further, the quilting point, as I theorize it, is a notion critical for separating a bare series from seriality.

Ending the Quilting Point's Relationship with Ending

As part of Lacan's return to Freud, the concept of *Nachträglichkeit* is threaded through his own notion of *le point de capiton*, or "the quilting point." However, *Nachträglichkeit* for Lacan does not refer chiefly to the retroactive emergence of a prior trauma that a neurotic subject had, as it did for Freud. Instead, *Nachträglichkeit* would become the structure of signification as such. Through his brief development of the quilting point, Lacan draws our attention to the retroactive determinative force that punctuation has on signification. The quilting point acts like the period at the end of a sentence, or in Lacan's example from *Seminar III*, the button in an upholstered chair. The button keeps the fabric (called "batting") inside the chair and also works to provide a level of design coherence for the chair itself. A period creates a single unit of meaning—the sentence, which can itself have multiple meanings—but the period needs to be there to conceive of meaning at all. Therefore, for Lacan, *Le point de capiton* is the meaning-making signifier for a given chain of signifiers.

To return to our earlier example of the traumatic cut of the end of the psychoanalytic session, Lacan's notion of the quilting point justifies and perhaps inspires his move away from the traditional psychoanalytic session established by Freud to his own "short" or "punctuated" sessions. For Lacan, the analytic session should not end because of the incidental and inevitable passage of time as it did for Freud but because the analysand ends up saying more than they mean, something that exceeds them. In ending the session at precisely this point, the punctuated session has the effect of "speeding up" analysis, allowing the analysand to make the breakthrough on their own, which removes the analyst from the assuming the role of "subject-supposed-to-know." What Lacan does not want is for someone to get bound up in this seeming continuity, seeking the validation of an external end that would grant consistency to their subjectivity. The word "narrative" is derived from the Latin word *gnarus*, meaning, in the infinitive, "to know."[2] This makes a narrator someone *supposed* to know. The overlap and resonance with the Lacanian "subject-supposed-to-know," a position whereby the analyst becomes, effectively, the fixed point of meaning for the subject in analysis, is too tempting to ignore. Put simply, eliminating the role of analyst as narrator—the someone one knows—is Lacan's aim with the punctuated session and the notion of quilting point. The quilting point—in this case the punctuated end to an analytic session—stitches the analysand's narrative together and grants them a point to look back from. Lacan, in this sense, is manufacturing *Nachträglichkeit*, attempting to introduce radical break into a seemingly continuous narrative. While Lacan never acknowledges this directly, the punctuated session seems intent with solving the "To Be Continued" cliffhanger problem of analysis that Freud identified in *Studies on Hysteria*. Put differently, enabling the perfunctory nature of the clock to end a session with a cliffhanger tacitly encourages the next session to pick up where the previous one left off, regardless as to whether that prior ending represented a meaningful path of egress for the subject to reckon with their symptom. Lacan's punctuated session, on the other hand, attempts to quilt the patient to their own narrative by forcing a confrontation with the unconscious.

The quilting point is the meaning-making signifier in a given chain of signifiers. As Slavoj Žižek explains in *Looking Awry*, the way we experience a narrative ending shows the effect of the quilting point. Žižek takes as his example the Hollywood legend surrounding the final scene of *Casablanca* (Michael Curtiz, 1942). As the legend goes, no one involved in the project could decide how the film should end, a disagreement that lasted as late as *the shooting of the climactic scene itself*. Everyone who has seen the film knows that Ilsa (Ingrid Bergman) eventually leaves Rick (Humphrey Bogart) for the hero of the French resistance, Victor Laszlo (Paul Henreid)—an ending that actually had been written, contrary to legend, long before shooting began. But this is more significant than a mere Hollywood history lesson; it is a useful illustration of how the quilting point functions. As Žižek writes,

> we experience the present ending... as something that "naturally" and "organically" follows from the preceding action, but if we were to imagine another ending—say for example, that Bergman's heroic husband were to die and that Bogart were to take his place on the plane for Lisbon together with Bergman—it, too, would be experienced by viewers as something that developed "naturally" out of earlier events.[3]

Žižek's point is that the appropriateness of *Casablanca*'s ending—and, indeed, any narrative ending—does not arise from the experience of a "linear 'organic flow of events'" but rather it emerges retroactively. The end stitches the narrative together, allowing us to perceive contingent narrative events as a single naturally flowing unity.

Žižek likely chooses a narrative to explain quilting point because Lacan does the same thing in *Seminar III*. Lacan chooses the first line of Racine's *Athaliah*, "Yes, I come into his temple to worship the Eternal Lord," to begin working through his idea: "*Yes, I come into his temple ...*, we have no idea where it might be taking us. It could well end up anywhere. *I come into his temple ... to arrest the High Priest*, for example. It does have to be completed for one to know what is going on."[4] Lacan is making an argument more intricate than it may at first seem. He is observing both the contingency *and* fixity of meaning, an idea he expresses lucidly when concludes his point by saying, "The sentence only exists as completed and its sense comes to it retroactively."[5] What's more, this is not just *any* sentence but the first sentence of a play. The first sentence of any narrative can establish where we are, who will be telling the story, and what is at stake (among other things). At the beginning of the sentence, "Yes, I come into his temple ...," there are a plurality of possible meanings. At the end of the sentence, there is only one.

There is, however, a nagging and significant problem with Lacan so closely entwining his formulation of the quilting point to the ending. Does the end always and only confer meaning to the beginning? The period at the end of a sentence is a clear example of punctuation but how do we know we are not punctuating meaning ideologically? How can we be sure we are not repeating an ideological series or giving new life to what we might call "a bad series"? In re-reading Lacan we can provide a strong answer to these questions where Lacan does not or, rather, where Lacan's formulation runs headlong into the problem.

Lacan overemphasizes the ending when he discusses the quilting point. It is not the ending which has the ultimate sanction on meaning but rather *the next term*. Meaning is structurally retroactive. As he points out, you do not understand this sentence until ... you read past the ellipse and get to the period at the end. Meaning is in negotiation until the *next* term. However, Lacan should understand this distinction between "end" and "next," as the primacy of retroactivity undergirds his idea of signification; that the signifier represents the subject to another signifier. The trick with quilting point is to find the term that arrests meaning on both sides—retroactively and prospectively. In other words, quilting in such a way that does not rely simply on the ending to confer weight and importance. To reach the full radicality of Lacan's idea, I argue, is to wed the quilting point to the point of castration, not a moment of confirmation or ending, such as the period at the end of the sentence. We need to quilt, simply put, at the cut of symbolic castration.

This idea of the quilting point as a retroactive and prospective cut is needed to help turn the breadcrumbs and sprinkles of Lacan's thoughts on seriality into a fully informed theory. Understanding seriality does not rely on "next" occurring as another scheduled iteration in an ongoing or experientially observable series but rather as a *next* that quilts. In any series we need to be able to locate a quilting point that demands retroactivity while at the same time signaling that something has transformed from that point forward.

Two narrative phenomena are directly relevant here: the anticlimax and the twist ending. Starting with the latter term first, it is not the twist as end itself that guarantees meaning but rather how the twist radically recontextualizes everything one previously read, watched, or listened to. The twist redoubles the narrative. It is not a linear endpoint that confers meaning, as Lacan discusses with Racine in *Seminar III*. It is a point which radically alters not just the text but our relationship to it moving forward. When we learn that Verbal Kint (Kevin Spacey) is Keyser Soze in *The Usual Suspects* or that Malcolm Crowe (Bruce Willis) is dead in *The Sixth Sense*, we flip the film narrative over in our heads. We have the same "oh my god" moment of recognition that characters in the film do. More important for the present argument, however, is how the twist-in-itself overwhelms the ending. The actual ending of each film—defining "ending" here as the final shot or series of shots—is made irrelevant by the twist that came before it. Upon learning the seemingly inconsequential Verbal Kint was actually international super villain Keyser Soze all along, FBI agent Dave Kujan (Chazz Palminteri) runs out to the street in a desperate attempt to apprehend the criminal he just let walk away. The final shot of a baffled Kujan scanning the street for Soze is pure anticlimax. After experiencing the shock of the twist along with agent Dave Kujan—who stared at the objects in his office recognizing that they were fodder for Keyser Soze's lies just as we did as viewers—this last image of the film doesn't last. It is end, yes, but it is not the meaning-making signifier. Likewise, in *The Sixth Sense*, the moment Malcolm Crowe learns that he is a spirit clinging to the material world persists longer in the mind of the filmgoer than does the actual end of the film. There Malcolm makes amends with his wife Anna (Olivia Williams) while she sleeps. He then seemingly disappears from the material realm when the film stock dissolves to white. The film then dissolves back into a brief clip from a wedding video of Malcolm and Anna kissing.

Twists are symbolically castrating: think of Kujan's face when he realizes *in his office* that Kint was Keyser Soze, or Edward Norton's shot face as The Narrator in *Fight Club*, or Luke Skywalker's face upon meeting his father in *Empire Strikes Back*. They overwhelm the endings because of this and become the chief meaning-making signifier, altering radically our relationship to meaning on either side of the twist. Lacan conceives this precise understanding of quilting point when he says, "It's the point of convergence that enables everything that happens in this discourse to be situated retroactively and prospectively."[6] Lacan's example of quilting point—the end of a sentence, the end in general—is at odds with this elegant definition he provides in the same lecture.

Lacan navigates into another inconsistency when he expands his look at the opening of *Athaliah* by working through the first conversation in the play. There he posits the fear of God is the quilting point. While, in the conversation, Abner *does* admit to fearing God and having no other fear, Lacan moves his notion of quilting point from the end of the sentence to an idea (the fear of God) that ties together a conversation between two people. It's likely Lacan chooses this tack as he is attempting to show that the psychotic has no relationship to the paternal metaphor. Where he errs is that he relies on already established meaning from outside a certain text to quilt that text's meaning. The radicality of Lacan's point is the impossible confluence of meaning's contingency *and* its fixity. Moving to an established meaning from outside the diegesis of a text to quilt that text's meaning obviates the radical dimension in Lacan's idea. In making "fear of God" into the quilting point we have the fixed meaning of a social and religious concept lying in wait to quilt anything. Here we have lost the dimension of contingency.

Lacan, in *Seminar III*, repeatedly links the logic of the quilting point to the narrative end. Žižek does the same thing in *Looking Awry*. The problem with aligning the quilting point with the end is that the concept becomes de-agentializing and potentially de-politicizing. We all lie in wait for the signifier to emerge that quilts meaning before we can say, "That's it! That's the end I've been looking for." Effectively, we become Chuck Berry in *Back to the Future*, waiting for a time traveling teenager to play his own music back to him before he can write it in the first place. We have to quilt—punctuate—at the point that does not confirm our subjectivity, the point where we perhaps feel uncomfortable and have to see ourselves as other to our symbolic selves.

The kind of quilting I am theorizing instantiates a new antagonism, a new terrain for the symbolic. We are not just making retroactive sense but destabilizing sense moving forward. We see a narrative example of this in Abbas Kiarostami's *Certified Copy* (2011).[7] Elle (Juliet Binoche), a French antiques dealer, and James Miller (William Shimell), a British non-fiction writer, develop a complicated bond during a day trip in Tuscany. Over the course of the film, it becomes increasingly unclear the nature of Elle and

Miller's relationship: are they strangers getting to know each other by exploring the existential deadlock of romantic relationships as such, say, like Ethan Hawke and Julie Delpy in *Before Sunrise* (1994)? Or are they estranged lovers coyly reigniting a long-term and intimate partnership by pretending to get to know each other for the first time? The film is continually and deliberately ambiguous in answer to these questions.

There is a clear moment, however, where this possibility is first made manifest. Forty minutes into the film, Elle asks Miller to expand upon a comment he had previously made about the inspiration for his book. Miller tells about a mother and son who walked fifty yards apart from each other in Florence everyday around the same time. The mother would always stride away from her son and the son would never do anything to catch up to her. At this, Elle starts to cry, saying bluntly, "Sounds familiar." When Miller asks if she knew the people from his story she replies, "I wasn't well in those days." It's unclear whether she cries because this story is profoundly reminiscent of her own relationship with her son, *or* she is in fact the mother in the story. Before this potential connection can be clarified, Miller receives a call on his cell phone and leaves the café, which leads to an exchange in Italian between Elle and the woman who is running the café. The café owner assumes Miller is Elle's husband. Elle does not correct her and indulges her reading on their relationship by building an image of Miller as an absent husband overly committed to work. The café owner asks Elle how long she and Miller have been married and she holds her fingers out briefly trying to count the years. Either trying to remember or making up the number on the spot she replies, "Fifteen years" and that they have a son whose birthday was last week and her husband, Miller, did not even bother to call him. When Miller returns to the café, she tells him in English that the café owner "mistook" him for her husband, and she did not correct her. He remarks that they clearly "make a good couple" and inquires what she asked him, as he does not speak Italian. Elle says she wanted to know why he does not speak Italian when his wife and son do and he replies, "they live their lives and I live mine, they speak their language and I speak mine; that makes sense doesn't it?" Hearing this Elle leaves the café in an offended hurry saying sarcastically, "Yeah, that makes a lot of sense."

It is only after the café owner "mistakes" Miller for Elle's husband that this ambiguous relationship starts to play out. Whether Elle and Miller previously had a relationship is not a question the viewer would entertain before this "mistake" and its continuance by Elle and Miller. After the idea is introduced and played with by both characters, suddenly everything that came before has new meaning (e.g., the beginning of the film shows Elle and her son getting Miller to autograph a copy of his book, they both sit in the reserved seats at the talk he is giving). Interrupting a phone call with her son, Miller says that "our presence can give comfort and pleasure to those around us." Elle shoots back, "Look who's talking about *presence*! When was the last time the three of us had breakfast together? When?" Miller replies, "I certainly can't remember the last time you came to breakfast in a good mood." Later in the same conversation, Miller says, "It's not really fair of you to give me this role of absent parent ... besides there's bound to be times when one parent or the other are away." Again, Elle presses him that he is never around and Miller replies, "So you're saying I've never been there?" Perhaps, like a good performer, Miller is embodying the "Yes, and" principle of improvisational comedy. Or, perhaps, as the film progresses, the thaw on the separate life he's been living gives way to a vulnerability he is unsure if he truly wishes to reclaim. Is Miller trying to learn to speak Elle's language? Not to learn Italian but to understand the way she thinks, feels, sees, and experiences the world. It is permanently unclear. What is clear, however, is the introduction of this problematic occurs almost halfway through the film and destabilizes the relationship between the characters for the rest of the film—both for the characters themselves and for the audience watching this relationship or meta-relationship play out. Again, we have both aspects of Lacan's idea here: a point which retroactively and prospectively alters meaning in such a way that we cannot go back to a time before the quilting point was introduced. The idea that Elle and Miller could be continuing a previous relationship or spontaneously making up a new one introduces a completely different antagonism to what theretofore existed in the film.

Quilting Point Unmastered

My engagement with the quilting point widens the stakes for the idea, charting a different path for it to move forward (and backwards). At this point, it's worth discussing why Lacan proffers it at all in the context of *Seminar III*. Understanding why the idea emerges *when it does* for Lacan will help us to see how and why it is relevant for thinking through formations of contemporary popular culture and how they inveigh upon the psyche.

Lacan's third seminar focuses on psychosis. For the psychotic, according to Lacan, the signifier exists with no possibility of it being quilted. The paternal metaphor has no purchase on the psychotic as they feel all attempts at social or cultural sense making to be coercive. It's important not to see this as a marginal phenomenon. The position of the psychotic is oftentimes dominant in discourse on popular culture. One need only pay attention to the Christmas tradition of pop culture articles decrying the portrayal of romance and relationships in the film *Love Actually*.[8] The angle is always the same in every article: these are not healthy relationships, and we need to stop celebrating this film about unhealthy relationships. Not being able to separate or acknowledge a split between the depiction of something in fiction with it being a recommendation for how reality should work is psychotic. The implicit idea is that if we stop romanticizing negative things people will stop desiring them which well and truly is putting the cart before the horse. Understanding the death drive and the psyche's primary inclination toward masochism shows that we desire that which undoes us first. We are not "taught" to desire that by culture. It'd be convenient if mass culture invented the symptoms of the psyche rather than giving name to them but, alas, unhealthy relationships and banal everyday masochism has always tarried with the subject.

One of the barriers to fully theorizing the quilting point has been thinking its history either with or against Lacan's later idea of the master signifier. Some intellectual histories or recapitulations of Lacan consider the quilting point as an idea sacrificed for this later and far more prevalent idea of the master signifier to emerge and develop. The idea of the master signifier can be defined as a signifier without a signified that, precisely because of its inability to concretely signify, works to hold together a web of otherwise contingent relations. The idea of Nation is, for these purposes, a perfect master signifier. Look at the following two sentences describing polar opposite perspectives on the state of the United States:

> For the good of the Nation, we need to rapidly curtail access to firearms, increase the welfare state, cancel onerous medical and student debt, and work to root out discriminatory practices in institutions across the country upholding class and racial divisions.
>
> For the good of the Nation, we need to rapidly increase access to firearms, disinvest from the oppressive welfare state, end anti-Christian religious discrimination, crack down on woke ideology on college campuses and in the news as a way to end practices that stoke divisions across the country.

Neither of these sentences should strike anyone as being inappropriate summaries of potential Democrat and Republican party platforms in an election year. It is not the litany of ideological differences that cohere either sentence; it's the master signifier Nation. Again, it is precisely because Nation does not by necessity refer to any one thing in particular that allows it to act as the glue for these divergent lists of political priorities. Because of its capacity to stabilize racist and classist violences, and justify the necessity for brutal regressive policies, I want to argue that master signifier is always conservative. Even if it can be employed to make sensible a list of Democratic or progressive policies, the internal structure that defines master signifier means it is a conservative concept.

Unfortunately, the idea of *new* master signifiers has often been seen as the way out of regressive political deadlock and the path to liberation. Fabio Vighi credits Žižek as the most influential purveyor of this idea in *On Žižek's Dialectics*. For Vighi, Žižek sees the cultivation of new master signifiers as a way to undermine the political flattening done by currently and historically operative master signifiers such as "democracy."[9] However, I think Žižek's own view on the master signifier is compromised by an early decision he made on the status of quilting point. In addition to comparing quilting point to narrative endings, Slavoj Žižek has repeatedly likened the function of quilting point to how the figure of the Jew operated for Nazi Germany.[10]

If we think of the figure of the Jew in Germany as the quilting point, then we give over this idea completely to conservative particularism. That, however, is the work of the master signifier.

Every master signifier is conservative. The master signifier is a signifier without a signified. The quilting point, however, requires a different relationship to signification. Master signifier organizes content under a banner. The quilting point does the work of snapping into dialectical relation a series. What Žizek describes above is not the retroactive *and* prospective quality of quilting point that Lacan mentions but, nevertheless, fails to insist upon. I am emphasizing the prospective quality of quilting precisely to steer the concept away from it simply becoming the period at the end of a racist sentence. The figure of the Jew for Nazi Germany is where signification stops. What's more, it works precisely because of the utter multiplicity of the conspiracy. Importantly this is not "Jewish people" but "the Jew" as an amorphous concept, at once the most brazen criminal element and the most secretive and cunning. This is even Žižek's point: the figure of the Jew always confirms the same vast conspiracy. There is no articulation of a new antagonism and no change to the symbolic by claiming that the Jewish conspiracy explains everything. Making the figure of the Jew the period at the end of every antisemitic sentence is a way of arresting signification yes, and this would seem to be in partial fulfillment of the quilting point, but it does so by reifying ideology. What's more, there is no risk and no cut of symbolic castration. What Žižek designates here is the work of the master signifier, not the work of quilting point. Every master signifier upholds status quo. Every quilting point—understood in the terms I am trying to develop here—heralds an upheaval of the prevailing situation and a direct threat to oppressive ideology and status quo. What I am proposing is that the quilting point should name the point of irreducible dialectical contradiction within in the symbolic and not just produce retroactive meaning. The quilting point must irrevocably unsettle future meaning from its point of articulation in a series *forward*. The quilting point cannot and should not be positioned as part of an implicit dualism. Regarding the quilting point as a two-sided process by which we have an understanding of an idea contingently which is then halted by the retroactivity granted us by some stable endpoint of meaning means all ideas are always laying in wait for the next cliffhanger. On the contrary, the quilting point is a dialectical concept at the heart of seriality saving it from being an organizational concept for the procession of material production.

In television screenwriting, a joke or statement that underlines the situation leading up to a commercial break is referred to as "a button." In sewing, buttons are also referred to as notions. In resetting the terrain for quilting point and insisting upon its retroactive *and* prospective influence, I want to return to Lacan's original example of literal upholstery and say that a quilting point is a button that moves us toward a philosophical notion. If a term, phrase, idea, political moment, movement, narrative (etc.) arrests meaning and produces a new and emancipatory series, then we have quilting point. If meaning is arrested and halted and what is produced is a recapitulation of already existing prejudices, then we have master signifier. The quilting point points to lack. The master signifier points away. The master signifier obscures a term, grafting it onto an expansive set of discourses, leaving the term untheorized as a way to reify and repeat already existing structures and prejudices.

As I have argued, the quilting point needs to make thinkable a new antagonism, a new terrain for symbolic relations hooked onto a castrating recognition that is easier to ignore than confront. It needs to hold that, in at least a minimal way, it's possible that we are ourselves the problem we are trying to address. To put it in very simple everyday terms, accepting the cut of the quilting point means moving from thinking "I am stuck in traffic" to realizing "I *am* traffic." People are not in *your way* when you go to work any more than you are in *their* way.

The Singular in the Series

The cut of the quilting point turns a bare series into seriality. Without steeling the quilting point against both the ending as the ultimate sanction on meaning and the master signifier as a bulldozing force flattening all fissures in a series, we lose a needed way to see seriality as radical. Theorizing seriality as a concept of dialectical relation is my primary aim. It is an aim that cannot be realized without tracing a path through Freudian and Lacanian ideas that are inflected by material serials (e.g., the Victorian novel, odds or evens) and psychical series (e.g., the structure of trauma and the recognition of meaning). By following these breadcrumbs and sprinkles, we are (re)creating a series where it has heretofore been difficult to find a cogent relation. Seriality cannot be theorized as wide category of human experience, knotting together material and mental life, without psychoanalysis. Likewise, many of psychoanalysis's most important ideas have been developed with recourse to serials and series, though this history has remained underexamined until now.

While inconsistent and needing development, Lacan's initial articulation of the quilting point is precisely what separates him from his contemporaries and what enables us to locate radical break in a series. He does not turn to the terrain of pure novelty to generate the creative or the new. Instead, he articulates something halting: the emergence of the internal and nonprescriptive or predictive series and a way to understand and arrest it. Even though he does not develop the notion of the quilting point after its introduction in *Seminar III*, even allowing for the concept to enter his thought is what enables Lacan to see the formation of a series as having radical and liberatory potential. Lacan lays the groundwork for us to articulate a radical notion of what I will call form. Freud was the first to posit how the psyche has serial form, which he saw through his work as an analyst. Lacan shows us how a series emerges coextensive with our symbolic experience. Across varied iterations of appearance, form is what remains stubbornly the same. Identifying form in this manner is central to extracting the seriality of a bare series. It is the difference from seeing and reckoning with seriality versus observing a procession of parts.

Form is what remains constant after stripping away differences. Form is what is immanent throughout content of different kinds. Form gives shape to content but increasingly we see content for itself, as Marshall McLuhan famously asserted. Lacan goes a step beyond McLuhan twenty years earlier by showing how even chance produces order—that pure chance itself has form. This makes Deleuze, in many ways, the best reader of Lacan. Many of Deleuze's most well-known ideas articulate an attempt to escape either the contradiction or constraint of form. Again, the "body without organs" is a body loosed from what "organizes" it. The idea is Deleuze's attempt to think a body without a subject ordered by the symbolic—an order from without—or from order within. With Lacan showing that not even chance can be considered radical difference, Deleuze imagines his project to be about creating absolute novelty. But his project stumbles—the shock of the new can get quite old—because he tries to imagine changes in content without changing form. To do this requires thinking repetition on the side of radicality rather than difference. Only Lacan offers us a way to see formal break. Derrida, Deleuze, and Sartre all try to find different ways to escape the serial framework that Lacan discovers. Of the three who depart from Lacan's position, Sartre believes in the possibility of radical content, but it is the limit of his formulation that demonstrates the problems with the idea. Sartre's dynamic collective doesn't emerge out of seriality but is an alternative to it. For Lacan, form itself includes breaks within it which create space for retroactive meaning through seriality. What's more, all three think that changes in content will alter the nature or construction of form. Understanding how form exists, how it operates, and how it persists is the only way to change form.

It is at these points of tension that the radical can rupture but we need to remain open to this possibility for it to emerge at all. It's the foreclosure of a notion of the unconscious that prevents Sartre (and Deleuze and Derrida) from avowing this position. What Sartre ends up arguing in *Critique of Dialectical Reason* is that we need radical consciousness and intent. His system cannot allow for or accept that people could do something that operates against their intention. Rather he needs people to change their intentions. The radical passivity he writes about early on in *Being and Nothingness* (which sounds suspiciously close to the unconscious of psychoanalysis) has evaporated.

We don't need a notion of "radical content" to change form. In fact, seemingly radical content often leaves form untouched. We change form by reorienting our relationship and tie to it. It's not necessary that within the domain of the popular will be something radical and transformative but that we can take up a radical and transformative stance relative to the popular. Rejecting the popular in favor of high art (what typically passes for radical content) does little to change formations of the popular. What we need to see, rather, is the radical in the popular as that which exceeds the content itself, pointing to something that would dismantle it. This is the problem of disavowing an unconscious. All we're left with is the necessity of fully conscious art and full intention that never gets full enough or pure enough. For these reasons, the next chapter will be pursuing our idea of radical form on the impure terrain of television.

4

Seriality at the Formal Limit of Television

In advancing a dialectical notion of seriality, I argue that seriality is not just a theory of successive parts, patterns, or installments. A series of relations can be apprehended in a singular part. To see how a series can exist in the singular—as in our "Strawberry Fields Forever" example from the Introduction—means thinking dialectically. This word—dialectics, used several times before now—will take center stage in this chapter's investigation of seriality as a formal homology. What is at stake for serial form in narrative is precisely what is at stake for seriality as an existential form, as the collision between television, Hegelian dialectics, and Sartrean seriality will show.

Form is most visible when we encounter some kind of limit. Seriality is the defining form of everyday life since the material introduction of the serial. Oftentimes the seriality of our lives feels like boring and rote repetition. A long middle. Just like a long-running television series, we live most of our lives not knowing when the end is coming. When we have an end, it becomes easy to turn everything into a three-act play. In other words, it's easy to have form when we have end. What I am trying to posit is finding form from the middle of an ongoing series, whether it be an ongoing material series (e.g., *The Simpsons*) or an unfolding serial crisis (e.g., climate change, the COVID-19 pandemic, racist policing, and gun violence in the United States). The only way to articulate form from the middle is through interruption or punctuation. It's the best way to alter meaning retroactively and prospectively, as Lacan says about the quilting point.

Nothing in the field of media punctuates in quite the same way a bottle episode does. The bottle episode is one of American television's truly unique forms. The term itself originates from the material production restrictions encountered by American television series in the 1960s. Leslie Stevens, producer of *The Outer Limits*, famously referred to "Controlled Experiment," a cheaply made and quickly produced episode of that series, as a "bottle show."[1] He remarked that the production team "pull[ed] an episode right out of a bottle like a genie."[2] Budgeting restrictions—funding that became "bottlenecked"—often meant that producers on *Star Trek: The Original Series* could not afford new sets, new costumes, or guest actors. This led to the production of episodes, such as "The Balance of Terror," where core cast members never left the U.S.S. *Enterprise* and rarely left the ship's bridge. The cast referred to these as "ship-in-a-bottle" episodes. Nodding to the production reality of *The Original Series*, *Star Trek: The Next Generation* titled a season six episode that mainly takes place on the holodeck, "Ship in a Bottle."

The stink of cheapness still tarries with the bottle episode all these years later. On pop culture wiki *TV Tropes*, for example, the entry for "Bottle Episode" stresses, in the first line, that "the point" of a bottle episode is to "take up as little money as possible."[3] It is true that this was the stated objective of the "bottle show" Leslie Stevens produced. Today, however, the bottle episode is no longer a form mandated by lack of funding.[4] *Seinfeld*'s "The Chinese Restaurant," where Jerry, George, and Elaine suffer an interminable wait for a table at a Chinese Restaurant before a screening of *Plan 9 from Outer Space*, was written as a deliberate experiment with staging an episode that unfolded in "real time." The interminable wait for the table was, in effect, the characters living through the run-time of the episode. More recently, cartoons such as *Family Guy* ("Brian and Stewie"), *BoJack Horseman* ("Fish Out of Water," "Free Churro"), and *Rick and Morty* ("Rixty Minutes") have used the bottle episode form effectively, testifying against the notion that bottle episodes are the last refuge for a swollen budget and are more deliberate explorations of constraint. Beginning an inquiry into the bottle episode from the perspective of the economic, however, reduces our ability to fully account for its narrative invention and existential intervention. As Alison Herman has recently put it on the popular culture website *The Ringer*, "the bottle episode is more central to TV than ever" but "its definition has also never been hazier."[5]

The task before us is not to exhaustively catalog all that a bottle episode *is* but to theorize what it does. Through its articulation of the limit, the bottle episode establishes a formal, narrative, and existential aesthetic that is unique to television. By trapping characters in closed settings such as a meat locker or an elevator, or locking them inside an apartment, the spatial constraint of the situation generates its own drama. My claim, however, is that what "bottles" characters is not physical space; rather, it is the shape of an intractable existential predicament. Bottle episodes constrain characters, forcing them to find ways out of their present situation that would ordinarily represent a social and structural impossibility. Far from simply being "cheap TV," a close study of the bottle episode shows that what began as a financially necessary production format is a complex theoretical form.

What's more, approaching the bottle episode in this manner enables us to continue our inquiry into Jean-Paul Sartre. Despite Sartre's disregard of Lacan, there is still more to work through with his formulation of the serial. One of the reasons I've spent so much time on Sartre (and will continue to) is his thought undergoes a radical revision between *Being and Nothingness* and *Critique of Dialectical Reason*. My wager is that attending to this shift will further open up our understanding of seriality. We do not need to move line by line or point by point to see the shift in Sartre across these texts. Paying close attention to the movement between how he writes about the coffee shop in *Being and Nothingness* versus the bus stop of *Critique of Dialectical Reason* will prove illuminating. By way of introduction, Sartre is far more Marxist in *Critique of Dialectical Reason* than he is in the prior major text. Since the subject is more a social designation in Marx and alienation is a pure negative, individual subjectivity drops out between café and bus stop. For our purposes, teasing out the consequences of this shift affords an opportunity to clarify crucial terms to the present inquiry, including alienation, contradiction (a term Sartre constantly conflates with conflict in *Critique of Dialectical Reason*), and cynicism. We can, and I would argue must, see that dialectical contradiction is an existential impasse. To do this work, we need Sartre and Hegel *together*—not at odds—using the friction of the gaps between them to bind them. The formal logic of the bottle episode works through the dialectical method of thought that unfurls in Hegel's *Phenomenology of Spirit*. The bottle episode form acts as a unique site enabling these two divergent thinkers to tarry alongside each other. Highlighting the contrast in their ideas shows why they must be thought together.

Jean-Paul Sartre regarded television with particular suspicion and animosity. While the influence of television on postwar society is typically played out as an American story, the story of television in France is just as affected by the Second World War. In 1937, France built a 30,000-watt television transmitter on the Eifel Tower, one of the most powerful in the world at that time. During the occupation of France by Nazi Germany, this transmitter was taken over and used to broadcast cabarets and newsreels to wounded Nazi soldiers in military field hospitals. After the war and until 1982, television in France was a state-owned monopoly, in direct contrast to the United States' corporate forward model. As we can see from the notes left in his unfinished *Critique of Dialectical Reason Volume 2*, Sartre fused the state monopoly of French television with the corporate model of American television to inform his understanding of television as a medium.

As we saw in the previous chapter, Sartre named seriality—a force coming from the outside to order and isolate human activity—as the biggest threat to collective political action. The bottle episode shows us that television at its most isolated offers a path to collectivity, a path that Sartre closes. The bottle episode also highlights how the singular depends on the series. Similar to how Sartre positions nothingness as that which being depends, the singular or the exceptional requires the series. A close study of the bottle episode form will uncover the relationship that the singular (or the seeming exception) has to serials and series.

From Cost-Saving Format to Dialectical Form

Easily approachable media objects are just as theoretically rich as opaque philosophical texts. However, in the case of the former, they are often dismissed precisely for their approachability and, in the case of the latter, for their opacity. Reading the dialectics of the bottle episode helps us apprehend the complexity of episodic television and the approachability of seemingly dense theory.

The bottle episode is the most singular, most radically self-contained form of television. One can watch a bottle episode without having any prior familiarity with a series because the internal dynamics of what is at stake in the episode is structurally clear. (Bottle episodes make for great teaching tools as well because one need not assign an entire season to talk about them.) They are perfect examples of Poe's dictum that a well-told story be brief and total. And yet, bottle episodes only mean anything at all because of their seriality. The drama they produce is only substantial because of prior arcs, interactions, and dynamics. What's more, bottle episodes affix and arrest meaning—even in series that have minimal narrative continuity between episodes. The bottle episode is the singular in the series.

Revelatory moments in bottle episodes, where characters move from isolated individuals to dynamic collective, are earned through a hardening of contradiction. This is the point of the Hegelian dialectic, the method which causes what Hegel terms spirit—the shape of the impossible—to emerge. In the nearly two hundred years since his death, however, the orthodox understanding of Hegel is as a philosopher of synthesis. This comes from reading his dialectical method as that which ends in an almost anodyne compromise, a "reset button" happy ending. Beginning in the late twentieth century but growing in prominence in the twenty-first, theorists such as Slavoj Žižek, Catherine Malabou, Rebecca Comay, Todd McGowan, Susan Buck-Morss, Adrian Johnston, and Terry Pinkard have pushed back against this tradition of reading Hegel as a thinker of synthesis. The bottle episode is an inherently dialectical form, but dialectical in precisely this understanding of refusing simple synthesis. In this way, the bottle episode and Hegel can be seen to have a reciprocal rather than transactional relationship. Hegel needs the bottle episode to help us explicate his dialectical method as generative contradiction. The bottle episode needs Hegel to help us arrive at a full theory of its formal invention.

Indeed, what I am interested in exploring is the unique art of television at its most limited. Bottle episodes work in the opposite direction of experimental television such as *Buffy the Vampire Slayer*'s "Hush" and "Once More with Feeling." Rather than expanding a storyworld to encompass something novel, bottle episodes take the old and familiar—typically a series' regular cast bottled in a recurring location—to generate the new, or what I refer to as dialectical revelation. This essay will look to NBC and Yahoo's comedy series *Community* (2009–2015)—a series renowned for its meta-referential bottle episodes—to ground its theoretical engagement.[6] In theorizing the bottle episode, we will continue to push the use of discrete media objects as a way for advancing a theory of seriality.[7] *Community* shows that the material and formal constraints constitutive of the bottle episode do not limit characters, storytelling, or storyworlds. Rather it is through a dialectical encounter with this limit that the new and transformative takes place, specifically, how collectivity emerges through bottled confinement. The limit itself is—as in Hegel's work—emancipatory.[8] Perhaps Sartre would not find much value in looking toward American television as a model for collective action, but we repeat structural mistakes in adopting this view. For one, everything must be dialectical—as in everything must have a point of tension within it that would undo it—not just the things one likes. If this is not the way we understand dialectics, then we miss the whole point of the idea. On this point, Sartre's dismissal of the unconscious and his move away from Hegel come back to the same thing: his system becomes increasingly founded on intentionality and cannot hold contradiction or death drive. Secondly, we must remember that during Sartre's lifetime French television was state owned. This doubtlessly influences Sartre's rejection of television. In an important sense, Sartre is responding to the domestication of the serial as seen on TV. This is no small thing. When one thinks of television as a medium controlled by the state, there is no possibility for TV to ever be radical. All it can ever do is reify the state. If you have no notion of the unconscious—or that people could do things against their conscious intention—then neither people working in television nor the medium itself could exceed ideological demands and break from it. However, as we will see in the case of the bottle episode, radical television form is not just possible but is becoming increasingly more popular and common. It is up to us to act in fidelity to its radicality and turn away from easy cynicism. Ultimately, this chapter will show how bottle episodes, as a medium-specific phenomenon of American television, are models for seeing how a genuine collectivity can only be formed through an encounter with the fecundity of the limit.

No television series embodies what the bottle episode does—what it effects and affects—more clearly than NBC and Dan Harmon's *Community*. Starting with "Cooperative Calligraphy" in season two, *Community* produced at least one bottle episode per season, including season two's "Advanced Dungeons and

Dragons," season three's "Remedial Chaos Theory," season four's "Intro to Felt Surrogacy," season five's "Cooperative Polygraphy" and "Advanced Advanced Dungeons and Dragons," and season six's "Basic Email Security," and—in many respects—the series finale, "Emotional Consequences of Broadcast Television." This chapter will focus on "Cooperative Calligraphy" and "Remedial Chaos Theory" because those episodes introduce novel constraints to narrative time and space that highlight the dialectical form of the bottle episode as such. *Community* helps to show that television is not simply a retreat for comfort viewing but can be both formally and existentially challenging. By theorizing television in this way, we gain an understanding of the relationship between the singular and the serial.

In "Cooperative Calligraphy," Annie Edison (Alison Brie) loses a pen in the study room. Except, it is not likely that *she* lost it. Far more likely, she thinks, is that someone in the study group stole it. As Annie puts it when Jeff (Joel McHale) limply says "sorry Annie" about her lost pen, "We passed 'sorry Annie' eight pens ago." The stakes are clear: the group has been taking advantage of Annie's kindness and scholastic preparedness and she is fed up with being used. For the entirety of the episode's twenty-six-minute runtime, Annie and the members of her study group—Jeff, Britta (Gillian Jacobs), Troy (Donald Glover), Abed (Danny Pudi), Shirley (Yvette Nicole Brown), and Pierce (Chevy Chase)—attempt to locate her pen. The episode brings tensions between each member of the group into the forefront. While there is a lot of physical movement in the episode, very little happens in terms of story. Annie loses a pen, accuses one person in the group of stealing it, that person is proved to *not* have the pen, and the accusations move to every member of the group—including the group eventually accusing her of secretly realizing she *did* in fact have the pen but was too embarrassed to admit it. The study room is literally torn apart trying to find it. Despite all the accusations, interrogations, and property damage, the pen is never found (though in a post-credits sequence later, viewers see Troy's missing pet monkey from season one in an air vent with a collection of Annie's purple pens). It is the fallout of the accusation—the idea that anybody could be the pen thief, including Annie—however, that brings the study group into intractable conflict. This is where the "action" of the episode is: in terms of character development nobody emerges from the study room unchanged. With no cuts to outside scenes (where a puppy parade the group is desperate to get to is happening) and the shifts in diegetic time occurring during commercial breaks, the episode seems to unfold in front of us "live" as the characters' relationships unravel and are reworked.

"Cooperative Calligraphy" is a self-aware bottle episode, as Abed remarks in the early search for Annie's pen: "This is starting to feel like a bottle episode." When Pierce accuses Abed of stealing the pen to make real life more like TV, Abed, who "has trouble reading people and says the wrong things sometimes," says that he "hate[s] bottle episodes. They are wall to wall facial expressions and emotional nuance. I might as well sit in a corner with a bucket on my head."[9] As a self-aware bottle episode, "Cooperative Calligraphy" makes frequent justifications for the stakes of the episode. Many of the characters are anxious to get to the puppy parade outside the library, where the study group is. The school dean, Dean Pelton, makes frequent loudspeaker announcements about developments in how adorable and exciting the puppy parade is. This is done to give the group even more reason to not be in the study room. Every four minutes or so in the episode, a character will tell another character in the room (and also the audience) what the importance of their investigation is. While looking for the purloined pen, the group finds little evidence of where it could have gone and who could have stolen it. But they find out a great deal about each other.

Pierce, who had recently broken his legs in a previous episode, is abusing painkillers. Shirley may be pregnant, and the father of the baby is in question. Abed, in an attempt to better understand the social dynamics of the group, has troublingly been charting the menstrual cycles of Annie, Britta, and Shirley. After the group effectively strip searches each other, Britta says something about Jeff's underwear, suggesting that the two of them have been having a casual sexual relationship on the side without the group knowing. What began as an annoying search for a pen that may have rolled away, as Jeff says at the beginning of the episode, turns into a serious existential interrogation of group trust. Annie opines that it seems "almost impossible" that any member of the group could be so inconsiderate as to not admit that they took the pen "after everything we've been through." It is true that it seems impossible after emptying each other's purses and backpacks, dividing the group by gender in the room and searching each other in their underwear, tearing into Pierce's casts to see if he was hiding the pen there, and ripping up the study room carpet apart, that anybody could have actually taken the pen. It clicks for Jeff that "actually it's *less* than impossible. Something impossible is *more likely*." The group eventually accepts Troy's earlier hypothesis that a ghost must have taken the pen. Here is where we see Hegelian spirit emerge.

To think dialectically, as Hegel understands, is to see the interdependence of things on their own internal opposition. Hegel develops this line of thought to its end point—absolute knowing[10]—in the whole of the *Phenomenology* but the Preface gives us enough to understand some key terms in Hegel's philosophical system. Spirit, for Hegel, is the motor of human endeavor, the prime mover of history. The question, then, is not "what" is spirit but *how* do we see it? Through what process? If it exists, how can it be shown? In the Preface, Hegel discusses spirit's relation to the subject, "tarrying with the negative," and how "authentic substance" is thinkable only through mediation. This is where Hegel codifies the "how" of spirit's emergence: "[spirit] only wins to its truth when it finds itself utterly torn asunder."[11] In thinking substance through negativity, in utterly tearing some *thing* asunder, spirit arises—opposite becomes apposite.

Spirit emerges from the process of dialectical interrogation, which pushes an idea through its own internal torsion toward what Hegel referred to as absolute knowing. As with many things in Hegel, absolute knowing is best shown through negation. We cannot mistake absolute knowing for a simple end or rest point for a line of inquiry. It is not a shorthand for enlightenment or a form of peaceful illumination where all conflict drifts away "like dross from pure metal."[12] Dialectical thinking is not taking an idea, finding an opposed external position, and then concluding, as the cliché goes, "perhaps the truth lies somewhere in the middle."[13] That cliché has been put to effective use in older television series. "Sammy's Visit," the classic episode of *All in the Family*, ends with Sammy Davis Jr. kissing Archie Bunker. While Sammy gets the final act/comment on Archie's racism, throughout the episode Archie's insensitive and offensive remarks are both upbraided and tolerated, usually through the studio audience laughter damning him one moment and redeeming him another. Or on *Cheers*, where Sam Malone is never totally wrong, but Diane Chambers is never completely right either. This type of tension-reducing middle ground is not the territory of the bottle episode or Hegelian dialectics. As Catherine Malabou writes, "Far from enforcing a violent stoppage of the dialectical progress, the advent of Absolute Knowledge will imply instead the exact opposite: its *metamorphosis*. Dialectical sublation will become absolute sublation—its own absolution."[14] What Malabou shows us is that what Hegel articulates with absolute knowing is a reversal of the above cliché: lying somewhere in the middle of an idea is the thing that would utterly destroy it.

Absolute knowing involves a subjective sacrifice: an encounter with the limit, a self-sundering.[15] Knowledge cannot be arrived at by stacking information atop of information (say, in the way Wikipedia entries proliferate) or by filling in a blank slate.

It is important to stress at this point that, in noting the way the bottle episode shows a proper understanding of Hegel's dialectical method, we are not just making an arbitrary point but are seeing him clearly as a philosopher of contradiction, rather than a philosopher of synthesis, and are—in a likewise move—seeing the same structure in the bottle episode. This is a key point for both Hegel and the bottle episode: we do not resolve or "synthesize" the conflict to move past it. We find a way to make the contradiction as intractable as possible. The emergence of spirit is not the inevitable consequence of contingent interactions (e.g., "this happens and then this and then this and now the problem is solved"). Nor is it the teleological end point of historical or narrative forces. Spirit emerges through contradiction as a point of relation that makes coherent a trajectory of meaning, the registration of which opens up new possibilities. Or, to put it in the language of "Cooperative Calligraphy," it is by reconciling oneself to impossibility that new possibilities emerge. Impossibility does not close down inquiry. The impossibility of the idea of a ghost *needing a pen* is irrelevant. When Dean Pelton looks at the destroyed study room at the end of the episode and asks, "What the *hell* did you people do in there?," Abed replies, "Something you and your puppies could only dream of, you non-miraculous sonofabitch." The emergence of spirit *is* a secular miracle. It is only through this hardening of contradiction that we can find a new way to relate to it, as the study group does in *Community*. Recognizing that what happens to the study group in "Cooperative Calligraphy" is them being "utterly torn asunder" (they are physically and emotionally stripped down) alerts us to how bottle episode, through forcing the relentless interrogation of internal antagonism, is dialectical. This is not the "simple synthesis" of characters being released from a situation with external constraints (such as being stuck in an elevator). It is the careful working through of intractable contradiction.

Television Aesthetics at the Limit

One of the ways television studies has been successful at defining the aesthetics particular to television—and therefore justifying its status as an object worthy of academic attention—has been through studying its most spectacular and experimental forms. In *Complex TV*, Jason Mittell writes of the "narrative special effect," a kind of payoff that the television serial offers that cannot be readily found in other narrative forms.[16] Jeffrey Sconce begins his influential 2004 "What If? Charting Television's New Textual Boundaries" by writing that the notion of television art "remains scandalous, a laughable oxymoron."[17] Sconce's essay argues for a particular kind of experimental standalone television art form, which he refers to as the "What If?" episode. "X-Cops," an episode of *The X-Files* that is also a played serious episode of *Cops*, is one of his chief examples. Sconce sees in such episodes a form of play with traditional expectations of American television—namely the expectation that what happens in one episode need not carry over to the next. Lynne Joyrich explores this common practice in "Epistemology of the Console." Joyrich shows how the explosion of the Connors' home in a Halloween episode of *Roseanne* both enables a theoretical consideration of what bringing queer sexuality into the heteronormative family sitcom would do (it would blow it up, literally) and allows for the suppression of that very same radicality, as the next episode of *Roseanne* has the Connors acting as though the previous episode never happened.[18]

Episodes such as these represent a significant deviation in television's expected storytelling aesthetic and serve as excellent sites to highlight what makes television a distinct artistic medium. The television episode, to borrow from Kathryn VanArendonk's "Theorizing the Television Episode," can have "more power" than the series as a whole.[19] Experimenting with convention can elevate the form of an episode, such as in Sconce's *X-Files* example, and can elevate the content of an episode to a level of theoretical critique, as Joyrich explains. It can even retroactively establish a relationship across multiple episodes and seasons, as in Mittell's narrative special effect. These ideas respond to a kind of maximalist experimentation made possible with television storytelling, expanding what an episodic television series can do in a way unique to television.

As Jane Feuer writes in "Narrative Form in American Television," "television as an apparatus differs in almost every significant aspect from film," TV's closest comparable visual medium.[20] In the essay, she emphasizes a kind of segmentation and discontinuity particular to television. Specifically, its proclivity to feature plots of disintegration of families (or synthetic families, such as a group of work friends) and the inevitable reintegration of that family. There is, as Feuer elucidates, a clear structural limitation here: "The [Norman] Lear sitcom [such as *All in the Family*] thus politicised the basic sitcom structure of a return to equilibrium and a new dilemma which would proceed in an endless circle until the series was cancelled."[21] Archie Bunker's liberal daughter and son-in-law cannot ever *really* rise up against his racism; otherwise, the entire premise of *All in the Family* would be uprooted. Sam Malone *has* to operate the bar Cheers in *Cheers*. Jerry Seinfeld cannot even get his apartment remodeled in *Seinfeld*. While Feuer sees that the constant rupturing of the family in a continuing serial can constitute a kind of "development," she does not believe that the reintegration imperative can ever lead to a critique of the nuclear family unit or synthetic family unit that, even today, remains a dominant premise for television.[22] Feuer helps us to articulate an important question: how can a television series—or any series—with such clear structural limitations ever present a radical break?

The answer depends on what we make of the word and idea of the "limit." What we see in Sconce's and Joyrich's essays, for example, is one kind of consideration of the limit of television form. A series such as *The X-Files* can play with its typical episodic formula to encompass many different variations, as Sconce notes, but it always returns to a kind of normality. The limit, in this case, can be transcended but only briefly. The kind of limit explored by the bottle episode, however, is not a wall that impedes progress, nor is it a hard end point. Rather, the bottle episode posits a limit that functions as an opening. It is just this sort of seeming paradox that is at the heart of Hegel's *Phenomenology*. This way of thinking contradiction as constitutive—as an impediment that is also an impetus—is what holds together the bottle episode as form.[23] In "Cooperative Calligraphy," we see this logic concretized in how Annie's pen moves from missing material object (a MacGuffin, perhaps) to a dialectical principle.

The Principle of the Pen

Before the study group becomes ensnared in a lockdown environment of mutual suspicion, Jeff tries to wriggle everybody out of the situation by reminding Annie that "It's a pen." As in, it is *just* a pen. Who cares? How much could they even cost? Why does it matter? Annie replies, "It's not a pen, it's a principle." Annie is speaking not just for herself but for the episode as such. Why should we, as viewers, care about a missing pen? Because it is a principle. When the group later turns to destroying the study room out of their failure to locate Annie's purple writing instrument, she suddenly agrees that it is *just* a pen.

While the pen itself may have lost its status as an item of principle for Annie, the principle of the pen has actually become bigger than her personal-particular investment in it. After Jeff says, "It's a pen now? It's not a principle?" he and Britta accuse Annie of realizing she actually *had* the pen halfway through her interrogation of the group. To prove she does not have the pen, she starts taking her clothes off. Jeff does likewise. At this moment, Abed stops the group from spontaneously stripping to say, "You're acting totally illogical. [pause] We need to divide the group by gender and search each other in our underwear." The joke, of course, is that the viewer is led to think that Abed will try to stop Jeff, Annie, and Britta from taking their clothes off but, instead, comes up with a formal process by which they can *better* and more efficiently search each other for the pen. Far from simply being a throwaway line, this joke encapsulates precisely what the formal logic of bottle episode demands. Abed, here, is deepening the contradiction that enmeshes the group, not turning away from it. In other words, he's embracing the principle of the pen. Rather than appealing to a kind of reason that would ordinarily dictate the group's actions, Abed further structures the shape of the dilemma.

What Abed understands is that the logic of the bottle episode emerges from within the space of the contradiction. It does not arrive from the outside. We can even see this internal dialectic emerging through a study of early shot-reverse-shot composition in the episode. The Dean arrives to give the group a "non-violent verbal reminder" of the Puppy Parade on the Quad, and, in his hands, he is holding an adorable pup. We see Annie and Britta make awed faces at the dog and, in the reverse shot, we see Troy about to say, "Aw, I wanna lick it."

On a first viewing this sequence seems almost perfunctory. It establishes an event outside of the study room that the group is eager to get to and, in just a moment, Annie will realize her pen is missing. It is true that there is a good deal of narrative set-up occurring in this short sequence but, more substantially, we can see a visual dimension to the dialectic in this shot sequence. Closer inspection reveals that the first shot is almost perfectly balanced. Jeff, on the viewer's right, and Annie, on the viewer's left, make an internal frame for Britta, who is in the center. The top of Britta's head is almost perfectly aligned with center of the frame, as we can see below. The balance in this shot, however, is about to be used toward deceptive ends in the reverse shot.

On the other side of the table we see, from bottom to top, Shirley, Troy, and Abed occupy the center of the frame leaving almost equal amounts of negative space on either side of them. The characters are positioned vertically in the center of the frame, with the top of each character's head above the person in front of them. Since the previous shot drew our attention to the middle of the frame, our eye is already in the center and moves slightly above where the top of Britta's head was in the previous shot when Troy says, "I wanna lick it." With the viewer's eye already in the center of the frame, the reverse shot moves it up slightly to Troy when he delivers what at first glance seems like a throwaway laugh line. At that precise moment, as viewers can see through magnifying the negative space to Abed's right, an actual monkey steals the pen.

Occurring to the viewer's left in seemingly unoccupied negative visual space, most viewers will miss what has happened. At the spoken narrative level, the conflict this sequence seems to have established is that the group wants to go to a puppy parade (except Jeff, who has a date). This is a conflict that is introduced literally outside of the frame. While we pay attention to the group paying attention to a puppy the Dean is holding, something else is happening *internal* to the frame. It is at this moment where outside and ordinary logic ceases to matter within the space of the study room since it does not even matter within the frame itself. The tight composition of this two-shot sequence seems to show us everything while it hides the impossible in plain sight. The Hegelian lesson, however, is clear: in order to see the impossible emerge within a bottle episode, we need to tarry with the negative (space).

Chaos and Contradiction

Hegel might say that fidelity to the contradiction attests to the truth of spirit. In the bottle episode form, this fidelity to contradiction is what seeds the ground for a different kind of collective to emerge from within bottled confinement. This is exactly what is at stake when Abed tells the group, at the end of "Remedial Chaos Theory," a season three bottle episode, that they must be accepting of each other's flaws and virtues because they are the same thing. As Slavoj Žižek writes in *Sex and the Failed Absolute*, "repetition brings out the obscene underside of the repeated term, Hegel focuses on the opposite case where a repetition causes idealization, the 'sublation' of a term to its higher level."[24] *Community* narrativizes this precise form of Hegelian repetition in "Remedial Chaos Theory."

In "Remedial Chaos Theory," the study group is gathered around a table at Troy and Abed's new apartment when suddenly the doorbell is rung by a pizza delivery person. No one in the group wants to go get the pizza. Jeff devises a plan to determine who will get up: he tosses a six-sided die into the air. The group member to his left starting with the number one will go to get the pizza. Before Jeff tosses the dice in the air, Abed tells him that he is creating "six different timelines." From there the formal invention of the episode is to have wildly different intragroup conflict play out depending on who leaves to get the pizza.

Here *Community* offers an exemplary case of the dialectical affordances of the limit. By removing group members one by one, "Remedial Chaos Theory" introduces gaps in the group's social order. In effect, it is the missing character (the person leaving the apartment to get the pizza) who determines the relational dynamic of the group. The way "Remedial Chaos Theory" handles the interrelation of these timelines is masterful, reaching its zenith when several Chekhov's guns—a scale model of the rolling boulder scene from *Raiders of the Lost Ark*, Serbian Rum that is "banned—banned! in Serbia," Britta smoking marijuana in the bathroom, and, of course, an actual gun—all fire at the same time. The point of the episode, however, is the emotional reveals in each timeline. Crucially, these reveals happen often when a character is not in the room. "Remedial Chaos Theory" shows that an absence can make its presence felt.

Shirley, for example, is revealed to be so generous and giving to the point that the group diagnoses her with a "baking problem"—constantly baking for the group to avoid confronting herself for, as Jeff says, "You aren't allowed to have baking things as an identity." But her "baking problem"—her being a "pie pusher" who "push[es] pies to get love"—is inextricable from her capacity to give and care for the group. Shirley's greatest virtue is also her fatal flaw. This contradiction utterly rips her asunder through the course of "Remedial Chaos Theory," and when Abed goes around the group to name each character's flaw and virtue, we can recognize that spirit has emerged. Abed, effectively, urges his friends to "tarry with the negative."[25]

At the end of "Remedial Chaos Theory," Abed halts the six different timelines from ever splitting by grabbing the Yahtzee die Jeff tosses before it hits the table. He tells the group that "chaos dominates enough of their lives" and—sublating the flaws of each group member—says "it won't matter what happens to us as long as we stay accepting of each other's flaws and virtues." The group must reconcile themselves to contradiction rather than attempt to overcome it. When Abed says, "flaws *and* virtues" we need to note that he proceeds to name only *one* thing about each group member, meaning this episode sees how flaw and virtue are intertwined notions: Shirley will always be giving, Annie will always be driven, Pierce will never apologize, Britta is "a bit of a wildcard," and Jeff will always be a "conniving sonofabitch" (meaning he will always resist how much he needs the group). Although it goes unmentioned by Abed, we can fill in from our knowledge of the gaps in other timelines that Troy will always be loving (he tries to say "You guys are my best friends" to the group in an earlier shown timeline) and Abed will always be concerned with the meta implications of what he and his friends do. The point is that one's flaw *is also* one's virtue and one's virtue is also one's flaw. It is not a spectrum—it is a limit. Someone who is giving, like Shirley, will always be *too giving* to the point that giving becomes pushing. Abed says, "we need to be accepting of each other's flaws and virtues." He doesn't say, "we need to make sure our virtues don't become our flaws," which is a comfortably liberal notion of moderation or the middle being the privileged location of truth. What *Community* shows is far more radical. A giving person or a kind person does not think "I should make sure to only be giving or kind in the right amount to the right people" because that is not what it means to be either giving or kind. One's virtues will always be excessive. One's flaws likewise.

By creating a space in the group dynamic, as this bottle episode does structurally by having characters leave the group one by one, we can see more clearly the complexity of their relation to each other and the dialectical relationship of flaws and virtues. We can also see, in Abed, a complete transformation from the character who claimed in "Cooperative Calligraphy" that he hated bottle episodes for their "wall to wall emotional nuance." There he twice urged Jeff to just give an "inspiring speech" to send them home, acting flippantly about the entire situation. Here, in "Remedial Chaos Theory," Abed's own inspiring speech gives the study group a new way to relate to each other—especially when he reveals that Jeff, the group's de facto "leader," used the Yahtzee dice to determine who left the room as a way to ensure *he* never had to get the pizza (e.g., "There are six sides of the die and seven of us"). When Jeff leaves the room, the group starts an impromptu dance party to The Police's "Roxanne"—finally acting as a collective rather than a series of people with individual side stories. Each study group member's relationship with Jeff is often at the center of *Community*'s episodes. By removing Jeff, the group loses its normal center of meaning. Even Jeff appreciates this. When he comes back into the room and spies the dance party, he sarcastically shouts, "See what happens when I leave you alone?" No one hears him over the music and the fun they are having. Jeff smirks, contented. This dance party, an almost physical manifestation of Hegelian spirit, carries extra meaning for us as viewers because we have seen the other timelines and know how easy it is for a group this close-knit to fall apart. In fact, we watch the apartment become torn asunder in Troy's timeline when all the various Chekhov's guns work in perfect orchestration to set fire to the apartment (a clear echo of the study room being torn apart in "Cooperative Calligraphy"). Spirit wins to its truth after the group has had an encounter with the limit. To confront the intractability of Hegelian contradiction entails the group reconciling itself *to* that contradiction. In "Cooperative Calligraphy," it is that something impossible is more likely to have happened than one group member having stolen a pen. In "Remedial Chaos Theory" it is that one's greatest flaw is at once also one's highest virtue. As Abed urges, it is only by recognizing each other's flaws and virtues *at once* that they can weather the chaotic randomness of life. It is only by paying fidelity to spirit—the result of radical dialectical revelation—and by acknowledging each other's internal limit that the study group can exist as a group (or community) at all.

From Series to Collective

Recognizing the relationship between Hegelian dialectics and *Community* is not enough to fully highlight the formal invention of the bottle episode heralds for television studies, however. Thinking the bottle episode through Hegel shows us a television form that argues a theoretically resonant mode of understanding the collective. This radical dimension of television form has remained underexplored. Television has more often been argued to be a deficit for realizing a politically potent collective than as an agent facilitating that change.[26] The bottle episode shows us otherwise. The bottle episode imagines dynamic collectivity forming through isolation and separation. This is the way the bottle episode narrativizes what I have referred to as dialectical revelation.

As we know from the previous chapter, Jean-Paul Sartre's *Critique of Dialectical Reason* explores the possibility of the dialectical transformation of a group into a stronger collective. Sartre's key term is seriality. Seriality, for Sartre, is that which separates people politically into artificially arranged groups and what keeps people from organizing as a collective. Again, Sartre's seriality needs to be thought of as a "series" of *individuals* grouped by capital and given superficial reasons to relate to each other. Sartre's most famous example of seriality—people in a queue waiting for a bus—shows "the intensity of isolation, as a relation of exteriority between the members of a temporary and contingent gathering, express[ing] *the degree of massification* of the social ensemble, in so far as it is produced on the basis of given conditions."[27] Rather than becoming a collective for Sartre, seriality is what keeps people a series of individuals.

Sartre finds the demands of modern life under capital produces groups of individuals who, by passively engaging in the same activity (such as waiting for a bus), are alienated from each other. This alienation is key for Sartre and it is the element that can turn a series into what he calls "group-in-fusion," a politically motivated collective. The group-in-fusion is predicated on the awareness that "everyone is the same as the Others in so far as he is Other than himself."[28] This is what Sartre means when he says that "members of the group are third parties."[29] The group-in-fusion must remain alienated from their circumstances, as "the most lively and united group is always in danger of relapsing into the series from which it came."[30] For Sartre, as Jameson summarizes, "the group-in-fusion emerges from seriality as a reaction against it, its subsequent development and fate governed by the danger of its dissolution back into seriality again."[31]

Sartre's formulation is totally at odds with how the bottle episode represents dialectical transformation of a group. Bottle episodes often find superficial reasons to constrain characters (that is one of their enduring features across genres and television history) and it is through this superficial frame that the larger existential breakthrough occurs. While Sartre sees that alienation is the key to group formation, he is wary of its "dissolution." For Sartre, the study group leaving the library room at the end of "Cooperative Calligraphy" would be tantamount to throwing away everything they just did to become a group-in-fusion. This split on what might seem like a minor point actually opens up an important consideration of how Sartre conceives of the dialectic as such. For Sartre, seriality is an aggregation of superficially connected particulars that can never form a collective. The only way a group-in-fusion can form is by overcoming seriality.

At first glance, it seems that the bottle episode does exactly what Sartre prescribes we do to escape seriality: finding a way out of a restrictive and alienating frame. The logic of the bottle episode, however, positions itself against this Sartrean idea. As Sartre writes, "*there is no such thing as an isolated individual* (unless isolation is treated as a special structure of sociality)," meaning seriality is so oppressive that the individual is always already implicated in the other.[32] For Sartre, this is a major problem. For Lacan, this is a fact of the symbolic as such. For Hegel, recognizing the individual as always already implicated in the group and the group being always already implicated in the individual is the condition of a radical kind of self-awareness. It does not close down the possibility of collective action but rather is constitutive of it. Sartre writes, "The reality of a praxis of a (fused) group depends on the liquidation (either simultaneous or subject to temporal dislocations which can be ignored) of the serial, both of everyone and by everyone in everyone, and its replacement by community."[33] This chapter has argued that the formation of a fused group depends on the isolation he associates with the series. In fact, that isolation is the vital first step toward reaching community (sitcom or otherwise).

As we see in "Advanced Dungeons and Dragons," alienation is the pre-requisite to new group formation. The episode opens with a fantasy genre-inspired voiceover telling viewers that Jeff has recently befriended another student at Greendale Community College, Neil. Normally happy-go-lucky, Neil has suddenly been branded "Fat Neil" by the Greendale community. As a result of this teasing nickname becoming his symbolic identity, Neil turns sullen and depressed (it is later revealed that Jeff is the first person to have called him "Fat Neil"). Worse, Jeff fears Neil is on the verge of suicide. Knowing that Neil is a devoted player of popular tabletop role-playing game *Dungeons & Dragons*, Jeff resolves to get the study group together to spend a session hopefully lifting Neil's spirits. In so doing, Neil's spirts *are* lifted but only after reckoning with Jeff's betrayal. To play *Dungeons & Dragons*, one needs to "role play," as in act according to a role in the game's world. This means not performing actions according to a code of ethics one would employ in their day-to-day lives but to commit to acting as, say, a morally ambiguous Rogue, an honest and dutiful Paladin, a charming yet secretive Bard, and the like. With each member of the study group acting *not as themselves* but as fictional *Dungeons & Dragons* personas (e.g., "Chester the Well-Endowed"), they then come together both as a group of fantasy role playing game players *and* a new dynamic collective that includes a recently introduced character. The group dynamic here makes the characters strangers to themselves, seeing themselves as other to themselves is required for the new dynamic to form.[34]

Reading the bottle episode as form, I find that separating a group into a series of individuals is the very precondition for establishing a dynamic collective. Further, the change occasioned by straining a group through the bottle episode means they coalesce as a group altered in such a fundamental way that there is no danger of relapsing into the collection of individuals they were before (we see this clearly in Abed's shift from bottle episode cynic to true believer). Rather than throwing off seriality—or escaping the bottle frame—I find that the bottle episode's constraint is a prerequisite to forming a "group-in-fusion." Where Sartre sees an impediment to the group—separation and isolation—the bottle episode shows its necessity.

The bottle episode shows how a group, already superficially connected (i.e., everybody just goes to the same school), can be separated—isolated—into a series of people (i.e., individual particulars) and turned into a dynamic collective through dialectical character interaction. The bottle episode structure—particularly as seen in "Cooperative Calligraphy"—renders characters physically inert. All "activity," such as strip-searching a group of friends to locate a missing pen, is pointless. Being active in a bottle episode pushes one away from having the ability to confront the self and the group. As it turns out, passivity and an openness to thoughtfully interrogate the self is necessary for the dialectical revelation to take place. What Sartre cannot see is the necessity of the limit in forming collectivity.

The conflict in bottle episodes is always deepened. It is not resolved, in the sense that a character can return to who they were when the episode began. Bottle episodes demand character revelation. What I have argued—and *Community* is consistent on this point—is that this moment cannot be walked back. These are not moments that can be overturned, as in the Conners' house exploding in *Roseanne*. Consistent with reading Hegel as a thinker against flat synthesis, dialectical revelations are moments that can only be used to move toward a new hardening of contradiction. In another characteristically meta moment on *Community*, Abed says of season six's "Basic Email Security" that it is the third in a "trilogy" of episodes where the group is forced to divulge secrets to each other. The first being "Cooperative Calligraphy"—an episode Abed refers to as happening in "what he now refers to as our Golden Age"—and the second being season five's "Cooperative Polygraphy," where the executor of the estate of Pierce Hawthorne submits the group to a lie detector test in the study room after Pierce's death. "Cooperative Polygraphy" gives us the diegetic reason for Donald Glover to leave the show, as Troy is gifted millions of dollars upon Pierce's death. Troy can claim the money on the condition that he sails around the world on Pierce's yacht. Troy never returns and the group (and series) would fill his absence with new characters in the show's final two seasons. And so, when Abed acts as the show's memory in "Basic Email Security" by recalling previous bottle episodes, *Community* is acknowledging how pivotal the bottle episode is in forging group dynamics with lasting consequences. As the crisis of the group's personal emails being leaked on the internet threatens to destabilize a nascent bond between Jeff, Abed, Annie, Britta, and new members Frankie (Paget Brewster) and Elroy (Keith David), "Basic Email Security" again demonstrates that the group owes its entire consistency to navigating these dialectical impasses.

Recalling VanArendonk, I think it is fair to say that if episodes stand out in a series and can, in some ways, exceed the memory of the series as a whole, then no kind of episode stands out more than a bottle episode.[35]

Bottle episodes open rifts and wounds in a group. They tear groups asunder, as we see in *Community*, and they leave a mark. Of course, not every series uses bottle episodes as direct textual references in the way *Community* does. However, since the structure of the bottle episode requires dialectical revelation, as I have been arguing, bottle episodes install memory in a series. The point is not that characters, having been through a bottle episode or two, will never quarrel ever again. The point is that being put through the ringer of bottled confinement makes a group closer and thus gives them more to lose because they—and the audience—remember. Importantly, even a moment of failed dialectical revelation can be seen as a success. In *Breaking Bad*'s "Fly," Walter White (Bryan Cranston) is about to admit to Jesse Pinkman (Aaron Paul) that he watched Jesse's girlfriend die and did nothing to stop it, but he cannot bring himself to say it. For viewers of the series, if they had not already earmarked the moment of Jane's (Krysten Ritter) death as the pivot for Walt becoming "Heisenberg," Walt's inability to speak it confirms its revelatory status. Here we see how the limit of expression can enable something to be expressed by something *not* being expressed. The limit makes Walt's nonexpression itself an expression, similar to how "Remedial Chaos Theory" turned character absence into presence as a way of understanding the study group as a social collective. Walt and Jesse—who at the point in the series where "Fly" appears—have stopped functioning as a group (let alone a collective) and are very much an isolated series of two people. Nevertheless, they do bond through the confinement in "Fly" and emerge more connected than they previously were. But crucially, this is a bond premised on Walt's nonexpression, his failure to deepen the conflict between him and Jesse. While a group does undeniably form here a collective does not. In the relief of collectivity's absence, however, we see the structure of the bottle episode further clarified. What we track here is the productivity of the limit and the imprint it leaves on a series.

No Series at the Café

The coffee shop "Meet Cute" is a hallmark of romantic comedies and sitcoms. The typical set up works like this: two characters who will become romantically involved bump into each other at coffee shop. Maybe someone takes the other person's order by accident, maybe they both grab for the last almond croissant at the same time, maybe one spills coffee on the other. No matter how it plays out, from these humble beginnings a heartwarming and/ or heartbreaking relationship typically results. Not too dissimilarly in terms of importance, the premise of a coffee shop meet-up serves as the jumping off point for Sartre's complex notions of subjective experience in *Being and Nothingness*.

Sartre, as the protagonist of this narrative philosophical example, walks into a café to look for his friend Pierre:

> It is certain that the café by itself with its patrons, its tables, its booths, its mirrors, its light, its smoky atmosphere, and the sounds of voices, rattling saucers, and footsteps which fill it—the café is a fullness of being. And all the intuitions of detail

> which I can have are filled by these odors, these sounds, these colors, all phenomena which have a trans-phenomenal being. Similar Pierre's actual presence in a place which I do not know is also a plenitude of being. We seem to have found fullness everywhere.[36]

Upon reading this—right off the bat—we are struck by the literary way Sartre paints this scene. He wants us to stand in it, look around, smell the air, and feel all the sensory details. Unsurprisingly, Sartre comes back to this scene again and again throughout the pages of *Being and Nothingness* and each time he does we understand more acutely another edge to the example. What Sartre is doing, besides painting a rich scene, is showing how entering *this* café almost overwhelms us with presence. The presence of the tables, the atmosphere, the sounds, the smells. Everywhere there is presence. Sartre details the scene in the way that he does because he will soon turn to showing us how an absence—nothing—is made-to-be.

All of the above contributes to a "ground" for Sartre. As he writes, "When I enter this café to search for Pierre, there is formed a synthetic organization of all the objects in the café, on the ground of which Pierre is give as about to appear."[37] There is, however, a problem. JP showed up late. Fifteen minutes late. He will not find Pierre. Maybe Pierre *was there* and left because he thought he was being stood up. Maybe he never appeared at all. Regardless, there will be no meet up (cute or otherwise):

> Pierre is not here. This does not mean that I discover his absence in some precise spot in the establishment. In fact, Pierre is absent from the *whole* café; his absence fixes the café in its evanescence; the café remains *ground*; it persists in offering itself as an undifferentiated totality to my only marginal attention; it slips into the background; it pursues its nihilation.[38]

Upon entering the café, we "seem to find" a "plentitude of being" but what's important to grasp is how this fullness of being can only appear on a ground of nothingness. Pierre not being present reveals the absence, the nothingness, that lies coiled in the heart of the café. Pierre not being there does not *create* the nothingness; rather, it *reveals it*. As Sartre writes, there is an infinity of people who are also *not* at the café, but he has no reason to expect them (movie stars, politicians, public figures of any kind, childhood friends, etc.). Their absence reveals nothing. Without a "real expectation" of them being present at the café, there is nothing revealed about the café nor about the ground of our existential phenomenological experience. The present absence of Pierre reveals what is at stake for Sartre's existential system of thought: nothingness is a primary and prior "for-itself." Sartre thinks that we typically regard the "in-itself" (or the plenitude of being he writes about in this café example) as what the world is. Nothing, we might think immediately, is only graspable when something has been taken away from plenitude. Consistent with his belief in a "pre-reflective *cogito*," Sartre believes in an original nothingness as the prior and primary term to any kind of phenomenological apprehension or experience.

Due to his focus on negation—and the negation of negation—it may seem like Hegel would be a partner in Sartre's existential investigation but like many others, Sartre reads Hegel as a philosopher of synthesis and, therefore, *not* someone who privileges or understands nothingness. We can see this when Sartre writes, "The true concrete for Hegel is the Existent with its essence; it is the Totality produced by the synthetic integration of all the abstract moments which are surpassed in it by requiring their complement."[39] And, just a few pages later, Sartre accuses Hegel of a synthetic operation in opposing "being to nothingness as thesis and antithesis."[40] This leads Sartre to deem Hegel a thinker who brings in conflict from the outside; specifically, he writes that Hegel "introduces negation to being from the outside."[41] While it is true that Hegel is avowedly a dialectical thinker, Hegel never once refers to his own dialectical method as comprising the Ancient dialectic of thesis-antithesis-synthesis and was, in fact, critical of the Ancient Greeks for employing this method of thinking. Hegel's dialectic is, as we have shown, premised with teasing out the consequences of internal contradiction (or a primary void, as Slavoj Žižek has argued) rather than finding the stable ground of synthesis after limply contrasting an idea with some external conflict related to it. Sartre even understands this logically, as he writes of his own investigation that "non-being is not the opposite of being; it is its contradiction," but imagines Hegel not capable of including this idea in his system.[42] Sartre imagines Hegel's dialectic to be binary and composed of bulwark oppositions where only synthetic compromise can arise to bring ideas together. Sartre writes a compelling tear-down of synthetic thinking, but this is not a takedown of Hegel as such since Hegel does not hold the precepts that Sartre criticizes him for, as we have shown already. As we saw in "Cooperative Calligraphy," the dialectical contradiction is inside the frame; it does not arrive from without. It does, however, make clear why Sartre is so opposed to the dialectic.

While Sartre's stance against the Hegelian dialectic (as he conceives it) remains consistent across the twenty years that separate *Being and Nothingness* and *Critique of Dialectical Reason*, in order to theorize his notion of seriality Sartre abandons the carefully won principles he established in that coffee shop. The café is full of literary life but, more importantly, it contains a revealing gap—Pierre's absence. The bus stop of *Critique of Dialectical Reason*, however, is just a bus stop. We no longer have the nihilating nothingness of the for-itself. Instead, we simply have the flat evident and surface nature of the in-itself. As Sartre says, the most important moment in the history of the in-itself is the emergence of the for-itself—just how the most important thing in the café is Pierre's absence, not anything in the plenitude of being that seems most immediate. What disappears is precisely *nothing*. The gap—the present absence, the nothingness that is coiled in the heart of being for Sartre—is not evident at the bus stop. In the way we have been defining dialectics, the café of *Being and Nothingness* is dialectical in nature. The bus stop is not. As we know by this point, for Sartre seriality comes from the outside—an external order. He has no space in his theorizing for what Lacan discovers: that a series forms internally, unconsciously, and coextensive with our own being in the world. While it's true that the idea of the present absence could potentially link Lacan's series to Sartre's café this not a stable or tenable connection. Despite regarding the phenomenological experience of the café as being structured by a gap in the series of people there, it's quite clear that Sartre and Lacan are proposing opposed notions of the gap and the series. In fact, by the time Sartre compiles the drafts and notes that would be posthumously published as *Critique of Dialectical Reason, Volume 2*, the existential gap in the café has evaporated. Sartre writes that "cafés project" as "ensembles without unity—but [are] still capable of fusing"; however, serialization prevents this from happening at all.[43] Seriality and its immanence have taken over the way Sartre sees the social to the point that he can no longer see the gaps that he previously saw as structuring absences.

Sartre misses that the gap in the series binds us to the symbolic and bonds us through the symbolic. In a very real sense, it is Jean-Paul Sartre and not me who first discovers and articulates that seriality is the existential form of modern life. The key difference is that Sartre sees this as a form that needs to be liquidated and escaped. I am arguing that it needs to be embraced. Sartre argues that it is alienating, that seriality ties every person together superficially, thereby preventing a meaningful politically active group to coalesce. I am saying that the superficial tie is a necessity to forming a politically active collective and, separately, that alienation does not obscure subjectivity but rather is the precondition for it and that we need to think these things at the same time. When Sartre discovers seriality as a concept, the existential subject completely falls out of his thinking. Seriality, as I am arguing, is the way that thinking the existential subject becomes sensible—with all the gaps constitutive of subject formation that Sartre disavows and forecloses. I've grounded this conception of the seriality of the subject through a media example (the bottle episode) and will now turn, a la Sartre, to a more mundane and everyday example to close the chapter.

It is hard to think of a wider spread and more isolating period of recent history than the COVID-19 pandemic. Especially during the lockdown portions of the pandemic, people were separated from friends, family, coworkers, and colleagues (as I likely do not need to remind most readers). It is likely that many if not all readers spoke with loved ones over Skype, Zoom, or FaceTime during the pandemic. At first glance these media communication platforms exacerbate our isolation and, indeed, loneliness. With our heads segmented by the camera into squares or rectangles, the form seems to highlight how cut off we are from the person we are speaking to. As a teacher, my work "in the classroom" was done exclusively through Zoom squares from March 2020 until the start of the 2021/2 school year. I like to make a lot of jokes as I teach and, in the Zoom environment, the possibility of knowing how any of those jokes landed with students on camera or off was impossible. At every turn there was a technological barrier to togetherness, even as our communication was aided. And yet—and yet—many times throughout the semester you could not have convinced me that we weren't together. It was not technology that brought my students together from Hyderabad, Hong Kong, Chicago, London, and elsewhere; it was investing in the idea that when we met *we were together*. I'm sure other people had different Zoom school experiences but, if we are to take Sartre seriously, there should be no structural way for people separated to come together around a common cause (in this case, learning). Were there times where I felt alone? Yes. Of course. When? When the students left. Never while we were together. In a reversal of Sartre's café, it is the ground of nothingness—of isolation—that enabled a plenitude of being and the formation of a class.

Just as Sartre's investment in the expectation that Pierre be present at the café reveals the centrality of an *a priori* nothingness, the above example reveals that separation and alienation are not barriers to community, a collective, or the formation of a group but, rather, are its precondition. Did these groups last? No. The class is always dismissed for the day. This is not the point. The point is what is the initial move needed in the formation of an active collective. It is, as I have been arguing, not shuffling off seriality but embracing it. We are often in series superficially brought together. Rather than imagining a pure position of group formation, as Sartre tries to, I argue it is far more radical to work with the superficial series as the ground.

We can do this work through investing in the superficiality of an initial connection, rather than decrying it. This is the basis of all attraction, the belief that there is depth in surface, rather than depth beneath it. It is precisely these superficial groupings that provide the unlikely points of contact and connection to foment and ground a liberatory politics. Meeting someone on the basis that you both like the *X-Men* is by definition superficial. At the 2024 Comic-Con in San Diego, over 135,000 people were in attendance. Over 200,000 people attended the New York City Comic-Con. Should convention planners allow space for it, any left-wing group would do well to organize at such an event. The very superficiality of such a gathering would seem to be at odds with organizing for human rights or against fascism. However, as we saw with the bottle episode contra Sartre, the superficial is a vital entry point to the serious and can even act as glue when discord threatens to splinter a group apart. This requires an investment in stepping beyond an initial and protective cynicism toward popular and mass culture.

Cynicism is by its nature stuck on the fact of the superficial, as it attempts to maintain pure and simple surface of its antonym in order to sustain its own surface-level position against it. It wants to keep everything at an arm's length and maintain a position of permanent distance. It does not engage with the superficial, merely sneers at it. The social cement aspect of seriality is founded on the superficiality of popular culture. Extracting and sustaining the depth of the superficial is what I take to be the political imperative of psychoanalytic inquiry and Hegelian dialectics. The political potential here cuts across all manner of social, education-related, and economic barriers, as the superficial is within everyone's grasp. Sartre's theory of the radical group-in-fusion is not. Effecting it requires a dogmatic kind of fidelity lest the affairs of the personal intervene to complicate or dissolve the group. This kind of group definition is too fragile to be sustained, to the point where the "proof" of Sartre's argument becomes the impossibility of realizing the kind of group he describes. We need instead, I argue, the logic of the classroom: you come together as a physical collective during a prescribed period of time but the work that is done *in the class* leaves an imprint that follows you wherever you go. Whether you are in the class or not. It's the impression of a certain form that is important—in this case the serial form and the idea that you are a bound series whether you are physically with others or not. It is not the impression of content. We'll take this idea into the next chapter when we look at social media, a communication method that presents as serial but is far closer to the kind of disconnected amalgamation that Sartre (erroneously) considers to be on the side of seriality.

The Emotional Consequences of Bottled Television

There is a further move to be made here in emphasizing the collectivizing movement of the bottle episode. This chapter has so far emphasized that Hegel helps explain the formal invention of the bottle episode, but it is also the case that the bottle episode opens up an unacknowledged aspect of Hegelian dialectics and the emergence of spirit: sincerity. This is another topic that, perhaps not coincidentally, divides Sartre and Hegel. For Sartre, sincerity is a de facto being-for-others, a performance of sentiment meant to placate other people. As he writes in *Being and Nothingness*,

"Total, constant sincerity as a constant effort to adhere to oneself is by nature a constant effort to dissociate oneself from oneself. A person frees himself from himself by the very act by which he makes himself an object for himself."[44] Sartre implicitly cleaves vulnerability from sincerity. We have a perfectly good word for the performance of a false sense of vulnerability that Sartre seems to be referring to: insincere. The sincerity of the dialectic and, indeed, the bottle episode, requires vulnerability and an openness to see oneself in a disfavorable light. Bottle episodes tend toward sincerity—by which I mean a heightened emotional tenor of truthfulness and openness among characters, without slippage between what is said and what is truly felt or meant—even in an insincere or ironic television series.

Community's "Cooperative Calligraphy" is an excellent case in point. Contra David Foster Wallace's well-known argument that television encourages disaffected irony through postmodern meta-fiction, *Community* acknowledges, in a meta-fictional way, that it *is* doing a bottle episode and through that acknowledgment of its form is able to deliver a sincerely affecting story.[45] Even the flagrantly insincere *Family Guy* featured an emotionally resonant episode where Brian and Stewie get stuck in a bank vault and—after a scene where Brian ingests Stewie's feces—the pair express feelings of genuine appreciation and love for each other. "Brian and Stewie" uses this clear obscenity as a way to raise the emotional stakes of the episode to a higher (Hegelian) ideal. When the pair are eventually released from the bank vault, Brian carries a sleeping Stewie out. It is the only episode of the series to end without theme music playing over the credits, as the catharsis of the ending is left to simmer.

It is not the case that bottle episodes *always* end with sincere expressions of feeling. *Seinfeld*, a series that famously had as its writers' room motto "no hugging, no learning," is an exemplary case but even here there is room to see the sincere in the insincere. "The Chinese Restaurant" ends with bitter irony as a table has just opened for the protagonists the moment they decide to leave. Even though "The Chinese Restaurant" ends on a bitter note, it is still heavy with character revelation. George shares a very intimate (and unfortunate) story of how impending intestinal distress doomed a romantic moment in his girlfriend Tatiana's "tiny apartment" and her "little bathroom." We also learn—mentioned for the only time in the series—that Jerry has a sister who, because of an ill-timed run in with a family friend named Lorraine, will surely find out about how he ditched plans with his uncle Leo to go see *Plan 9 from Outer Space* with his friends. Elaine expresses clear existential angst when she says that, as a child, she was so excited to go to a new restaurant and "see food you'd never seen before" and now, as an adult in her thirties, she feels "like a big sweaty hog waiting for them to fill up the trough." We also see, in his absence, the role of Kramer in the group. The idea that Kramer had a rich life outside the apartment building that included hanging out with Jerry, George, and Elaine had not yet taken root on the show. In "The Parking Garage," a bottle episode written the following season, Kramer's purchase of a discount air conditioner at the mall is what binds the group together. Remembering his absence in "The Chinese Restaurant," the later bottle episode is a sincere apology for excluding Kramer from the earlier bottle episode.

Interestingly, in both of these examples, for insincere series to make a sincere gesture it requires the presence of what Julia Kristeva would call abjection. The abject is located in the social breakdown between that which is recognizably self and that which is recognizably (and terrifyingly) other. Abjection represents a barrier to reconciling oneself to a symbolic situation that appears totally alien or objectionable (seeing the dead body of a loved one, for example). What happens in abjection is a "casting off." In the *Seinfeld* example, Elaine describes herself as a "sweaty hog," confronting the distance between her idealized childhood self and the bodily horror of her adult self. In the *Family Guy* example, Brian eats Stewie's feces (a scene which does not appear in syndicated version of the episode, testifying to the idea that this moment of confronting abjection cannot be incorporated in symbolic reality). Both examples involve the casting off of bodily fluids, perhaps literalizing the purging of insincerity that the bottle episode requires.

In looking at sincerity in the bottle episode and in the dialectic, I hope to make clear that Sartre—while he represents the relationship of the individual to the collective and the function of the serial to an opposed end—helps to emphasize the existential aspects of Hegel's philosophy. For Sartre, a series of people is something to be overcome. Seriality makes us isolated and we need the group-in-fusion to break out. In fact, even *sincerity* is something that needs to be overcome and done away with according to Sartre. As he writes in *Being and Nothingness*, "Total, constant sincerity as a constant effort to adhere to oneself is by nature a constant effort to dissociate oneself from oneself. A person frees himself from himself by the very act by which he makes himself an object for himself."[46] For Sartre, sincerity disassociates one from oneself. Sartre sees being sincere as a being-for-others, a separation in the heart of the self. What the kind of sincerity we have been tracing shows is rather a radical kind of vulnerability in the face of both self and other. This Hegelian reading of the bottle episode underscores that the bottle episode forges a new way of relating to the self and the group. In short, the bottle episode as form enables and deepens character and group confrontation, thrusting characters into a new relation with self and other. Further, understanding the richness of the bottle episode form teaches us something: namely, how connected we are *but only through this isolation*. In other words, it is only by becoming "a series of people" that we can see collectivity. Advertisements have long attempted to monopolize this genuine collectivity to make it seem false but understanding this idea through the dialectical sincerity of the bottle episode shows us more. In a literal way, we need to move past seeing the bare appearance of this idea in a car commercial to see the social truth it is attempting to hijack.[47] A sincere kind of openness to the dialectic is needed to be able to brush past the easy and comforting cynicism that seeks only to sustain a dissatisfying relationship to oneself and the world.

Unbottled

The notes to *Critique of Dialectical Reason, Volume 2* end with a short treatise on television. Sartre believed that, in bourgeois society, owning a television was a "cultural enrichment" that causes impoverishment.[48] The idea is that owning a television demarcates a certain kind of attainment and carries with it status. Sartre even sees aerials or TV antennas on houses as symbols avowing a certain kind of wealth, status, and surface connectedness to mass culture. The problem for Sartre is that this was a prescription from the bourgeoisie to the proletariat and attaining this kind of technological sophistication ensures one will be forever indebted to bourgeois culture. To sustain this view, Sartre subscribes to a thesis of scarcity, writing in a representative paragraph that "in the field of scarcity an increase in the number or power of my neighbors has the result of increasing the precariousness of my existence."[49] While this, effectively, is the thesis of the contemporary conservative movement, Sartre is not endorsing it. He is attempting to lay out the immanence of this relation and the importance in rejecting it totally. As we have been tracing out, the issue with Sartre's formulation is that this is not a dialectical relationship. It's relevant to mention that French television was state-owned. Sartre responds to the domestication of the serial as seen on TV through the television as a device. When one thinks of television as a medium controlled by the state, there is no possibility for TV to ever be radical. All it can ever do is reify the state. If one thinks of television even as only *primarily* ideological rather than *completely*, the medium itself can exceed ideological demands and break from it. We can see this in examples of radical television form such as the bottle episode.

One of the temptations in arguing for television as art has been to dismiss the influence of the economic or mitigate it in some way. When minimizing the role money plays in television art, scholars have tended to argue that the TV artform transcends its economic situation.[50] Others argue that the interests of financial stakeholders and audiences are actually the same thing.[51] Sartre forces us to be more Hegelian and see that the nakedly capitalistic dictate that occasioned the bottle episode is inextricable from its art.[52] Rather than confirming the idea that capitalism is a creative force and should, in some way, be venerated, the bottle episode teaches a profoundly anti-capitalist lesson: that only through alienation and separation can we fully encounter a genuine collective. By foregrounding that who a character is for others is not the same as who they are from themselves, bottle episodes posit a confrontation with self and other that cannot be overcome by mere hugging, crying, and theme music. The bottle episode uses economic limits, spatial limits, character limits, as a way to exceed them. American commercial television has been characterized by Jason Mittell as operating on an "infinite model of storytelling," in that, "a series is deemed a success only as long as it keeps going."[53] The bottle episode represents a challenge to this notion, as its whole reason for being is to engage finitude and the limit at economic, structural, narrative, and emotional levels. Bottle episodes represent points of break within a given series architecture. They are points of no return that halt the insistence on infinity that the economic apparatus of television—American network television especially—insists upon.

What's more, and in contradistinction to Edgar Allan Poe's thoughts on the singularity of self-contained content, the bottle episode form highlights how the singular depends on and affects the serial and how the series as such is graspable in the singular. Not every series has seriality—this logic of impossible connectivity and retroactive causality Lacan points us to recognize through chance relations. Not even every television series has seriality. Some shows, such as *I Love Lucy* or *Gilligan's Island*, are referred to as "amnesia" television by critics, meaning that the characters are unaware that they have done whatever they are about to do once or several times before. (Lucy, famously, gets stuck in a meat locker twice.) The instance of a television series that has the most seriality is the bottle episode. Paradoxically, bottle episodes are often considered self-contained departures from what a series ordinarily does. However, as this chapter has argued, it is through the bottle episode that we can best see how seriality arises in a series. This idea will be crucial to hang on to as we turn our attention from television and the televisual seriality that began to proliferate in the 1950s and 1960s, to the so-called Digital Age: streaming media, social media, and the serially social situation we are living in right now.

5

From Film Serials to Streaming Television, or the Gaps in the Gapless

While the roots of the television serial can be traced back to the serial form's inception in nineteenth-century print culture, its more immediate influence came from the big screen. Not from the development of the feature film, however, but from its matinee supplement: the film serial. Within twelve years of the turn of the twentieth century, as Alan G. Barbour notes in *Cliffhanger: A Pictorial History of the Motion Picture Serial*, "there were thousands of nickelodeons and movie palaces dotting America's landscapes. An immediate problem arose as to how to satisfy the demands of theater owners for new product—especially product which could draw fans to one person's establishment at the expense of a competitor's."[1] The answer to this dilemma would appear first in 1912. Two years before Cecil B. DeMille would produce and direct *The Squaw Man*, Hollywood's first full-length narrative film, the Edison Company produced *What Happened to Mary?*—a series of one-reel episodic narratives distributed to movie palaces and nickelodeons. Released alongside the print serial version of the same story published monthly in *McClure's Ladies World*, *What Happened to Mary?* became the first successful film tie-in and established a form audiences would come to know as the film serial.

Film serials or "chapter plays," seen in their original context, acted as theatrical glue. The fifteen-to-twenty-minute episodes would be screened before and/or between feature films. Often appearing between a double feature at the cinema, new film serials would be screened every Saturday alongside newsreels, which were invented by Pathé, the French production company behind massively popular and hugely influential serial queen melodrama *The Perils of Pauline* (1914) starring Pearl White. The popularity of silent cliffhanger serials peaked in the mid-1920s.[2] The transition to simultaneous sound serials was a challenge for a media format that had previously sustained itself on being cheaper and quicker to produce than a feature film. However, the sound era would lead to the serial film's golden age. The 1936 merger of Mascot, Monogram, and Liberty Pictures that resulted in the formation of Republic Pictures is generally recognized as the beginning of the Golden Age of Serials. While the serial queen melodrama dominated the silent era, the sound era would come to be dominated by superheroes, science fiction, and westerns.[3] Republic, Columbia, and Universal Pictures would produce films that captured the rapt attention of audiences. Just like the case of *What Happened to Mary?*, film serials would continue to act as a site for cross media confluence, as some of the most enduring and serials were adapted from comics (e.g., *Dick Tracy*, *Flash Gordon*, *Superman*, and *Batman and Robin*), pulp magazines (e.g., *Zorro* and *The Spider's Web*), and radio broadcasts (e.g., *The Shadow*, *The Green Hornet*, and *The Lone Ranger*), presaging our current media landscape of interconnected serial universes and cross-platform product development. However, the rise of television would mortally wound the production of film serials. After the release of *Blazing the Overland Trail* on August 4, 1956, the American serial film industry would shut down for good.

In significant ways, the current state of streaming film and television services such as Netflix, Hulu, and Disney+ shows us how the forces that once propelled film serials to their golden age have simply found a new media technology. Comics and pulp serials play an influential role in determining the value of almost every streaming service. Disney+ is the exclusive home for the Marvel Cinematic Universe films and television series. Netflix has invested in importing and adapting Japanese anime (e.g., *Neon Genesis Evangelion*, *Attack on Titan*, *Avatar: The Last Airbender*) or anime style series based on existing videogame intellectual properties (*Castlevania*, *Cyberpunk: Edgerunners*, *Arcane: League of Legends*). Amazon is expanding its hit meta superhero commentary series *The Boys* with *Gen V*. HBO Max and Warner Bros. are desperately hoping their forays into the DC comics universe can return the same fervent passion that Batman and Superman enjoyed for Columbia Pictures in the 1940s. Finally, the so-called "docuseries" first made popular by Netflix (*Making a Murderer, Tiger King*) blends the genre expectations of a documentary film with the cliffhanger-inspired true crime investigation format first made popular by the *Serial* podcast. Simply put, the venue may no longer be the nickelodeon and the genres may now be hybridized, but streaming television capitalizes upon and attempts to sustain the very same formal appeal that previously defined film serials.

The hallmark of the film serial form was the cliffhanger. While the history of the cliffhanger begins in literary fiction, the narrative technique of suspending the consequences of a dangerous even death-defying scenario is the most distinctive and omnipresent feature of the film serial. Whether we are talking about Pathé's *The Perils of Pauline* (1914), a silent serial queen melodrama, or Universal Pictures' *Flash Gordon Conquers the Universe*, a sound and color sci-fi serial (1940), the cliffhanger punctuates the serial film installment. While the cliffhanger form remained central to the appeal of the film serial throughout its lifetime, it's arguable that the appeal of streaming television is precisely the *elimination* of the cliffhanger—a structural foreclosure of the serial gap. While it is true that Netflix (and other streamers) are intent on producing seemingly gapless entertainment, the following look at Netflix's sci-fi/ fantasy series *Stranger Things* will show that the reality is more complicated. Streaming television is an overlooked analogue for viewing the legacy of the motion picture serial, as streaming series are published under the exact same pressure that Barbour noted above: streaming providers have to meet a demand for product and must provide a product that values their service at the expense of others. No streaming television provider has been more influential on this front than Netflix.

When film serials ran initially—weekly—the excitement and enthusiasm that audiences of the 30s and 40s greeted each new installment presaged the coming age of television, its distribution, and its viewing practices. From the standpoint of formalist aesthetics, however, film serials more closely resemble the binge series that Netflix has made popular rather than traditional television. Film serials, seen in their original environment, acted as instances of interruptive closure within a double-feature film viewing experience. They were examples of filmic content that, being cliffhanger oriented, created and sustained themselves through gaps. Just as *Flash Gordon* filled a gap in time before a feature, it created and sustained a narrative gap for several weeks. Today it is difficult to re-create this context for film serials. While one can self-pace a film serial to avoid bingeing an episodic narrative as though it were the unbroken unity of a typical feature film (landmark features with intermissions such as *2001: A Space Odyssey* notwithstanding), the form we have these films in today are as a bound volume—as effectively long features. As a bound serial, Columbia Pictures' 1938 serial *The Spider's Web* is three hours and forty minutes long. The invaluable fan restoration and enthusiast website/community *The Serial Squadron* implores viewers new to film serials to *not* watch them from beginning to end—the way one would a feature film. Contemporary media connoisseurs recognize this viewing practice as a binge. The question of whether *The Spiders Web* is better watched with self-paced gaps or binged is not the concern of this chapter. Further exploring the bound totality of previously interstitial and episodic narratives is, however, as it raises important questions for the serial gap. If this gap is as immanent as I am claiming, then we need to look at what happens when the gap is diminished structurally by an archival release that cannot replicate the original. The way I have theorized the gap that breaks and binds seriality will need to be durable enough to withstand reference to some serial production with minimal or no evident interruptions.

No One Steps in the Same Stream Twice

The "in the air" quality of seriality we previously saw in the early to mid-1800s and 1900s emerged anew in the early 2000s. With the mainstreaming of broadband internet, technology would again change the terrain for the serial. Broadband internet speeds enabled the advent of streaming media. Through rearticulations of television, radio, and news media in guises of streaming television, podcasting, and social media, seriality was again pushed to the fore as the glue holding together the pop cultural social tie.

Despite changes to the appearance of traditional media industries, the serial form would remain stubbornly central. It is this immanent quality of seriality that has convinced detractors such as Sartre and those who follow his line of argumentation that seriality is the form of capital's accomplice, the root of flattening cultural hegemony. Sartre's biggest issue with seriality occurs here with his accusation of it being on the side of flattening ideological continuity—a numbing and unceasing sameness. As I have argued so far, Sartre's sweeping objection to seriality is only sustainable if we imagine a series to be a totality. Seriality, therefore, must be thought of dialectically and as a gapped form. With the bottle episode, we see how something most singular—most self-contained and total—can be at once most serial. With this chapter, I aim to show how our focus in discussion seriality needs to be the gaps within a series rather than the gaps between its installments. It is easiest to see this in a television series, so I will continue to work with TV but by looking at a different format: the binge series.

If seriality is the crushing and coercive kind of continuity that Sartre and others imagine it to be, then there would not be a more ideological form of popular seriality today than the Netflix binge serial. Netflix embraced what it saw as a shift in viewership and turned it into a model for television distribution. Based on an extensive survey of users, Netflix declared binge watching television as the "new normal" in 2013. According to this survey, 61 percent of US users reported that they binge-watched their favorite programs.[4] Bingeing, defined as watching two to six episodes of one show in a single sitting, was also an act that a full 73 percent of those "bingers" said they felt good about.[5] In the least likely corporate agreement with Jacques Lacan of all time, the binge model championed by Netflix was offered initially as something that solved the problems of network television seriality. Here the "linear model" of television is Freud's session with beginnings and ends determined externally by the clock and Netflix is offering a punctuated session determined by the viewer. (The important difference being that the analysand/viewer's unconscious determines the length of the session, not conscious clicks from an on-demand menu.) With a binge series there are no annoying ad breaks, no waiting for new episodes, and no being told by a TV network *when* to sit in front of your TV or when to set a digital recording time. There are no obvious gaps, no clear sites for interruption or irruption. Total ideological flattening (some might argue).

Ten years later, it is evident that Netflix's approach to content creation and distribution has irrevocably altered how we view television. What's more, Netflix's model for releasing original television has vexed serial narrative scholars due to its refusal of a traditional serial television release structure. Jason Mittell writes that Netflix has taken the "TV-on-DVD box set" premise and used it as a structure for its entire streaming network approach. This, for him, complicates the status of Netflix shows as serial, since "forgoing the gap-filled serial broadcast experience altogether ... [raises] the question as to whether these multi-episode narratives can be considered serial at all."[6] While Netflix series have many of the traditional interruptions we come to expect from broadcast television in its episodes—act breaks, episode breaks, and skeuomorphic cuts to black as though there would be a commercial break—it is missing the clear and regimented temporal breaks between episodes that has long been heralded as the defining feature of television serial narrative, as—with rare exception—all Netflix original television programs are released with every episode available immediately.

Contra Mittell, the question we should raise is how is something like Netflix's *Stranger Things* still serial? Despite appearing to offer gapless ideological entertainment, where can we see the gap and how can we articulate a notion of radical rupture despite the seeming flat continuity of the Netflix serial? Formulating the questions in this way moves us from treating seriality as though it is only a material quantity (e.g., serial narratives, serial tweets, serial iPhone updates, serial commodities) and moves us toward considering it as a theoretical construct that psychoanalysis is uniquely capable of taking on.

Cliffs, Then and Now

In considering these questions, I want to return us to Freud binge-reading *Daniel Deronda*. Freud read a bound volume copy of *Daniel Deronda*, rather than reading it in its initial eight-part serial print run in 1867 (when he would have been eleven years old). One might be tempted to say that this no longer makes the novel serial. My position is that the serial gap cannot be eliminated by printing *Daniel Deronda* as a single novel or releasing a television series such as HBO's *The Wire* in a single DVD/Blu Ray boxset. Believing only in seriality as a momentary and transient phenomenon makes it elusive. Further, it disobeys one of the cardinal rules of seriality: that meaning can only be apprehended retroactively. I've argued throughout how ironclad the rule of retroactivity is for governing serial meaning. This book is a self-contained bound volume but even in this paragraph we can see what retroactivity can do to repeated material. In the first chapter, I referenced a snippet from Freud's letter to his wife regarding Eliot's *Daniel Derona* to show how Freud may have first had pause to consider repetition compulsion through his voracious consumption of serial novels. Here I am positioning that same letter and that same late-night narrative binge session of Freud's alongside a reference to the now commonplace aspect of watching streaming television (or, indeed, any television). The phenomenon of staying up well past a reasonable bedtime to finish bingeing a narrative is so ubiquitous that eye-drop brand Visine recently built a whole radio, print, and television ad campaign around it.[7] *Just one more episode*, the ad commands.

But Freud does not just show us a conveniently analogous way to binge a serial text. He helps us see that when one is caught up in the temporal gaps of a serial—the cliffhanger of analysis or the cliffhanger of Thomas Hardy—it is the psyche that takes the hit or "suffers more." When it comes to bingeing a serial, however, it is the body that suffers more. The Visine ad confirms as much, showing a man who is practically self-harming in order to stay up to watch more episodes of his favorite shows streaming on Hulu. While the ad conjures up a hyperbolic portrayal of binge-watching, it nonetheless touches on such a common response to streaming media that sleep studies have tried to raise the alarm about how deleterious this audience practice is.[8] It seems commonplace to observe that binge-watching is a result of technological advancement colliding with viewer preference (the ideological approach Netflix favors). Freud shows us that it is the serial form itself that occasions this response, and it has aroused the passions of audiences since the Victorian era.[9]

One might argue that the binding of a serial narrative takes something vital away from audience members who experience a serial text long after its initial run of publication. In other words, Freud's bound volume reading experience is not serial in the same way that 1867 readers experienced *Daniel Deronda*. Jason Mittell focuses on the ephemeral aspect of communal viewing of television serials with precisely this idea in mind.[10] I understand and appreciate the value of this approach, as it pulls us back to one of television's medium-specific differences from film: its liveness. However, such a viewpoint elides the ontological cut of the serial. In other words, a cut text *stays cut*. For this reason, I am reluctant to agree with the idea that the serial is best realized or understood by way of accounting for audience engagement during a serial text's original and simultaneous unfolding. If the serial gap is truly the constitutive aspect of seriality—as Mittell, Sean O'Sullivan, Frank Kelleter, and other narrative theorists have argued—then this gap cannot be eliminated by printing *Daniel Deronda* as a single volume, or by extension, releasing *The Wire* in a single DVD/Blu Ray boxset. *Daniel Deronda* is forever marked—cut—by seriality. This cut cannot be healed. Put differently, when a volume is bound it is bound by its gaps. The binding does not erase the holes in the whole. The gap will appear somewhere else. The attempt to overcome the gap through binding just places the gap elsewhere. Sometimes it is even placed in the body of the audience rather than the body of the text, through dry eyes and lack of sleep.

As in our example, Freud clearly reacted to Daniel Deronda's cliffhanger-like "real time" learning of his own mysterious lineage. Believing that serial narrative only has form as a momentary and transient phenomenon makes it too elusive to be the object of an extended academic inquiry. This relies on one of the cardinal rules of seriality: meaning-making that can only be apprehended retroactively. This even more closely mirrors an audience's actual relation to a serial text, as audiences are always getting caught up in serial narratives long after the original publication date. This is the rule of seriality, rather than the exception. And, just like Daniel Deronda's discovery of his Jewish heritage, the signs are more clearly graspable retroactively than linearly. If the serial is only graspable in the transient dispersal of a currently running narrative, then one must conclude that serials only have temporary form and once they are released become just another episodic and self-contained story. What, then, distinguishes the serial *after* its initial release? What does the mark of seriality look like? How can something bound and seemingly self-contained from the get-go evince seriality? Netflix's popular series *Stranger Things* helps us to address these questions.

Stranger Things is a sci-fi/horror series set in the 1980s, taking place in Hawkins, Indiana, a fictional US town. Hawkins is a hotbed for supernatural activity and the first season of the series inaugurates its trademark narrative technique of juxtaposing parallel storylines. Season one focuses on the mysterious disappearance of Will Byers, a young boy, with the equally mysterious appearance of a young girl with telekinetic powers named Eleven. Over the course of the first two seasons, the citizens of Hawkins learn of illegal activities and experiments of a paranormal laboratory, the Hawkins National Laboratory, who are hoping to tap into the power of what the show calls "The Upside Down," a dimension of space and time that seems to mirror that of the "real world" of Hawkins. The notable difference between this world and Hawkins is that it is crawling with supernatural creatures that the Hawkins Lab is attempting to weaponize. The second season of the show foregrounds how Will is still affected by the Upside Down and how Eleven decides to investigate her own origins. Both plots come to a head in the liminal space between season two's "The Spy" and the following episode, "The Lost Sister." "The Spy" ends on a cliffhanger that would have caused any audience member to "suffer more," as it becomes clear that Will has been manipulated by the Upside Down. Since one can simply proceed to the next episode on Netflix without even watching a series' opening credits, resolving the tension installed by a cliffhanger is seemingly a click away. Anticipating an end and not getting it is no big deal because absent from the Netflix series is the temporal delay long heralded as the constitutive of seriality. It does not matter if the characters have five minutes or an hour or a week to rescue another character, if the *viewer* has enough time to watch the next episode the tension will resolve itself. Traditional serials accomplish the cliffhanger by way of installing an almost mandatory wait time—the same kind of temporal gap that Freud writes about in psychoanalysis. What *Stranger Things* season two does is accomplish a cliffhanger *while giving viewers a whole episode to watch*. I call this "a gap filled with content," an inviolable gap independent of release schedule temporality.

"The Spy" ends with a season-changing event that leaves many of the series' prominent characters in imminent peril—in a traditional cliffhanger situation. It is important to stress that viewers of a binge series do not expect a cliffhanger to be a "real cliffhanger." What creates the cliffhanger is *not* that *Stranger Things* interrupts a scene, nor is it that the episode pivots away from the previous action entirely.[11] What creates the cliffhanger here is twofold. "The

Lost Sister," the episode following "The Spy," does *not* pick up on *any* of the previous episode's story lines. Secondly, and more importantly, the Netflix viewer is virtually unaware that it is even possible to introduce a cliffhanger in a streaming series. One of the great myths of Netflix as television producer is that it has freed itself—and viewers—from the shackles of the network schedule. Ted Sarandos, Chief Content Officer of Netflix, upholds this myth when he says in a 2013 press release, "Netflix has pioneered audience choice in programming and has helped free consumers from the limitations of linear television."[12] The notion that a popular Netflix series would engage in a "dirty trick" typical of traditional television is almost beyond belief, given how Netflix has positioned itself in contradistinction to traditional broadcast methods of storytelling.

Anticipating the radical content-filled cliffhanger of "The Lost Sister," *Stranger Things* season two introduced a false cliffhanger earlier in the season. Between "The Pollywog" (episode three) and "Will the Wise" (episode four), *Stranger Things* cuts in half a dramatic sequence where Will Byers attempts to confront the demon creature that has been stalking him. "The Pollywog" ends with Will screaming at the creature to leave him alone. Rather than take orders from a child, the supernatural being dives into Will's mouth, possibly (for all the viewer knows) killing him, and the episode cuts to black. "Will the Wise" then begins immediately on the other side of this cut, with Will alive but with the creature seemingly possessing Will's body. *This* is the expected kind of cliffhanger on Netflix. Certainly, an episode might end in such a way that a viewer is required to move on to the next one, but the viewer can simply watch the next five minutes of the next episode to instantly resolve the tension. "The Lost Sister" refuses to allow *Stranger Things* viewers to evade the "To Be Continued" and the registration of the interruptive gap—the cut of seriality. In other words, "The Lost Sister" introduces a proxy for the week-long or months-long gap that viewers of traditional television serials experience.

Unsurprisingly, "The Lost Sister" is, by some distance, the show's worst-rated episode by viewers on IMDb (i.e., until the final season's ratings are settled). Having to watch a character-based episode that not just interrupts the tension produced by "The Spy" but seems to rip *Stranger Things* away from every single urgent storyline has been met by widespread annoyance. The following is an excerpt from a review of "The Lost Sister" by the user tggrif, whose comment is rated by other IMDb users as being most helpful (read: most representative). It is titled "Why did this exist? Save yourself the trouble and skip it!!":

> This episode was such a jumbled piece of garbage. I love this show (excluding this episode), and the episode was written in a vacuum probably for the sole purpose of one or more spin-offs. It doesn't even feel like it's on the same time line, nor does it feature any of the other main characters doing anything important.
>
> I dug my IMDb account out of the graveyard just to review this monstrosity ... This is just such a train wreck that I have to speak against it, lest it become more common in the future. As subscription television becomes more popular and common it should not need to relive the historical downfalls of traditional TV and the reason we cut cords in the first place.[13]

This IMDb user's comments are extraordinary for a number of reasons. The first is that tggrif, in panning this particular episode of a Netflix series, affirms the "consumer choice" model of television that Netflix is chiefly responsible for creating. The user even warns against *any* Netflix series from writing an episode such as "The Lost Sister," associating the structure of *Stranger Things* season two with "the historical downfalls of traditional TV." If the register of these comments seems unnecessarily high (e.g., a bad episode of television is maybe not a "monstrosity"), we should recall Netflix executive Ted Sarandos's comments that Netflix has "free[d] consumers."[14] A cliffhanger episode such as "The Lost Sister" is a reminder that one cannot be freed from the spectre of a serial interruption. As Freud shows, the interruption causes the patient to suffer more than if the session—or serial story—came to a complete and self-contained end. The binge model mitigates a number of non-narratively mandated interruptions, as previously discussed, but it cannot turn serial television into a gapless five or ten-hour movie. Film is a far more radically self-contained medium. To think of streaming television as simply a long movie is to ignore the ongoing interruptive aspects that simultaneously break and bind it. It is to imagine the erasure of the gap. As I have argued, erasing the serial gap is formally impossible.

The second insight we should take seriously from this user's assessment of *Stranger Things* is that "The Lost Sister" shows the stakes of being confronted with serial narrative design in a binge series. For the IMDb user (and many others), the confrontation of "The Lost Sister" is the forcible look "behind the curtain," so to speak, to peek at the mechanism of serial narrative. In other words, we can categorize this as a clear confrontation that there is no subject-supposed-to-know. As the IMDb user sees in "The Lost Sister," there is no benefit in the episode other than interrupting the overarching narrative of Will Byers and company dealing with a new threat from the Upside Down in Hawkins, Indiana. There is even the cynical suggestion in the comment that the episode is intended to establish a spin-off series for which there is no evident basis. In effect, there is no benefit apart from the suffering it incurred. The result is narrative trauma.

What distinguishes "The Lost Sister" is that it radically reconfigures the viewer's understanding of the shape of *Stranger Things* season two. The virtue of "The Lost Sister" is in its capacity to manipulate, misdirect, and mislead. The cliffhanger, recalling Freud, *should* cause the viewer, reader, or listener to "suffer more" than if the story had simply played out for another five minutes. A cliffhanger is simply not worth talking about if our investment in the narrative is not upset in some way. Worthwhile narrative should always raise our expectations for it. When we feel let down or betrayed, we know that the narrative has "worked" and become more significant for us than a mere passing story. Freud wrote *Studies on Hysteria* in 1895, but the notion that the "To Be Continued" (or cliffhanger) causes suffering is just as prevalent today as it was at the end of the Victorian era. *Stranger Things* creates an interruptive gap within a serial publishing model that seems intent on eliminating them. That the interruptive gap comes by way of providing content is, to me, a radical gesture. Finding a way to introduce a serial gap into the binge structure shows the supposed "user control" (or mastery) over a Netflix series is illusory. This is something the IMDb user recognizes but categorizes it as a negative. In fact, this loss of mastery is doubled: the user has no control over the narrative and, it appears, neither do the showrunners (why else would they write such a "jumbled piece of garbage" other than that they don't know what they're doing?). We also see that significant interruptions can arise in narratives *seemingly liberated* from such interruptions. The *Stranger Things* example shows that the serial gap is not a relic of a bygone era of network television programming but is the single inerasable element of the serial. It appears even—and especially—where it would seem not to exist.

Left Hanging

Seriality, both in media and psychical formations, constantly confronts us with interruptions—sites of resistance—to continuity. In *The Interpretation of Dreams*, Freud writes "… *whatever interrupts the progress of analytic work is a resistance*."[15] Lacan amends this line in *Seminar I* by saying, "Everything which suspends/destroys/interrupts the continuity … of the cure is a resistance."[16] These sites of resistance do not stop analysis; rather, they are the precondition for it. "Resistance," Lacan observes, "is produced at the moment when the speech of revelation is not said."[17] This is what the cliffhanger does. It punctuates an end through interruptive closure but leaves revelation for another day.

"Revelation," as Lacan says, "is the ultimate source of what we are searching for in the analytic experience."[18] We might say the same of the serial fiction experience. Lacan believes that it is in these moments of resistance that the analytic work takes place, as "The ego makes itself manifest [in analysis] as defence, as refusal."[19] Psychoanalysis says, do not look to the end—look to the gap. When we look to the gap, we find our quilting point. Only by acting as a way to apprehend the deadlock of symbolization and signification can quilting point do its work. Quilting an absence, as *Stranger Things* does, is a concrete example of the way this can operate. Rather than saying that resistance and refusal prevent revelation, Lacan's point is that speech is already itself resistant to meaning and non-total. The resistance of the gap is also the revelation of the gap. For Lacan, "it is often what appears to be harmonious and comprehensible which harbours some opacity. And inversely it is in the antinomy, in the gap, in the difficulty that we happen upon opportunities for transparency."[20] Lacan uses the word "antinomy" where contradiction is perhaps more appropriate because he is hitting on the paradox of a clear opacity, the clarity of obscurity. Nevertheless, this psychoanalytic approach to seriality looks precisely at this "antinomy in the gap," this constitutive confrontation. While Lacan does not grant "the gap" primacy in his system, my wager is that its primacy is nonetheless there. Further, there is much to be gained by formalizing a conception the gap as the site in a series that breaks it as it binds it. This gap is material and external and is internal and existential. We need to think of gap not as a one-off occurrence common to many different relations or structures but a site of torsion in the psyche that is always already serial.

6

Social Media against Seriality

While Netflix appears relatively gapless and questionably serial, social media would seem replete with gaps and completely serial. We should not let appearances get the better of us. Per a previous example, the dialectical logic of the bottle episode shows that through isolation and superficial connection, things Sartre argues are the enemy of politically potent thought and organization, the possibility of a dynamic community emerges. Reconciling oneself to the existential, psychical, and political contradiction brought about by having to navigate novel constraints and confinement as a group opens an unexpected gap in the subject and the other. Given that all social media platforms foreground the coincidence of group interaction through the constraints of the short form (e.g., a character limit, a time limit, a post limit), we might expect social media to be a site that follows or at least enables the logic of the bottle episode to flourish. However, moving the dialectical lesson of the bottle episode or the binge model cliffhanger from fictive worlds to our own is symptomatically difficult. Social media is structurally opposed to dialectical recognition, to seeing the series in the singular. Indeed, social media regularly demonstrates an almost collective group resistance to the kind of dialectical recognition our television examples make graphic.

As every person who has even a tangential relationship to social media implicitly understands, social media platforms privilege what I call "shock and aww" content. Facebook, X (formerly Twitter), Instagram, TikTok and others all employ algorithms that are purposed with highlighting for users either deliberately upsetting images and ideas or upsettingly adorable pictures of puppies and kittens. The undergirding algorithmic logic of social media platforms is concerned with showing users content that will elicit in them a strong immediate reaction. In plain terms, social media platforms want to repeatedly show users newer and newer things that they will either love or hate. These practices make all manner of financial sense. Divisive content drives what is commonly referred to as "engagement" (e.g., liking, commenting, reposting something) and engagement drives the monetization of content through pay-per-click ad sales and the sale of larger caches of data to advertisers. However, this merely explains why and how social media is profitable for the social media companies themselves. It does not explain why the common everyday user is invested in social media as though it is making us money. It's my contention that the more intoxicating appeal of social media for all of us is that it privileges what in philosophical terms we would call the particular over the universal. In so doing, it makes what appears to be a serial medium a self-contained nonreflective silo. The appeal of social media, in short, is that we do not encounter seriality and do not have to reconcile ourselves to dialectical contradiction. There is a tremendous amount of enjoyment to be had in *not* encountering ourselves and social media is replete with this enjoyment through its mobilization of the particular.

The particular is an idea at the heart of nominalism. Nominalism is the belief that, as Paul Guyer puts it in his reading of Immanuel Kant, "the only objects that there are are particulars, not universals."[1] Hegel criticizes nominalism in both "The Concept" and "Judgment" sections of *Science of Logic*, writing "superficial nominal definitions [...] are of no interest here" due to how the nominalist renders things in the world and resulting phenomena a "mere accident."[2] In simplistic terms, Hegel is pushing back on the logic of "case-by-case basis" which refuses connective tissue between even alike things, let alone unalike things. As a thinker of immanent dialectical contradiction, it is unsurprising that Hegel occupies an antagonistic stance toward nominalism and the logic of the particular.

While the nominalist Kant of Paul Guyer is not my preferred way of reading Kant—the transcendental aspects of Kant's project alone, I think, resist reading him as either purely or predominantly nominalist—it is nonetheless a pedagogically helpful starting point. The merits of Guyer's argument will not be subject to analysis here; rather, I want to highlight how the appeal of the particular that grips Guyer is the same as that which grips anybody who scrolls through their social media feed. Put differently, the very same lure to the particular that pulls Guyer is homologous to the appeal of social media. By lure I mean how the nominalist particular offers a way to sew up inconsistencies at the expense of engaging with contradiction. The continued expansion of social media is undergirded by our demonstrable preference for the particular, as seen in how we willingly slid from interfacing with the World Wide Web (emphasis on the connective tissue of "World Wide") into interfacing with the internet through social media apps, or engines of algorithmic siloing. The particular makes more immediate sense than any notion of the universal, which is why the "shock and aww" constant novelty of social media algorithms has leaked so thoroughly into the way we think about everyday life. To think the universal, one has to see oneself in a web of basic commonality that is much easier to ignore. We feel "seen" by the particular—by the algorithmic silo—in a way we feel overlooked by the universal. The fantasy of constant novelty and the endless refresh of social media platforms prevent us from moving toward seriality. This chapter will attempt to uncover ways to reverse that movement. Further, I will show why this is an urgent intellectual issue.

Memory Insufficient

At the level of bare appearance, social media seems serial. The "tweetstorm," the threads, the evolving discourses—and counter discourses—that spillover to many different internet communities all seem ripe for being yoked under this concept of seriality that I am developing. The issue is that the kind of series that drives social media is radically against the logic of radical causality and connection that I have been developing thus far. Social media seems serial but only presents us with a constantly unfolding "now" that bears little resemblance to any past, even the extremely recent past.

Top trending terms and issues from one month to the next—even one week to the next—evaporate and become nonsensical. There is no memory in social media from which to forge a serial tie beyond being able to dig up someone's old tweets, confront their current hypocrisy, and pithily retort, "this you?" This kind of *Gotcha!* aims at rooting out hypocrisy, not locating contradiction.

Hypocrisy is a tendentious error in logic. It is a mistake somewhat purposely made—an unconscious choice and a conscious choice not to reconcile oneself to the unconscious choice. No instance of hypocrisy rises to the level of our example from *Community* where we see, amazingly, that one's best quality is their worst quality, their worst quality is their best quality. The *gotcha!* aspect of social media does not make for serial glue nor social cement. What social media is so good at is getting its users and participants to buy into a logic of the immediate before they even engage with it. Recently, Elon Musk formalized the "gotcha" aspect of Twitter with the Community Notes feature. While his reign over X has been absurd, the Community Notes feature is universally adored, as it allows X users to add context to a misleading tweet. Proponents of the Community Notes feature would point to the potential for users to mitigate the damage of misinformation on the platform by effectively adding asterisks and addenda to prominent tweets. All this does is enforce the idea that "gotcha" is coequal with truth on social media. Social media—both structurally and in popular use—does not aim at the pursuit of contradiction. Rather, it encourages users to get wrapped up in playing whack-a-mole with hypocrisy, attempting endlessly to get the final word to end all final words.

While X, as a platform, currently serves as the world's richest man's fascist-friendly loudspeaker and is worthy of intense political scrutiny, Twitter is more of interest for staging the theoretical drama I am looking to play out. As we'll see, Twitter structurally eliminated the kind of dialectical recognition that is at the heart of seriality. The memory of Twitter endures culturally as an almost prelapsarian social media space. Every day users wish X could go back to the way "Twitter used to be," opining that things will improve dramatically when/if Elon Musk sells the platform. However, we should not be nostalgic for a method of meaning reduction that dampened by necessity the retroactive revelations that seriality instigates and instantiates. There is more to learn from how the particular was prized under Twitter than there is to understand today from Elon Musk deliberately directing traffic to and away from certain terms and posts. Understanding the structural ways in which Twitter resisted seriality is crucial to understanding the infinite particularity of social media as a media form. The point is that even without fascistic meddling, social media proliferates the particular.

Software engineer Brian Feldman incidentally quantified the particularity of Twitter when he tracked top trending terms for the year 2022 and compiled them in a calendar for the project whatshappening.online.[3] Despite similar terms or the same people trending on different days throughout the year, it is almost always for different reasons. The radical discontinuity of social media, specifically Twitter (and now X) as a platform, is made graphic with this experiment. For example, French philosopher Voltaire amazingly became a top trending term on January 31, 2022. It's highly unlikely that even "extremely online people" will remember why. An anti-Dr. Anthony Fauci tweet by US Representative Thomas Massie falsely attributed Voltaire with a quote that he used to criticize Fauci and the United States' pandemic response Fauci helped to craft and lead. (Incidentally, the actual quote attributed to Voltaire was not even something he said but rather came from a 1993 pro-Nazi radio broadcast by American white nationalists.) The appeal of social media lies in its radically disconnected, cloistered, and seemingly self-contained form. This, at bottom, is the appeal of the particular.

Not only does social media seem serial but it also seems de facto social. A platform such as Twitter is as public and "social" as a country club. That one can do *socializing* on Twitter does not necessarily make it social. That one can make certain information *public* does not make it a public space. A public space does not require you to register a monetizable account to enter. It does not ask you to spend money to continue to stay there. It does not harvest data from you to make money for itself to avoid requiring you to directly spend money in order to stay there. Twitter did all of these things (and X has continued them while adding more). Twitter was not a public space. And yet—and yet—it is precisely the privacy of a place such as Twitter that enables people to feel that they can speak to a public or on behalf of a public. In fact, heads of state used Twitter to issue valuable pieces of news to citizenry. They did not, crucially, *only* use Twitter because that information is, again, not actually public. It is not free to access. One needs a considerable amount of technology and stable internet to be able to see it. I am not required to have an account, internet connection, or smartphone to enter a park. (Perhaps this will change or is changing and, if so, we will all be the worse off for it.) My presence in the park does not make money for someone—in fact, it does the opposite. People simply existing in a park does damage to it. To be in a park is to take from it. One needs to engage in a secondary act (donations of time or money, etc.) to be able to give back to a park. Accessing material at the Library of Congress, for example, takes away from it. Not just physically touching special collections of old manuscripts with white gloves, even accessing older digital material, say to play a Colecovision videogame on its original hardware, causes "bitrot"—literally a rotting of the digital material (bits). This is what it means for something to be in public and accessible by the public. As Sartre might have liked to observe, we bring our nothingness to a park and leave it a worse place for the experience. This, I would argue, is the contradiction at the heart of the public that private spaces like Twitter do everything they can to avoid. The public is a site of universal lack which is why the more brazenly authoritarian second Trump administration has concerned itself with shrinking the public. Libraries are exemplary public spaces because they accept everyone's lack. Capitalism sells a fantasy of private plenitude. Desiring the public, by contrast, is a direct threat to the undergirding premise of capitalist expansion and accumulation.

Contra Sartre, what any mass or public needs to collectivize is a sense of its banal internal seriality—the mundane and utterly ordinary surfeit of commonality across a group. A public can form and exist in private spaces but it needs a dynamic connection to form through gaps between people and within each person as subject. Social media, however, is premised precisely with tamping down the ordinary, highlighting the particular, and making the constant appearance of wild exceptionality seem the governing rule. This is what is so exhausting about social media. Every day is begun as though the previous day did not exist. How can a bare series of particulars move toward radical seriality in this environment? It is here where we need to develop a precise understanding of universality.

The Universal in the Series

Recent philosophical and theoretical approaches to the social have portrayed universality as a brutal form of flattening that comes from a necessarily white-Western perspective and is often the enemy of radical and emancipatory politics.[4] In this reading of the universal, it imposes a "one-size-fits-all" idea on everybody regardless of whether that one size fits anybody. It sweeps all people into a single container that serves majoritarian interests. For this reason, the universal has been rejected by the academy, particularly in the United States. José Esteban Muñoz famously attempted to navigate this academic allergy to the universal through his idea of the "pluriversal," defined as "being singular plural."[5] Simply put, universality is a bad object.

This allergy plays out in the mainstream as well. It can be seen in the popular mentality displayed by conservatives toward COVID-19 safety guidelines and regulations such as vaccine and mask mandates. Conservative posturing typically drapes a hysterical conspiracy of ever encroaching "globalism" (never capitalism) over its employment of the particular, but in its most banal formulation the notion inheres that California is different than Alabama and what works there is not what will work in wherever "here" happens to be. However, this view is not simply a political binary. Indeed, many of the scholars and theorists who avow an anti-universal political program consider themselves left wing. To further show how pervasive the appeal of the particular is, California Governor Gavin Newsom employed this very same pro-particular anti-universalist line of thinking in public comments against the idea of lockdowns and mask mandates on March 18, 2020, just one day before issuing the first statewide lockdown in the United States. As Newsom told reporters:

> We're not some small isolated state. We're a nation-state… Clara County's conditions are extraordinarily different than Tulare. Extraordinarily different than Madera. Or Colusa. And so, while it may be fanciful and comforting by perception standards, for some [who want] one size fits all, that's not the world in which we view the reality on the ground. There's no community spread in some communities, there [is] significant community spread in other communities.[6]

What is always obviated in this kind of argument is the web of agreement and commonality necessary to even begin to disagree with something. It's not very likely that the COVID data Newsom had available on March the 17th was vastly different from the data he had available on March the 18th. What he had to be convinced of was to move from thinking on the terrain of the particular (i.e., COVID spread is not the same in every area of California) to thinking on the terrain of the universal (i.e., COVID itself is immanent and every area of California needs to take the same precaution). Newsom had to reconcile himself to the demand of the universal rather than operate in the safe non-conflictual terrain of the particular. It is no surprise that as the pandemic wore on the particular became more closely aligned with conservatives where the universal became operative, for a time, on the mainstream left. The pull of the particular is such, however, that lockdowns, mask mandates, and vaccine mandates were abandoned the second it became politically expedient to do so, rather than existentially beneficial.

For Hegel, the universal operates quite differently than an appeal to flattening or "one-size fits all." As he writes in *Science of Logic*, universal judgment works "in such a way that the singulars are at the same time expanded to the universality of the species."[7] It is only by going through the expansion of the singular to the universal that changes "all humans"—a flat aggregating of particulars—to "the human being," a universal.[8] The idea of expanding the singular rather than accumulating or aggregating particulars is the basis of Hegel's universality.

The singular in the series, like the bottle episode, is representative of it while also being dependent upon the series. In other words, it can stand at a remove from a series—it can be lifted up and examined as an object unto itself without reference to the surrounding series—but cannot be extracted from the series as though the series surrounding it does not exist. Hegel prefers the term singular over the particular for his explanation of how universality works because, for him, inherent in the singular is an always already weddedness to group existence whereas the particular is excised from any group connection. It's the movement of singular to universal that Hegel is invested in and it's here where I want to offer a slight but significant deviation from Hegel that maintains the spirit of his idea.

There is no reason to cordon off the language of nominalism to get to universality. Far from being a semantic or rhetorical objection, I hope to show that including the language of nominalism into Hegel's thinking can introduce a dialectical reversal whereby the particular suddenly unlocks universality. Where the particular seeks siloed individualization and nonintegration to any series, the singular is a link in a signifying chain that can be representative of a series. The universal transforms the series. Based on all of the above, it does not seem wise nor even arguable to attempt to include the particular in a notion of universality which is precisely what I am going to do.

Structurally speaking, the universal has to be the enemy of the particular, given that the particular insists on the utter separateness of phenomena and a denial of connection. It is my contention, however, that while the universal has to be the enemy of the particular, the particular does not *have* to be the enemy of the universal. Due to Hegel's own allergy to the particular he roots his definition of the universal in an expansion of the singular rather than seeing the dialectical opportunity of the particular. In doing this he falls victim slightly to nominalist logic by merely positing *another* way of seeing the world and its relations between things. By avoiding the terminology of nominalism—preferring the singular over the particular—Hegel misses an opportunity to dialectically reverse the logic of nominalism using its own terms.

Indeed, we can use the particular to effect universality. What is required is recognizing the universal as a particular element or idea in a given series that fundamentally changes all other particular elements. To put it plainly, *the universal is the particular that changes all particulars.* The universal, in this view, transforms the way all parts relate to each other and to a whole. This is one of the consequences we should extract from Hegel's idea. To recall the quilting point, what I am looking for with the universal is an idea that re-quilts an existing field of relation such that the previous way of thinking that relation is obliterated or made irrelevant.

The Particular That Changes All Particulars

Examples are the engine of theory, and, while helpful, Hegel's own example of how the universal works leaves some questions. His example does not show exactly how a particular can change *all particulars*, which is what we are looking for in our definition of the universal. Fortunately, Ta-Nehisi Coates's memoir, *Between the World and Me*, demonstrates exactly how profound the movement from the particular to the universal—understood as the particular that changes all particulars—can be. Further, Coates shows us that the universal is not some dead relic of German Idealist thought but that it has urgent contemporary import.

Coates's book takes the form of a letter written to his son, as he charts the development of his own understanding of the world, grappling with the people "who believe they are white," and what it means to be black in a country that everywhere threatens the black body. At one point in the book, Coates recounts a life-changing experience he had while at Howard University. There, he learned, "Serious history was the West, and the West was white. This was all distilled for me in a quote I once read from the novelist Saul Bellow … 'Who is the Tolstoy of the Zulus?' Bellow quipped."[9] As Coates writes, the lesson he learned from Bellow's racist question is that "Tolstoy was 'white,' and so Tolstoy 'mattered,' like everything else that was white 'mattered'."[10] A rhetorical question such as Bellow's, if we can even grant it the dignity of calling it a rhetorical question, conjures up the precise figure of the universal that is often rejected by scholars. The history of the world is the history of the West, to follow the line of logic undergirding Bellow's racist question. Bellow imposes that history in considering any other culture and uses that to belittle or erase any non-white and non-Western culture. Bellow's is a colonizer's logic. It is easy to see how and why something like this would be tarred with the label "universal."

Indeed, in response, Coates sought "the Tolstoy of the Zulus" and found her in Queen Nzinga, a figure whose resistance to the Portuguese occupation of Central Africa in the sixteenth century is detailed in the pages of Chancellor Williams's *Destruction of Black Civilization*. For Coates, Nzinga demonstrated "the kind of power I sought … My working theory then held all black people as kings in exile, a nation of original men severed from our original names and our majestic Nubian culture."[11] Here, Coates found a particular answer to Bellow's question. At this point in Coates's intellectual history, his understanding of the project of equality was to look for the unacknowledged equal of Tolstoy, in answer to Bellow's dismissive statement.

Coates indicates, however, that his thought would undergo a massive revision. "I discovered an essay by Ralph Wiley," recounts Coates, "in which he responded to Bellow's quip: '*Tolstoy* is the Tolstoy of the Zulus ... Unless you find a profit in fencing off universal properties of mankind into exclusive tribal ownership'."[12] We see here an echo of the radical potential of the quilting point: a retroactive reversal of an existing series against the march of status quo. At this moment, Coates realized the seduction of nominalism. He writes his "great error" was in "accept[ing] Bellow's premise" confining Black culture, literature, and identity to the logic of the particular.[13] Instead of "proving" Saul Bellow wrong by finding the Tolstoy of the Zulus, Coates realizes that the more effective task is to undermine the premise of Bellow's statement entirely. This is the task of universality: finding the particular element that overturns or irrevocably alters all other attempts at formulating a logic of the particular. In this revised thinking, Coates demonstrates the movement toward understanding the universal. In this case, it is the idea that Tolstoy is "the Tolstoy of the Zulus." The premise of such logic can be undermined by insisting that the universal is that which changes all particulars, not that to which an aggregate of particulars adds up to. The universal instead is the particular that changes *all particulars*, as we have said. To put it another way, when Coates answers Bellow's racist question that Queen Nzinga is Tolstoy of the Zulus, he stabilizes and legitimizes Bellow's question. When he adopts Wiley's position that *Tolstoy* is the Tolstoy of the Zulus, he makes Bellow's remark utterly irrelevant.

What is particularly compelling in Coates's encounter with the universal is that it had nothing to do with Hegel, which gives greater weight to the idea that developing Hegel's understanding of the universal leads us to a concept that is—in a profoundly common sense—"universal." This demonstrates how to think universality in a way that is not totalizing or flattening. The universal is an idea available to be seized by anybody. It belongs to no one person in particular, and it is not the provenance of a country or Western white intellectual hegemony. To further bolster this fact, it's arguable that Hegel is not even equal to his own formulation of the universal. Susan Buck-Morss, in *Hegel, Haiti, and Universal History*, shows how Hegel's notion of universality was shaped by the Haitian Revolution, in which—as Buck-Morss's original research into Hegel's reading uncovers—Hegel took sustained academic and personal interest.[14] However, Hegel's understanding of the revolution in Haiti is betrayed by his later racist comments on Africa. As Buck-Morss writes:

> in an effort to become more erudite in African studies during the 1820s, Hegel was in fact becoming dumber. He repeated his lectures on the philosophy of history every two years from 1822 to 1830, adding empirical material from his reading of the European experts on world history. It is sadly ironic that the more faithfully his lectures reflected Europe's conventional scholarly wisdom on African society, the less enlightened and more bigoted they became.[15]

Buck-Morss is right to argue that Hegel's insights into universality occur historically with his embrace and understanding of the revolution in Haiti. In fact, her goal in highlighting Hegel's knowledge of the anti-slavery rebellion in Haiti is to "[rescue] the idea of universal human history from the uses to which white domination has put it."[16] Extending her point, the Coates/Wiley example demonstrates exactly how anti-racist universal logic can be. That Hegel fell victim to the racist particularizing of Africa in the late 1820s means he also failed to understand the universal. To not put too fine a point on it, what Hegel failed to see is that the universal is the universal of the Zulus.

Slavoj Žižek, in *Disparities*, takes up Hegel's discovery of the universal and argues the necessity for reclaiming it in terms similar to Buck-Morss's call above. Žižek notes that "humanism and/or the thought of the Subject are both falsely universal, the form of universal human subject that they sustain relies on a hidden norm (privileging Western white males) and thus excludes others who do not fit its implicit unitary model."[17] This is, of course, Saul Bellow's position which Ralph Wiley undermined. Following Žižek, we see that "the 'concrete universality' of a certain phenomenon or field is not so much some universal feature shared by all its elements but rather a gap, antagonism or obstacle which holds this field together."[18] Identifying the presence of the gap and its organizing influence is central to universal logic and, indeed, will be crucial to understanding the serial gap and how it influences and orders a series. To tease out what Žižek means, I return to Coates's example above. The gap or antagonism that held together Bellow's pseudo-rhetorical question is not just the racism that separates African art and achievement from serious Western White art (to paraphrase Coates) but the racism that prevents recognition of Wiley's formulation of the universal. That is, that Tolstoy is the Tolstoy of the Zulus. Wiley's counter to Bellow brings the gap in the field to the fore. Rather than playing by Bellow's rules, Wiley flips the game board.

As we have seen, Žižek seizes a way of conceptualizing the gap that brings it into line with Coates's revelatory encounter with universal logic: rather than thinking of, say, a chain of metal links as being tethered by the metal links themselves, we need to move to see that what connects them is the gap, the supposedly empty space in the middle of each link. It is not the "universal feature" of the rounded metal that connects the chain; it is the gap itself. Elevating this seemingly open space in a series of chains to having an active role in shaping the look and legibility of the chain alerts us to the nature of the gap. In other words, the gap is not mere absence. The gap is a kind of present absence that binds the chain together, as we have said.

When we think about the serial gap, therefore, we must approach it with this understanding. The serial gap is not a neutral or blank space that acquires definition through the discursive practices of single or group actors (audiences, content creators, critics). The serial gap is an active caesura, an antagonism. It curves meaning and symbolization around it and makes its absence felt. In this way, the serial gap is not just immanent but, in a meaningful sense, universal. It is through the gap in serial relations that a particular can emerge that changes all particulars. The particular that changes all particulars instantiates a radical change in a series. It makes it impossible for the parts in a series to relate to each other in the same way that they did before.

There may not be a better example of the particular that changes all particulars than the Black Lives Matter political movement. What Black Lives Matter did, has done, and its legacy continues to do is show racism as a structural and systemic antagonism and *not* as a group of disconnected extreme instances perpetrated by individual actors that we can only understand on a "case-by-case basis." The terrain of the political has shifted as it regards conversations on systemic and structural racism. We can see this in the US conservative movement's attempt to villainize the thought that racism could possibly be in the bedrock of American institutions and everyday interactions. This turn has seen its ire focused on Critical Race Theory and a tendentious distortion of Diversity, Equity, and Inclusion initiatives as an apparently oppressive force dividing the country. Critical Race Theory's core argument is that racism is so intrinsic to American life that an attack on racism will be interpreted as an attack on America itself. And what has the regressive right done to dispute this idea? They have acted in conformity with this thesis and tried to attack the thesis. Even in the attempted negation and overturning of everything Black Lives Matter has done to change the very language of the politics of racism in the United States, we can see the transformative change Black Lives Matter has effected to the series of relations that govern the political both in the United States and in countries all over the world.

The Persistence of the Particular

Anyone who has ever lost a loved one should understand what I am saying about universality. When losing someone forever alters one's heart, we see in the realm of the existential what it means for the particular to change all particulars. When someone takes a piece of your heart, everything becomes harder. It's difficult almost to the point of impossible to psychically confront all the ways that any one person is bound up in our psyche's everyday functioning until we feel the palpability of their absence. The mundane tragedy of this is it's easier to understand how much someone meant to you in death than it was in life.

Something as common and cruel as losing a cherished loved one should mean universality is common sense. Yet this is hardly an accepted position. Even more so, it has required the work of this chapter to reach something that could possibly be considered a common sense definition of universality that is resistant to co-optation by regressive interests. As I've argued by way of extending Hegel's insights, the universal is the particular that changes all particulars. The universal is not the particular that continues the operation of existing relations in some novel formulation; rather, the universal represents a permanent challenge to status quo. Again, the universal changes a series of relations such that they cannot relate to each other the way they did before. Social media operates on and is sustained by an obverse logic and it is this logic that is much closer to common sense than the lesson of radical and emancipatory universality. More often the reverse of the logic of the universal is widespread on social media platforms such as X, Facebook, TikTok, and Reddit.

In a March 2021 interview with *Yahoo Finance*, Walter Isaacson, author of *Steve Jobs: The Exclusive Biography* (among other publications), articulates one of the popular grievances against social media. As Isaacson sees it, algorithms that drive businesses like Google, Facebook, TikTok, and Twitter "push us to be more and more extreme" and "tend to incent people to get enraged and pass along misinformation."[19] How to mitigate this, according to Isaacson? Tech giants should take more responsibility for what their algorithms privilege. While Twitter took steps to more actively police election and vaccine misinformation through such initiatives as Birdwatch, a crowdsourcing program that encourages users to add more context to certain tweets,[20] Facebook took darkly comic steps to further empower its most destructive users.[21] As Center for Humane Technology founder Tristan Harris told the US Congress in April of 2021, central to how social media companies sustain their business models is "creat[ing] a society that's addicted, outraged, polarized, performative and disinformed."[22] Leaked internal Facebook documents showed that parent company Meta understands their business model at the problematic level that Harris does … it's just that, to them, this is a PR problem that they have no idea how to solve.[23] On this story, a headline from the excellent media watchdog group *Fairness & Accuracy in Reporting* argued: "Facebook Puts Engagement and Growth Before the Health and Welfare of Democracy." This sentiment is no doubt true, but to reach a consistently pertinent question we have to invert the clauses: why shouldn't Facebook put engagement and growth before the health and welfare of democracy when democracy puts engagement with and the growth of capitalist enterprise ahead of the health and welfare of democracy? Demanding social media companies adhere more strictly to a code of personal responsibility informed by a nebulous notion of democratic morality is unlikely to change anything material about the way social media operates. What's more, it misses that this purportedly dark underbelly to social media is the *raison d'etre* of its entire appeal.

The problems of social media are made manifest in accounts like these: it's making us angrier, less informed, more isolated and—most alarmingly of all—it represents an existential threat to democracy. Supposed solutions to these problems—offered both in documentaries such as *The Social Dilemma*, and by tech pioneers such as Sir Tim Berners-Lee, and progressive politicians such as Alexandria Ocasio-Cortez—tend to focus on individual actions: We should delete the apps, own our own data, never click on recommended videos, and realize that we are the product.[24] If predatory algorithms succeed by individuating people—selling people "choice" and "options" as it harvests user data—then an entire online ecosystem arranged through the logic of that design can neither be meaningfully challenged nor effectively understood at the level of the individual alone. Transformative action addressing social media can only occur after we understand it at the nexus point of where the collective impinges on the individual.

It'd be convenient if the problem of the nominalist particular on social media was simply a problem of social media. Instead, it's a proxy for how resistant the psyche is to seriality and the universal. It's not enough to know or be aware of the resistances to seeing a problem in a certain way; one must find a way to incorporate the resistance itself into the project of addressing the problem. In other words, knowledge of the problem is not enough. Freud attacks this issue and anticipates many contemporary misunderstandings and accusations made against psychoanalysis in his essay "'Wild' Psycho-Analysis."

The essay begins with a brief narrative account of a conversation Freud had with a new patient, a woman in her mid-forties, who had told him about the brazen advice given to her by a younger physician. She had recently divorced her husband and, after the divorce, reported experiencing severe states of anxiety. This young physician proceeded to tell her she clearly just needed to have sex and should do so either with her ex-husband, a new lover, or with herself. After delivering this cartoonish impression of psychotherapy, the young physician then claimed his prescriptions followed Freud's own discoveries and were thus, effectively, licensed by him. Bearing in mind the possibility that this account was embellished, Freud nonetheless writes an essay purposed with shutting down the disturbingly dispassionate kind of "analysis" displayed by the young physician described in the story. The point of psychoanalysis as a therapeutic practice is not to listen to someone describe difficulties they may be having with ordinary everyday functions for a few minutes, shake your head, and then say, "Mhmm, you have a little thing called *Oedipus Complex*. Might have heard about it? Here is the prescription." Freud criticizes this practice and dubs it "Wild Psycho-Analysis," an attempt to alleviate the torsion of the psyche through the process of knowledge dispersal alone. As Freud writes, "If knowledge about the unconscious were as important for the patient as people inexperienced in psycho-analysis imagine, listening to lectures or reading books would be enough to cure him. Such measures, however, have as much influence on the symptoms of nervous illness as a distribution of menu-cards in a time of famine has upon hunger."[25] There is no syllabus for the unconscious. Accumulating knowledge alone—about anything—does not cure the symptom. Knowledge accumulation or consciousness raising is often the explicit or implicit prescription for the ills of social media, as seen above.

Social media shows us in increasingly graphic ways that the idea of the social *itself* is a problem. What's more, social media practitioners seem to be aware of this and their prescriptions to address the problem do nothing to address the social. Rather the supposed solutions reify the problem itself. It's worth delving deeper into how commentators on social media see the issues social media is beset by. Only then can we see how mired in the particular social media is both as media platform and as a site of discourse generation in contemporary culture. We will continue to refer to Twitter and X as our extended example. As stated earlier, my aim is to show that the structure of siloed particularity is intrinsic to X/Twitter's functioning and its mass appeal regardless of who its headmaster is. Furthermore, it is only by interrupting this particularity that any supposed problem unique to social media can be properly addressed.

To do this work, we will need to revisit one psychoanalytic theory's primary gambits in interrogating the effect the social has on the individual psyche. Psychoanalysis argues that the social is an injunction on the individual. Freud's *Group Psychology and the Analysis of the Ego* and *Civilization and Its Discontents* look at the tension generated by the collision of the psyche and the social. The fact of the social itself is a problem for the psyche to grapple with, according to Freud. This way of engaging the problems of society proceed not from discrete problems of the social but rather accepts the social, the instantiation of the social, as itself a burden on the individual psyche.

Responding to attempts by his contemporaries to understand the relation between the social and the individual, Freud opens *Group Psychology and the Analysis of the Ego* by entertaining the possibility that "the social instinct may not be a primitive one."[26] By this Freud means that people are not born with the intrinsic inclination to operate socially in the same way as, say, herd animals or honeybees. Despite this positioning Freud is not open to the notion that the social is *so alien* to the human psyche that the injunction of a group completely changes the psychical structure of the subject. He begins *Group Psychology* by critiquing Gustave Le Bon's notion of mob mentality and the obliteration of the individual that he argues takes place in the group. For Le Bon, certain groups incite desires and behaviors in an individual that they would have shown no prior inclination toward. Freud pushes back on this assertion, highlighting that for psychoanalysis:

> it would be enough to say that in a group the individual is brought under conditions which allow him to throw off the repressions of his unconscious instinctual impulses. The apparently new characteristics which he then displays are in fact the manifestations of this unconscious in which all that is evil in the human mind is contained as a predisposition.[27]

Freud is underlining that, to even operate in the social sphere at all, a kind of repression has to have taken place. One cannot do *exactly* what one wants all the time in every situation; otherwise, one will find themselves on the outside of the group. If certain attitudes shift within the group at large, Freud offers, one may find an opening to display behavior and activity that they would have otherwise repressed. For Freud, the key point here is that the social is always already inflected and injuncted on the individual subject.

It's not likely that Walter Isaacson or Tristan Harris have Freud in mind when they speak about the problems of social media but there is a case to be made that Freud is addressing their concerns about Facebook and Twitter directly when he writes, "Inclined as it itself is to all extremes, a group can only be excited by an excessive stimulus. Anyone who wishes to produce an effect upon it needs no logical adjustment in his arguments; he must paint in the most forcible colours, *he must exaggerate, and he must repeat the same thing again and again.*"[28] As distressingly timeless as these words have turned out to be, what Freud helps us to see is that we have a psychical investment and implication in the social and that this positioning creates friction. This is no small thing. As we saw in the survey of public commentary above, discourse on the ills of social media tend to reject precisely this positioning and focus on a unidirectional model where powerful tech companies are doing things *to us*. Uninterrogated is the potential for us as subjects of direction to be adopting a psychical position as desiring that which undoes us. As Freud writes in *Civilization and Its Discontents*, "The fateful question for the human species seems to me to be whether and to what extent their cultural development will succeed in mastering the disturbance of communal life by the human [drive] of aggression and self-destruction."[29] This discussion of social media and its problems is directly relevant to the problems of the social and the psyche that Freud saw fomenting in 1930.

In the Algorithm Less Than the Algorithm: Psychoanalysis and the Social Tie

In 2020, Twitter commissioned a self-study of its algorithm to see if it favored one kind of political content over another.[30] A popular right-wing talking point is that social media algorithms favor left-wing content and that conservative voices are dampened or effectively de-platformed because of this. Twitter's self-study proved the opposite. Twitter found that their algorithm significantly privileged conservative content over anything left of center. The study offered no explanation as to why and how this might occur but simply confirmed what every even vaguely online person already knew. The findings of this study are importantly different from the similar seeming revelation that, after Elon Musk took over Twitter, stories related to the "Ukraine Crisis" were dampened on the platform. In the case about Twitter's self-study yielding the revelation that right-wing traffic was privileged over left wing, the issue was not related to any direct line code or operator interference but problems that are more endemic to the architecture of social media as such.[31]

As I've argued to this point, the logic of social media is a logic of the particular. The particular de facto favors conservative politics which seeks to excise everyday phenomena from the structure in which they occur. There is no such thing as structural violence or systemic violence in conservative thinking. This is why whenever American cops murder an unarmed Black person, the conservative media complex rushes to smear the character of the victim. They are looking to particularize the event as a way to avoid seeing it. This draws attention away from the system that enabled the disgusting act and, unsurprisingly, these kinds of stories spread like wildfire on social media. The universal, being on the side of left and liberatory politics, solicits our attention to the systems that enable abuse and the structures that uphold vicious status quos. Recommendation algorithms work to amplify certain kinds of contents over others. The very nature of algorithmic logic as such requires excising a part from a whole. If the universal functions the way that I am presenting it—that it looks for the hole in status quo that keeps status quo impossibly cohered—then no tech company algorithm will ever "by accident" amplify left and liberatory content. The algorithm will always circumscribe a problem. It will always ask us to pay attention to the problems of social media and never the problem of the social itself.

The social that social media inveighs upon the user is an amalgamation of particular interests. The idea that a group could emerge from this foundation to fundamentally or radical alter a social media platform itself is not a structural possibility within those platforms. We do not need a more or better representative social media, as is often the popular prescription, but rather to disinvest from the idea that social media represents a social at all. Overinvesting in social media's capacity to represent "the people" also—almost paradoxically—leads to an undermining of our agency relative to social media. Ed Finn writes in *What Algorithms Want* that "the most powerful corporations in existence today are essentially cultural wrappers for sophisticated algorithms."[32] At tech companies such as Facebook, X/Twitter, and Google, the algorithm they employ is so complicated that there is no single person who knows how it works or why all of it works the way that it does. Engineers are employed to work on, maintenance, and develop just portions of an algorithm. Apple experienced a now-forgotten scandalous rollout of its Apple credit card where women with better credit histories than men were either denied a credit line completely or issued much smaller lines of credit than less qualified men. One of the high-profile applicants this affected was Apple cofounder Steve Wozniak and his wife.[33] Apple assured its credit card holders that the company did not know why their algorithm was guilty of gender discrimination. Since no one person knows how the whole of the algorithm works, it is likely that this is true, though this cannot reassure anyone. Rather, it draws our attention to how ideologically entrenched misogynist assumptions find their way into the supposedly objective data processing of an algorithm.

Understanding that no one person knows how the algorithm works does nothing to demystify it. Further, there is political danger in believing that while no one may know the algorithm, the algorithm *itself* knows. We cannot regard the algorithm as a "subject supposed to know." What Lacan's axiom "there is no subject supposed to know" means is that there is no person or entity that can guarantee the consistency of our subjectivity. Recall the child of Lacan's "Mirror Stage" looking back at its parent to make sure that they are, indeed, seeing themselves in the mirror. We long for this kind of confirmation in all manner of everyday interactions far beyond childhood (e.g., the cashier smiling at us, our boss saying we did a good job, our friends expressing that they miss us). We even desire this dynamic in things we claim scandalize us. We often hear expressions of everyday paranoia, "I was just talking about buying something to a friend and then I saw ads for it on Instagram. Do you think they're listening?" etc. The problem here is twofold: (1) We are attempting to turn the algorithm into the "subject supposed to know" with this stance and (2) If the algorithm is supposed to be operating in a clandestine manner yet *we can notice the algorithm working* then it has failed. If the algorithm fails to anticipate without raising suspicion, it fails to seduce us into libidinally investing in its supposed necessity. When one imagines the creation, curation, and distribution of algorithmic content as a perfect totality, one misses the actual points of break and torsion that allow for resistance to take place. I insist here that a psychoanalytic approach to social media highlights and foregrounds precisely these moments of break and failure. Rather than capitulating to the supposed dominance of the algorithm, we instead open the possibility of turning what has recently been seen as a deadlock for democracy into the site of transformative political work.

It is more important than ever to see the structural problematics that social media instantiates as being separate from the will of a petulant CEO or invasive algorithms. This work must be done carefully and precisely. The Twitter of former CEO Jack Dorsey et al. cannot be treated as a prelapsarian public space that has been ruined by Elon Musk. To avoid this error, the first move, as I have tried to articulate, is to theorize the social itself. We cannot take the social for granted or imagine it in an adjectival sense for a specific kind of media engagement. What I have tried to do is make concrete how the social and the individual are inseparable, interdependent, and conflictually constitutive of each other. Where Freudian and Lacanian psychoanalysis is vital in this conversation is that they approach and understand the social *a priori* as a problem, as Hegelian contradiction, as constitutive subjective friction. As Freud puts it in *Civilization and Its Discontents*, "It almost seems as if the creation of a great human community would be most successful if no attention had to be paid to the happiness of the individual."[34] And yet, as Freud understands, the individual compels attention be paid to their happiness. It is much more appealing psychically to separate the individual subject from the social or to blame the social for dragging down the individual subject than it is to see that the subject is socialized *first* and it is this prior socializing that causes the subject to exist at all. The social—particularly the social of social media—is a site par excellence from which to interrogate this primary dialectical tension. The turn toward the "great human community" Freud mentions, or, to put it in a word, collectivity, requires giving up an idea of the social as a springboard for personal action and the acquisition of freedom as though it is a consumer good.

Social Media Now

Social media is interested in a constant now, an infinite procession of particulars. The particular represents a logic of pure individuation and separateness. It is uncluttered and unencountered by contradiction. Psychically, the particular is far more preferable to invest in over the universal. To think seriality means to commit to universality, to reconciling oneself to contradiction as Abed does at the end of "Remedial Chaos Theory."

There may not be a better example of a series without seriality than scrolling through Twitter. In many ways, social media as a form is sustained by proliferating the exact opposite action of the bottle episode: it succeeds at isolating us in such a way that the silos we find ourselves in never cross contaminate. Social media effects Sartre's version of seriality. What drives social media is the enlarging of the individual, not understanding oneself as part of a larger group through contact with a wider public. Algorithmic siloing is successful at limiting collective imagination. We can name "Academic twitter," "furby TikTok," and "cottagecore" as highly specialized singular containers but cannot imagine "worker TikTok," "plebcore," or "prole twitter." These categories seem so big—seem to encompass so many people and so many experiences—that it's hard to imagine that they exist at all. These groups cannot be sold things or marketed to because, in a meaningful sense, they are all of us.

Social media does not and cannot represent a model for solving any problem of the social since it takes for granted the category of society and obscures its constitutive conflictual character to exist at all. This tension of the social is also its glue. Social media dramatizes this tension, but it appears as a disconnected series of individual conflicts rather than something that coheres a whole. If we can, collectively, move to see how social media operates against the social—against seeing the seriality of everyday life—then we've made a move toward seeing the existential stakes of the situation.

Identifying the particular that changes all particulars radically alters our comprehension of a series. We have to quilt at the gap, the point where mastery fails. That point is the particular that changes all particulars—the universal. Without being able to see the gap in the subject we cannot see the gap in the social. Without acknowledging the present absence of the gap constitutive of existence as such, it's easy to miss the gap in something like the algorithm. Imagining the algorithm or developments in AI to herald the coming of an all-knowing outside is a belief that can only be sustained by conceptualizing our subjectivity to be a whole and knowable math equation of cultural experiences + genetics and familial influences. As subjects we are divided unto ourselves. The gap in our subjectivity breaks and binds us and bonds us to the social.

There is no seriality to Twitter/X. Every day people fight battles against the same things as though the previous day's battles had not occurred. This is because Twitter/X, and social media in general, is a nominalist medium. The algorithmic privileging of the particular—and every user's investment in particularity—guarantees this. As a popular meme has it, everyday there is a main character on social media and the goal is to *not* be that person. The particular is on the side of "and then." By this I mean, there is *this* main character and then *that* main character and then that main character *and then* (etc.). This would be an example of a particular that *does nothing* to change other particulars. The structure repeats the same on Friday as it did on Thursday. Worse than that, it's often hard to remember who the previous "main characters" were because of the relentless immediacy that social media privileges. Social media gives a surfeit of particulars that we can take, leave, and take again.

Social media is not serial. Psychically speaking, the appeal of social media lies in it being a case-by-case medium with little to no connection between trending cases. This is what makes the breakthrough of #MeToo and #BlackLivesMatter stand out so much: they forced Twitter users to remember. Transformative left wing political movements always wield universality in this way. They pierce—present tense—the infinite particularity that sustains the medium. It is the seriality of these movements, again, confronting people with a series that they would prefer to ignore or disavow, that make them successful. Regressive interests will always try to particularize and silo a protest movement that aims at universality and emancipation. We see this today in the struggle for trans rights and Palestinian liberation. This is exactly why we should fight for universality, for the particular that changes all particulars. To put it differently, these hashtags and protest movements served as the underlying thesis for organizations to collectivize. This collectivizing confronted America with a series it preferred to ignore.

We badly need the clarity universality brings to a series when it comes to thinking through the suite of platforms that comprise what we think of when we say "social media." The disparate nature of these platforms, despite Silicon Valley monopolies, makes them inherently resistant to seriality. On the one hand, it is because of social media's utter particularity that these social and reparative justice movements stand above it and remain in the public psyche. On the other hand, it is this same thirst for the particular, for the immediacy of now, for the relentless novelty of a constantly updating present, that imperils these same movements philosophically. At the practical level, I do not think there is any way to reorganize social media according to seriality, universality, and contradiction, given the way it privileges content and sustains itself as platform. Social media outrage is a constantly moving target. The feeling of righteous victory that comes from "destroying" someone on X or Facebook is great for X and Facebook but is no model for establishing a resilient social justice movement.[35] Monetizable engagement with the non-contradiction of nominalism, of the separable particular, builds nothing. We merely keep running the same cynical circuit.

Theoretically speaking, however, we can reorganize our orientation and position *to* social media. We can reconcile ourselves to its internal functioning of algorithmic bias in a different way. What I mean by this, is that thinking in terms of contradiction instead of hypocrisy, the universal instead of the particular brings us to a different set of questions: How do we have a social media that doesn't lose the social? How do we enlarge online spaces in a way that doesn't privatize a public? How do we collectivize a mass from a public disconnected by the particular? How do we form a radically connected series? How do we mobilize the universal? Attempting to answer questions such as these affords us the opportunity to break status quo—the infinite series of particulars. It requires a different way of thinking the public. It requires memory. It requires more than the simple proliferation of information—even "correct" information—since that does nothing to cure the symptom. It requires an ethics more substantial and subjectively difficult than looking for and delighting in "*gotcha.*"

7

Radical Repetition

Seriality is a form of radical connectivity and causality. When understood in this way, we can grasp the homology between the material serial (such as a Victorian novel or television series) and the existential serial (climate change or systemic violence). This chapter wishes to engage directly the following pertinent questions and obstacles to seriality, namely what prevents seriality from emerging in a certain series? In other words, what keeps things a string of particulars with no apparent intrinsic connection? What encourages the faulty logic of case-by-case basis to coalesce and dominate? It'd be compelling and perhaps even comforting to say capitalist ideology is the answer. In some ways this is Sartre's answer. Seriality, as we know, is Sartre's name for how capitalism separates and alienates. Sartrean seriality is disconnection. Giving the credit or placing the blame on an outside force preventing us from seeing a web of congruity and commonality across various phenomena has the effect of letting us off the hook for our role in sustaining the dynamic. This view refuses the elementary understandings of the unconscious and the primary masochism of the drive (e.g., that we have a predilection toward participating in and repeating dynamics that do us damage). What's worse, there is a backdoor way that this becomes de-agentializing. In simplistic terms, the only way to leave a bad relationship is to see our role in sustaining it.

It is my contention, however, that any series—including the bad relationship—can have its succession arrested, quilted, and altered. Where Sartre names seriality as an existential evil, a logic of ceaseless repetition, I am arguing for a properly dialectical approach (one that refuses Sartre's claim that Hegel's dialectic is a monism) that sees seriality as a retroactive logic of radical transformation. Sartre can only see seriality as superficial succession. As I argued earlier, it is often the case that the superficial can serve as the site for the retroactive intervention of seriality. In *The Science of Logic*, Hegel takes great care to play out the relationship between what he calls the "bad infinite" and the "true infinite." Hegel's distinction between "the bad infinite" and the "true infinite" further illuminates how the superficial is inextricable with the serious.

The bad infinite is any logic which regards ideas of finitude and infinity as two sides of the same coin. The error here is that we can only alternate between either position. As Hegel explains:

> This bad infinite is in itself the same as the perpetual ought; it is indeed the negation of the finite, but in truth it is unable to free itself from it; the finite constantly resurfaces in it as its other, since this infinite only is with reference to the finite, which is its other. The progress to infinity is therefore only repetitious monotony, the one and the same tedious alternation of this finite and infinite.[1]

For Hegel, it is not the procession of similarity that makes a series bad, as it is for Sartre. Rather a series is bad when we invent reasons for dialectical thought to be foreclosed. The bad infinite refuses to see the finite and infinity as "one process."[2] Without this insight we are left to alternate between the two ideas without meaningful intersection.[3] The bad infinite, then, is the unlimited sprawl of "and then." It knows no conflict with an internal limit, nor with contradiction. The bad infinite never encounters itself. It is reason expanded infinitely without encountering the deadlock of subjectivity. We see this logic at work most prominently in contemporary capitalism, which seeks to expand and—through this expansion—provide no opportunities for the subject under capitalism to encounter themselves. The bad infinite is sustained by finite and infinite operating as a duality. It is, structurally speaking, a non-dialectical relation. Sartrean seriality is a dead ringer for the bad infinite as Hegel describes the concept. In the same way that seriality for Sartre subsists on spreading inertia, Hegel writes that the bad infinite is "motionless self-sameness."[4] We can never move toward dialectical revelation if we see things according to the logic of the bad infinite. The true infinite, for Hegel, is "bent back upon itself."[5] Every bad infinite can be bent back upon itself through seriality.

Understanding the structural division between the bad infinite and the true infinite is the antidote to the tyranny of the particular. However, rather than distinguishing between phrases such as "the bad series" and "the true series," I will employ the terms the infinite series and seriality. The infinite series, like the social media algorithm that prizes user engagement over anything that might quilt it retrospectively and prospectively, propels a similar dynamic into ceaseless iteration. Interrupting an infinite series with an element that would bring it into seriality is the goal.

Mounting a project such as this is no simple task. It is easy to become attached to an infinite series. We might think of this in the everyday terms of a bad relationship with a romantic partner, friend, family member, or work colleague. Worst, we may see the exact same *kind* of deleterious dynamic play out in relationship with completely different people in completely different settings in completely different points in our lives. This would be the bad infinite or infinite series of the toxic relationship.

In a less personal though no less serious example, we interact everyday with the bad infinite—the infinite series, the endless procession—of contemporary capitalism. All the time capitalism offers differences without distinction from another. Micro advances in technological sophistication, such as new model iPhones, Smart Televisions, or Electric Vehicles become markers of progress to the point that they substitute culturally for advancements in social or environmental justice. It can be intoxicating to become wrapped up in a procession of content changes and conclude that formal interruption is not possible. In short, we feel every day the infinite series of capitalism. Letting that convince us the cynical thesis that there is nothing to be done just helps it do what it does. This is one of the chief ways that we participate in and help sustain that which destroys us.

Being Duped

We are not simply observers to serial phenomena; rather, we perpetuate and participate in them. While, materially speaking, my effect on the changing climate when I buy a plastic bottle of Coca-Cola is tiny when compared to Coca-Cola CEO James

Quincy's for proliferating the production of these same plastic bottles. Nonetheless, I am included in this dynamic. My material participation matters far less than my nagging sense that nothing can be done to fundamentally alter its present relation, so why not continue it? It is easy to flee to the self-preservation of cynicism in these moments, feeling inundated by the particularity of contemporary capitalism and the numbing crises of the world. The abuses that capitalism requires to function encourage adopting a cynical stance toward the world which, simultaneously, helps capitalism do what it does by making any alternative response to the abuses of the world seem *a priori* insufficient and therefore pointless. Cynicism is a protection against disappointment that artificially and devastatingly limits the horizon of what is possible. However, it's appeal is not difficult to understand.

The appeal of cynicism as a thoughtful and perhaps even ethical response to the modern world is perhaps best articulated by Friedrich Nietzsche, who writes "Cynicism is the only form in which base souls touch upon that thing which is genuine honesty."[6] To say that this view has become generalized in contemporary society is an exercise in understatement. Why I'm interested in targeting cynicism is that it is easy to say that the deniers (capitalist dupes) and the grifters of deniers (capitalists) are the reasons why the problems in our world persist. I think this would be tremendously convenient if it were true. It would mean that knowledge is capable of curing the symptom. We know that knowledge alone produces no such cure. We know that when flat earthers inadvertently prove that the earth is round that they do not forfeit their position. What must be said at the outset is that I do not think nor am I arguing that cynicism is *causal* for the dynamics that it sustains. What I argue here instead is that once a deleterious dynamic arises, a serially cynical response helps to sustain the dynamic rather than meaningfully challenge it. Cynicism sets up a bulwark against the universal. The cynic favors the particular, claiming implicitly that there are *only* particulars and no authority exists that is good enough to crystalize a just and fair world or, more mundanely, even make a good popular film. Cynicism often works in tandem with nostalgia, its opposite. Where nostalgia attempts to sustain an originally satisfying relationship, cynicism seeks to sustain a dissatisfying relationship. Nostalgia allows the cynic to enjoy the past because nothing in the present could ever measure up to it. Cynicism is a protection against disappointment that artificially and devastatingly limits the horizon of what is possible.

Recognizing the pervasiveness of cynicism and its place in the social as the often-popular substitute for critical engagement is crucial to seeing two things: (1) how cynics routinely disregard subjectivity and (2) it is cynicism that guarantees the Sartrean series of a numbing repetition, not seriality itself. Seriality, understood as a gapped and dialectical logic, offers the antidote to this position as it requires the trauma of self-recognition that cynicism keeps at arm's length.

The cynic maintains a clear division between themselves and the world phenomena they imagine to be other to themselves. As Hegel writes in *The Phenomenology of Spirit*:

> We have therefore to see how *pure insight* and *intention* reacts *negatively* against the other opposed to it that it finds before it.—Pure insight and intention, which react negatively, can, since its concept is all essentiality and there is nothing outside it, only be the negative of itself. As insight, therefore, it becomes the negative of pure insight, it becomes untruth and unreason and, as intention, it becomes the negative of pure intention, becomes a lie and insincerity of purpose.[7]

Hegel's point is that a position of "pure insight" extracts itself what it is opposed to. One of the most important and foundational philosophical arguments Hegel makes in *The Phenomenology of Spirit* is the necessity of self to see itself as other, subject to see itself as object. A position of pure insight cannot accept contradiction—not even the mundane but profound contradiction that one's best quality is their worst quality, their worst quality is their best quality, as we saw with *Community*. The cynical position refuses this fundamental gesture and attempts to adopt a position of purity.

Hegel has another name for the folly of hewing to a position of logical and existential purity in *The Phenomenology of Spirit*: The Beautiful Soul. The Beautiful Soul refuses to be dirtied by dialectics, opting for clean lines between the Good—additive and morally productive pursuits—deleterious ones. The Beautiful Soul is the height of imagined moral clarity and cannot admit that self-sundering or contradiction could possibly be the path to philosophical discovery. While this idea of Hegel's hinges on the side of morality, Lacan's idea of "the non-duped err" is its twin on the side of logic.[8] For Lacan, to say "the non-duped err" means those who claim to be too clever to be "duped" by, say, an advertising campaign, a salesperson, or a social media influencer duping themselves. This imagines that one can occupy a position of meta-language, or a position *outside* the symbolic order. To think that one exists at a remove from the way the rest of the world works is the fundamental gesture of cynicism. To imagine oneself *outside* discourse, politics, or ideology is to adopt a cynical position. Cynicism is best understood thusly: where pessimism is the gesture of expecting the worst to happen, cynicism is *needing* the worst to happen. "I'd love for there to be a socialist president of the United States, but it simply can't happen" is an example of distressingly common American cynicism—one I have been guilty of partaking in many, many times. The most common defense of cynicism is that one is "just being realistic." This view absolves one of the structural problems with cynicism. In order for one's cynical position to remain solvent one *needs* the present political situation to remain immovable. Contradiction becomes the stopping point for the cynic. Rather than reconciling oneself to the contradiction and using that recognition to move toward another deeper antagonism (as in Hegelian dialectics), the cynic seeks to preserve existing conflicts, even though, consciously, they believe they are doing the opposite.

Feeling Bad on Demand

Cynicism is often positioned as a fundamental critical step, one that creates necessary distance between oneself and an object. Taking this position in different ways, both Peter Sloterdijk and Michel Foucault turned their critical attention to cynicism during the early 1980s. Sloterdijk, in *Critique of Cynical Reason*, regards cynicism as "enlightened false consciousness" and sets up Diogenes's *kynicism* as its antidote.[9] According to legend, Ancient Greek philosopher Diogenes lived in a barrel and owned only a single wood spoon. Avatar of the unalloyed or unattached life, Sloterdijk casts him as a model for how to live a politically engaged life at a remove from the material world while not fully divesting from society completely. Sloterdijk sees cynicism as the gateway drug to nihilism or, more specifically, the idea that citizens in modern society can do nothing to effect change or even marginal improvement in the world. This, he argues, is the precondition for fascism to arise in a society. While the angle Sloterdijk takes on cynicism broadly travels along similar existential lines as this chapter—as is his understanding that cynicism underwrites ideology ("hegemony," in his phrasing)—his conception of *cynicism* is not a rejection of cynicism but is rather its half-measure, a middle position between idealism and nihilism. Sloterdijk still accepts the premise that something like cynicism is needed to create critical distance. Foucault has even more praise for Diogenes and the cynics, however. While Sloterdijk attempts to separate Diogenes's method from cynicism, in *The Courage of Truth*, Foucault knots them together. For Foucault, "there is no privacy, secret, or non-publicity in the Cynic life" which he finds liberating.[10] Foucault outlines how *parrhesia*, or radical truth telling, underlines the cynic's entire existence. This extends not just to speech acts but to living an exceedingly public life, including the performance of sex in public. In effect, Foucault argues that the cynic confronts society with what is most natural and must human, which is why he says that the cynic is "responsible for humanity."[11] "The cynic," Foucault claims, "addresses all men."[12]

Even Sloterdijk's and Foucault's approving examples of cynical practice, however, show how the cynical position depends upon status quo remaining status quo. For all the discussion of the radical gestures made available through the unalloyed life, the cynic needs society's restrictions to underwrite their alleged radicality. A Lacanian formulation against cynicism shows that, to put it bluntly, one needs to see themselves within politics to be able to critique it. One cannot abscond to a "non-political" space and be able to participate meaningfully in political discourse. In other words, contra Foucault there is no non-social place within the social. One has to see where, perhaps, one is part of the problem by relying on the problem to grant consistency to one's actions. This is why Slavoj Žižek has classed cynicism as a position that delights in upholding ideology as it imagines itself opposed to it.[13] It exchanges a detached "too cool for school" posture for a genuine threat to the status quo symbolic situation. What's more, it releases one from responsibility. When one is cynical, one effectively removes themselves from needing to pay any debt to the thing they are being cynical about.

One of the crucial things to understand here is that the cynical or hysterical position does inhere within it genuine insight. This is, again, the lesson of Hegelian dialectical contradiction. We need to remember how Hegel discovers even within the pseudosciences of physiognomy and phrenology key insights. To put them in plain language, we may have moved past the notion that, for example, the red hair sticking out of a mole on the face of Chaucer's Miller in *The Canterbury Tales* demarcates something conclusively negative about the quality of his soul, but it is still very much the case that we often take appearances—particularly a person's physical appearance—to harbor some deeper truth. One only need to think of how much pressure we put on first impressions or how much currency "dumb blonde" jokes have to know that the core tenets of physiognomy are still with us. More famously, Hegel interrogates the already disproven and debunked science of phrenology to help him arrive at the notion that "spirit is a bone." What he means is that we need to see thought as concrete as the phrenologists regarded a bone. In effect, Hegel reverses phrenology: where they saw in bones a theory, we need to regard theory as material as the human skull. We can see, in miniature, Hegel's entire dialectical method: the truth that we arrive at through a rigorous intellectual exercise (i.e., the dialectic) should feel as true and as proximate to us as stubbing our toe on the coffee table in the middle of night. It should feel as concrete as our skulls.

The cynic, however, is unable to make this dialectical move. Complaint is, as we saw above, begins a foundational mode of inquiry for psychoanalysis. The problem occurs when one remains stuck in the complaint, unable to partake in the ordinariness of the everyday. Cynicism accomplishes nothing as much as a constant rearticulation of a dissatisfying relationship toward a person, object, idea, or the world in general and is, at bottom, an attempt to sustain this dissatisfying relationship. It's this aspect of cynicism that links it so closely to hysteria. We may even be moved to consider cynicism a mass hysteria, only instead of inciting people toward an outbreak of activity they otherwise would not have done (say, hoarding toilet paper on or around March 2020), cynicism inclines people to a permanent shrug of the shoulders. It is more tantalizing to remain rooted to the cynical point. Cynicism is by its nature subtractive. But it mistakes this refusal for engagement. The cynical position leaves the thing it is being cynical about fundamentally untouched since the cynic refuses to be duped by participating in it. Thus, we can see what is really at stake structurally with cynicism: maintaining the solidity of the cynic's own position rather than altering in any way the material conditions or social and intellectual dynamics of the world. There is nothing to do but to feel bad.

As with Hegel being able to distill a kernel of dialectical wisdom from the junk science of phrenology, the task before us is to find within cynicism the seeds of that which would undo it. To be anti-cynical is not the same thing as being optimistic. Nor is the prescription to cling on to a nebulous notion of hope. Turning to popular media to work through this deadlock will provide us a double benefit: it is easy to be cynical toward popular media. It is harder to see within popular media a strategy against cynicism. We gain the chance, therefore, to practice anti-cynicism in our investigation of sources that it is easy to be cynical about.

Pixar Films and the Collectivity of the Cut

One of the common stories told about Pixar's industry importance during the early portion of their rise to prominence is that their arrival heralded the death of the traditionally animated film.[14] Nearly thirty years after the release of *Toy Story*, we know that this is not the case completely. It is true that *The Little Mermaid* (1989) was the last hand-painted cel (short for celluloid sheet) animated film and *Winnie the Pooh* (2011) was the last hand-drawn film for the company before dismantling the hand-drawn animation division in 2013.[15] More recently, Disney's *Wish* (2023) promised to blend hand-drawn watercolor style with computer animation. Regardless, *Toy Story* certainly heralded a movement in technology and production toward the computer-animated film and away from hand drawn animation. More substantively, and much less discussed, the Pixar film moved away from stories of individual attainment and moved toward stories of collective action. By contradistinction, the Disney Princess film tends to be about an individual and their exceptional rise to greater social or existential riches (oftentimes literally). In the Disney Princess film, protagonists typically struggle against a barrier preventing them from realizing an individual or personal particular ambition. We can see this in the stories of Snow White, Cinderella, and Ariel. Even in Disney films without a princess figure at the center, the trajectory is similar. The Radcliffes and their Dalmatians must overcome Cruella de Vil and Simba must avenge his father's death to become the leader he was born to be. Many of these are good films and some even classics, but the evaluation is irrelevant. Structurally speaking, however, they all center individual uplift and attainment.

The Pixar film, with few exceptions, tends to move in the opposite direction. *Monsters Inc.* (2001), for example, makes the principle of moving toward collective understanding away from the attainment of the individual quite direct in its plotting. The film takes the commonplace childhood fear of monsters living in their closets and turns it into the reality of a scream-driven energy economy for a world of cartoon monsters living on the other side of children's closets. After seeing the flaw and danger in the scream energy economy, protagonists Mike (Billy Crystal) and Sully (John Goodman)—frequently the "Top Scarer" at Monsters, Inc., a prestigious individual award—successfully advocate for and implement the structural change of aligning monster society on a children's laughter-based energy economy over the traditionally venerated value of individually harvested screams. I do not say this with even a hint of tongue-in-cheek, but rarely do films aimed at adults present the necessity of moving away from extractive capital to dual power do so as elegantly as *Monsters Inc.* does.

None of this is to say that the path to individual attainment or the enlargement of the individual is *never* a storyline in a Pixar film but rather that these pursuits are complicated in a way not seen in the Disney Princess Film. The individual path in a Pixar film is often represented as "doing the easy thing." In *Toy Story 2* (1999), the easy thing would be for Woody (Tom Hanks) and Jessie (Joan Cusack) to live as prized toys in a museum collection. The difficult thing is to face the possibility of being abandoned by a child and face the trauma of becoming a disfavored or forgotten toy. For Jessie, she has to be convinced to face this possibility for the second time in her life. Jessie must move to accept the potential of being abandoned again—must accept the possibility of the cut—for the greater reward of discovering a wider toy community *and* the rediscovery of what a child's love means.

Jack Halberstam and Lilian Monk Rösing have each contributed valuable theorizing to the subject of Pixar films and computer-animated films generally. In *The Queer Art of Failure*, Halberstam coins the phrase "Pixarvolt," emphasizing the radical alternative societal groupings and oftentimes utopic transformation common to recent children's animation from Nickelodeon television series such as *Spongebob Squarepants* to *Monsters, Inc.* Rösing furthers this discussion by bringing Lacanian psychoanalysis into the fold. In *Pixar with Lacan: The Hysteric's Guide to Animation*, Rösing deftly shows how Pixar films help us to understand how human life and the psyche is animated or given life (e.g., the way the pun operates in *A Bug's Life*, the way the rat operates at the heart of the human soul in *Ratatouille*). Refusing to accept the intended audience of these films as a cap on their theoretical complexity, each stress the revolutionary aspects of contemporary children's animated cinema.

In the Pixar film, the protagonist is typically faced with a choice that either damages their social symbolic identity or threatens their very existence. In a future where humanity has left earth to live in a spaceship flotilla due the earth becoming uninhabitable, trash collecting robot Wall-E repeatedly sacrifices himself to bring humanity back—nearly losing his life in the process. The ship's captain plays no small part in this, as well. After being told by the artificial intelligence system of the ship that humankind will not survive on earth, the captain shouts, "I don't want to survive, I want to live." Again, the refusal of the easy thing and the acceptance of a cut against one's current symbolic status are characteristic of the Pixar film. The protagonist accepts this damage for the good of the community or for someone outside themselves. We have a return here of the quilting point that transforms a subject or situation retroactively and prospectively. We likewise have a return to the death drive of a new vulnerability theorized earlier.

For these reasons, the typical Pixar protagonist, not unlike the great American socialist Eugene V. Debs, would be ashamed to admit they had risen from the ranks. Rather, when they rise it is with the ranks, not from them. This is precisely what is at stake in *Cars* (2006). Lightning McQueen (Owen Wilson) begins the film as a brash and selfish racecar singularly motivated to win racing's ultimate prize, the Piston Cup, by any means necessary. Through a transformative extended stay in provincial backwater Radiator Springs, Lightning learns not only the error of his ways but how to *desire differently*.

On the last lap of the Piston Cup, Lightning uses a braking drift technique he learned from watching retired racer Doc (Paul Newman) in Radiator Springs to pass his rivals. Taking an insurmountable lead, Lightning has time to relax before crossing the finish line and see that behind him embittered perpetual runner-up Chick Hicks (Michael Keaton) has executed an illegal driving maneuver that causes his rival The King (Richard Petty) to suffer a catastrophic accident. Rather than winning the race and ignoring what has just happened, Lightning incredibly stops right before the finish line, waits for his cheating rival to pass him, and then returns to the crumpled heap of The King to push him across the finish line in what will surely be his last race.

This is where I want to realign dialectically the cynical position: believing in the effectiveness of collective action is, indeed, childish. As in, even children understand that a solitary hero or anti-hero is not going to change the way a system works. Lightning refuses to rise from the ranks if it means his victory comes at the cost of another's destitution. At the film's end, he sacrifices the easy victory and the fulfillment of his career goals for the sake of a competitor's dignity and to show Doc, Sally (Holly Hunter), and everybody from Radiator Springs that he has fundamentally and irreversibly changed. Simply put, Lightning acts not for himself but for community. Lightning even performs a dialectical reversal on Doc Hudson's cynical line about the Piston Cup simply being "an empty cup." He doesn't stop short of winning because he realizes that Doc was right and that the Piston Cup is just a meaningless material possession. He stops short because he recognizes that to win with The King lying in a smoky heap would repeat the violence done to Doc during his career. He refuses to accept an empty cup. He chooses the less tangible but more meaningful reward of acting in a way that snaps into dynamic collective relation the disparate communities represented in the film.

Again, it's easier to be cynical about these films and these ideas. It's fiction. This is for kids. The "real world" doesn't work that way, we might say. It's easy to affirm the cynical position through recourse to the "real world." In so doing, one gets to dismiss not just the films themselves *but the idea of collective action as such*. It's cute that the toys in *Toy Story* band together to save their friend, someone can say, but this is a movie for children. The challenge, as I have been trying to argue, is to take this childish logic seriously. To see that these films are not simply about endowing "feelings" to inanimate objects—as a commonplace criticism of Pixar's film holds—but that they stage a radical kind of sincerity that we scoff at and brand impossible in our own lives and in the modern world. It is my claim that adopting a position of childish openness is absolutely crucial for sustaining a politics of collectivity that meaningfully challenges the infinite series of capital.

Japanese Role Playing Games: *Final Fantasy VII* and Psychical Revolution

Role Playing Games have a history almost as long as popular gaming itself. In 1976, Will Crowther and Don Woods released *Colossal Cave Adventure*, a text-based game made for the DECsystem-10 mainframe computer (also known as PDP-10). The game is considered a forerunner for both the adventure and Role Playing Game genres and was recently remade by adventure game trailblazer Roberta Williams for all modern gaming systems, testifying to its continued importance and place in the industry. The early-1980s saw games such as Richard Garriott's *Ultima I* (1981) and Andrew Greenberg and Robert Woodhead's *Wizardry: Proving Grounds of the Mad Overlord* (1981) move beyond the text-based format and employ an open-world design (as in, not a linear progression of discrete levels) that continues to define the genre even today. Significantly, these games would also import fighting classes or "roles" from tabletop RPG *Dungeons & Dragons* (*D&D*). The basic classes or roles of fighter, cleric (healer), wizard (magic user), and thief are present and, in the case of *Wizardry*, the morality alignment of evil, neutral, good is also taken from *D&D*.

For Japanese studios Enix and Squaresoft, these western games would prove inspiring. In 1986, Yuji Horii (writer), Akira Toriyama (art), and Koichi Sugiyama (original soundtrack composition), co-created *Dragon Quest* for Enix. The game, featuring a young would-be-hero who needs to restore Light to his world's kingdom by defeating a dragon and rescuing a princess, released to massive success in Japan, selling over a million and a half copies on the Nintendo Entertainment System (NES).[16] While success in the west was less forthcoming, the game helped to establish what has colloquially been referred to as the "JRPG" or Japanese Role Playing Game by western audiences and games journalists. As opposed to computer games such as *Ultima* and *Wizardry*, *Dragon Quest* was released on the NES, a home videogame console. From the late 1980s into the early 90s, videogaming would move increasingly from public spaces, like arcades, to home spaces and would see the home gaming space increasingly dominated by gaming consoles like Nintendo's. *Dragon Quest* helped to clarify what a home console gaming experience would look like. Further, *Dragon Quest*'s gameplay mechanics such as turn-based combat, accumulating allies to act as party members, random battle encounters, experience points, and leveling up may not have been invented for the game itself but they were nonetheless combined in a way that is now genre standard. Despite the relative simplicity of the NES's sound chip, Sugiyama's soundtrack for *Dragon Quest* was dynamic, as was the manga style art produced by Toriyama (creator of famous manga *Dragon Ball*). All these elements—being home console based, turn and party combat based, having a sweeping emotive soundtrack, having lively manga or anime-inspired art—have come to define the JRPG genre.

Still, it would not be until 1997's *Final Fantasy VII* that Japanese Role Playing Games would break into the Western mainstream. Few videogames begin as memorably as *Final Fantasy VII* does. With the camera tilted up, the player looks at what appear to be white dots far away in the sky. The soundtrack gives the impression of ambient wind, and the camera seems to be floating amongst the stars. At the precise moment that the player intuits a zoom in, the camera drops; the white objects in what appeared to be sky turn imperceptibly to green and then a quick dissolve into a close-up of woman's face staring straight at the player. The woman, holding a basket of flowers, seems to have been staring at a leaky pipe emitting a green mist down an alley. As she walks away from the alley, she heads toward a bustling city center. Still looking at the woman holding flowers, the camera pulls back. A motorcycle and then a car zip past as the camera pulls all the way back to a god's eye view of the sprawling city of Midgar. The camera rests on this wide view of the city for just a moment before a crosscut to the wheels of a locomotive. The train wills the camera back toward the industrial metropolis it just left. Gathering pace as it zooms back into the city, the camera eventually brings us to a top-down view of the train we had glimpsed only through quick crosscuts. The train and the camera arrive at their destination. Now fixed at a ground-level perspective of the platform, the player suddenly sees two figures leap off the train and attack station attendants clad in a red uniform. After two more people hop off the train, in the near ground a blond spiky-haired man with a huge sword somersaults from the top of the train onto the platform. This is Cloud Strife, the game's protagonist. He and his friends are will soon commit an act of eco-terrorism designed to damage the Shinra Corporation, the world's dominant capitalist fascistic force, whose expansionist energy needs are sucking the lifeblood of the planet dry.

Cloud's is a story of failure and loss. He is repeatedly forced to confront his own castration in a dynamic mid-game sequence taking place both within the planet's Lifestream and Cloud's psyche where the player literally fuses Cloud's tripartite broken psyche together. Most videogames put the player on an "empowerment curve." Most games unfurl knowledge so that one knows more as the game goes on. With *Final Fantasy VII*, "knowing more" makes the player less certain. Learning more about Cloud completely changes the way we see him. *Final Fantasy VII* asks the player to consider: Why save a broken world? Why not let a broken world break? Why even save a broken person? Maybe it would be better for everybody else to leave a failed and broken person. The game is, in a very precise sense, a rebuke to Bartlebyan ethics and suggests that in a time of collapse and catastrophe "I would prefer not to" is insufficient to encourage a system to break and thereby bring about structural change.[17] Rather than starting with this position, the game grows into it, placing Cloud's trajectory of reconciling himself to the contradiction holding his consciousness together alongside his understanding of the wider existential stakes of the planet.[18] For much of the game, Cloud is other to himself. His interiority is meaningfully not his. Cloud's literally split subjectivity serves as a nice videogame example of the psychoanalytic position that no one is their own person. The other is always already there.

As with Pixar films, Japanese Role Playing Games (JRPGs) almost always position themselves against cynicism.[19] JRPGs take this positioning even further, often positioning cynicism *itself* as the social enemy that needs to be defeated alongside the main character's quest. *Final Fantasy XIV*, in fact, quite literally makes the final boss of a 300+-hour epic concretized cynicism. In *Final Fantasy IV*, the central protagonist begins the game by robbing sacred items from people "othered" by an oppressive Empire and begins to question whether he is on the right side of this supposed conflict. In *Final Fantasy VI*, the characters unwittingly bring the entire world to ruin. In *VII*, the characters actively question whether the cost of their eco terrorism is worth the loss of life it incurred. These games routinely stage the question, how to engage and then sustain the revolutionary spirit?[20] Exploring the question, "are we in the right?" is a feature of the genre's storytelling across its history. If we adopt a cynical approach, we have no capacity to even ask the question, "are we in the right?" let alone answer it. We are never more wrong at an ordinary or banal level than when we are cynical.

The Radicality of Repetitive Sameness in Seriality

JRPG protagonists are almost always part of a transformational collective working against a villain who is looking to expand the particular in its oneness to everybody. Naturally, in line with the cynical critique that all Pixar films do is grant feelings to inanimate objects, the reductive view of the JRPG tendentiously holds that all one does is gang up with a bunch of teenagers to save the world. It is true that a group of teenagers *do* end up saving the world in many of these games—usually by killing god or a godlike stand-in. Oftentimes this genre casts a group of outsider agents working on behalf of the collective interest at structural odds against capitalism or a system that hyper-privileges the individual.

It is the predictability—the repetitive sameness—in the JRPG's genre structure that brought it unfair and jingoistic scrutiny from the west. However, it is this very repetition of structural anti-cynicism that underlies the genre's radicality. In other words, it uses repetition to interrupt the infinite series and turn it back on itself. It's worth putting this position through a bit of a theoretical ringer. We previously showed, through the bottle episode, how the isolation of seriality that Sartre makes the enemy of politically active subjectivity must be refigured to serve as the very precondition for radical dialectical transformation to flourish. The JRPG will help us perform a similar move in redeeming repetition. Crucially, the redemptive arc for repetition will have to be charted in contradistinction to Gilles Deleuze's understanding of repetition and difference.

For Sartre and Gilles Deleuze, repetition is a vulgar term. As Sartre puts it in *Critique of Dialectical Reason*, "How can one fail to see that 'reification' comes to man through recurrence, that is to say, precisely as that which makes him act as Other than himself and which determines his real relations on the basis of relations between Others?"[21] What Sartre is saying here is that repetition, "recurrence," in his phrase, solidifies a status quo that makes us relate to each other and to ourselves through rules outside of our own choosing. Why do we say, "Good, you?" when someone passing on the street asks us, "How you doing?" It's because recurrence has reified an utterly surface relation between us and the passerby and the passerby to us. For Sartre, this reified relation would evidence how existentially compromising the modern world is. We have mass-produced goods with no intentional variance between them and we, likewise, have mass-produced social interactions with no intentional variance within them and—more importantly—no potential for radicality.

Gilles Deleuze is at his most Sartrean in *Difference & Repetition*, as he explores the play of differences, their relationship to repetition, and the emergence of the new. Deleuze rejects repetition as sameness for much the same reasons that Sartre rejects seriality. The separation in their approaches, however, is important: rather than rejecting repetition *as such* the way Sartre rejects seriality completely, Deleuze sees repetition as the affirmation of difference rather than as the return of the same. "Repetition is never a historical fact," as Deleuze writes, "but rather the historical condition under which something new is effectively produced."[22]

The generation and production of the new is central Deleuze's project, "every idea is a multiplicity or a variety," he writes at one point.[23] The consequence of this argumentative move, however, is that it leaves Deleuze with no theory of repetition beyond its support role in generating difference. One might intuit from the title that difference and repetition would be set up as each other's *anstoss*—Fichte's term meaning both obstacle *and* impetus—or Hegelian contradiction as we have been tracing it (e.g., that one's best quality is their worst quality and vice versa). This is not how opposition works in *Difference & Repetition*. Difference, in Deleuze's theorizing, is able to overcome anything. As Deleuze writes, "Instead of the enormous opposition between the one and the many, there is only the variety of multiplicity—in other words—difference."[24] In fact, Deleuze is clear early on that contradiction exerts no purchase on his idea. As he writes, "Our claim is not only that difference in itself is not 'already' contradiction, but that it cannot be reduced or traced back to contradiction, since the latter is not more but less profound than difference."[25] Difference exists in noncontradictory space for Deleuze. Part of the reason for this is because of the way Deleuze reads Hegel. Deleuze begins a representative section of *Difference & Repetition*, by writing that, "according to Hegel, 'contradiction' poses very few problems."[26] Deleuze's reading of Hegel positions him much closer to Kant (as is well-known, Kant is a philosopher Deleuze has greater affection for). This grafting of a Kantian position onto Hegel is particularly evident when Deleuze writes, "Hegel determines difference by the opposition of extremes or of contraries."[27] However, Hegel's departure from Kant occurs at precisely this point: there are not antinomies of reason (something and then its extreme), but rather reason *is* this encounter with its own contradiction. As discussed earlier, the dialectic for Hegel is held together through the interdependence of things on their own internal torsion.

Deleuze, however, needs to read Hegel as a "distorter of the dialectic" to buttress his own theorizing of difference. In a move similar Sartre's, Hegel ends up the foil for Deleuze but this cannot be the Hegel who says spirit emerges through the subject tarrying with the negative. In order to write, "Negation is difference, but difference seen from its underside, seen from below. Seen the right way up, from top to bottom, difference is affirmation"; Hegel's negative cannot in any way be seen as productive because Deleuze's theorizing in *Difference & Repetition* is built on a bedrock of Hegel's supposed non-contradiction and non-negativity.[28] Like with Sartre, Hegel needs to be the purveyor of philosophical and existential status quo for Deleuze. The problem is that, as we have already shown, this runs counter to the principles of Hegel's entire project, particularly in *Phenomenology of Spirit*. Put simply,

Deleuze needs Hegel to be his villain, but the villainy Deleuze needs is not in Hegel; it's generated only by the necessity of Deleuze's own argument.

We earlier saw, in Chapter 2's discussion of Lacan, how repetition is generated even through pure chance, and that rules, impossibility, and a symbolic order can emerge from nothing. The rules that govern a series form through the dialectical relation of its elements. As opposed to Sartre's insistence to the contrary, there is no outside force that produces the order here. Even something predetermined, such as a coin having two sides, does not predetermine the order that is generated from the series of coin tosses. In a reversal of Deleuze, just as a microscopic analysis of falling snowflakes will show their internal structural similarity despite individual uniqueness, the play of differences guarantees repetition. Repetition inheres break and structural contradiction. Again, as Lacan shows, the structural contradiction within chance operations is that repetition will emerge, and that pure chance is not possible. We see here what Deleuze and Deleuze inflected analyses of popular culture and the political are truly resistant to: form.

We previously defined form as that which remains stubbornly the same across varied iterations of appearance. Form—any form, whether it be cultural, political, or narratological—takes its shape through a series of repetitions. Without a theory of repetition, Deleuze has no theory of form. Or, rather, form becomes the very thing Deleuze abhors: a serial order emerging in the symbolic that must be escaped. The task is not to rescue difference or novelty from the scourge of repetition, from the emergent danger of form, but to see how repetition—even mundane and ordinary sameness—is radical. We can have no notion of radical form without making this move.

Deleuze exerts a large influence on game studies despite having no sustained theory of repetition (apart from repetition being disguised difference or the motor for multiplicity). At a fundamental level, mundane and mechanical repetition is at the root of all videogame playing experiences. One hits the same buttons in the same order to produce the same on-screen effects. JRPGs heavily incent the player toward repetition. One returns frequently to the same towns, dungeons, and item screens. One even fights many of the same grunt-type enemies before bosses. It's my contention that the JRPG offers an ideal site from which to see this radicality considering how often the genre uses repetition to critique cynicism. As I've been arguing, most often this occurs in the form of the genre itself.

Sometimes, however, this argument appears directly in a game's content. "Don't you want to linger in the endless now," *Xenoblade Chronicles 3* protagonist Noah is asked by a seemingly interdimensional and/or timeless being. Monolith Software's 2022 game foregrounds what is effectively a damning critique of capitalism. In the game's world, young people are born to live ten years in service of a never-ending war. Then they die and their bodily essence returns to something called a Flame Clock. Colonies, the game's name for discrete warring factions, keep fighting each other to increase the status of their Colonies and to fill their Flame Clocks. (The Clocks need to "eat" life force of people killed with the juiciest life force, so to speak, and the juiciest life force is that which gets released from the body during a war killing.) Why is the world this way? A cabal of influencers behind the scenes called "Moebius" are responsible for pitting the world's people against each other. The point is to keep the world in a constant state of battle—giving everyone "something to live for," which is, of course, the license to die in service of one's colony. As the protagonists find out during the game, they have lived these same lives of warring existence dozens if not hundreds of times: every time they die in excruciatingly new ways, their consciousness is erased and put back into a system that sees them reborn anew. (Though there are traces of their past lives accessible to them, as Eunie remembers encountering the "true evil of the world" during a past life through a traumatic re-encounter with a Moebius.) In a rebuke to Deleuze, the shock of the constant new is the oppressive force that the characters in *Xenoblade Chronicles 3* attempt to overthrow. What they want, effectively, is a chance at having the mundane repetition that we often complain about in our own lives. The mundane and the ordinary becomes the biggest threat to the game world's ruling order.

The hegemonic and fascistic force in the game's world—Moebius—are not motivated by power but rather cynicism and enjoyment. They enjoy watching the protagonists muddle through their lives in benighted ignorance. What's more, they do this in a theater. What *Xenoblade Chronicles 3* understands about authority that most highbrow media gets wrong is that power is an insufficient explanation for why the world works the way that it does. Enjoyment and the maintenance of a cynical super-egoic "now" is what keeps the world spinning like a record that has found the perfect run-on groove. *Xenoblade Chronicles 3* asks and stages a vitally important Hegelian question: How do we move away from the lure of immediacy? In the game's term, how do we break out of "the endless now"? What does it take to imagine a radical act from within a structure that privileges, extols, supports, and demands cynical sameness? Embracing the ordinary becomes a radical act against a world that demands constant newness. Amazingly, the game even dramatizes the protagonist Noah, in one iteration of his life, choosing cynical sameness—the endless now. The game presents this as a fork in the road with the character choosing the right over the left. It's not likely that is meant to be as politically provocative as it is but the right—or conservative—path is the path of cynicism, sameness, and endless now. Any series which perpetuates an endless now, a relentless gapless present, lacks seriality.

The appeal of conservativism *as such* arrives here: in the relentless now, one never has to solve the problems of the future or face the seriality of existence. One can relentlessly solicit the now. The conservative alternative to takes on the environment or school shootings or racist violence is always to atomize the situation, focus on who is complaining and not the what of the complaint or critique. But here is where our complicity often lies: in being absorbed in what the regressive right has to do or say about anything, we confine ourselves to attempting to eradicate the problems of the immediate, rather than solving the problems of the present.

Breaking Relentless Immediacy and the Endless Now

When it comes to violence, the serial exists only at the level of the individual in the public imagination. In other words, we speak of serial killers, but rarely would the phrase "serial killers" be used to refer to systemic or structural violence. These ideas exist as separate phenomena. To imagine and properly reckon with this violence we need a serial memory. The radical continuity and connection it takes to imagine structural violence as a serial killer is made the point of a videogame such as *Xenoblade Chronicles 3* and is evinced by a character like *Final Fantasy VII's* Barret. So how do we characteristically miss it in our own world?

We tendentiously ignore or repress the seriality of the world's most pressing existential or social concerns. As Freud writes of repression in the "The Neuro-Psychoses of Defense," the ego works to turn a "powerful" excitation "*into a weak one*, in robbing it of the affect—the sum of excitation—with which it is loaded."[29] Turning a powerful idea into a weak one, or turning a serial phenomenon into an evental one, is as good of an answer we are going to get to the above question. It is so much easier to imagine that happenstance has curtailed us than that we are repeating an odious personal series (e.g., dating the same kind of partner who presents the same kind of trouble that we do not want to face). Taking Freud's idea that the basics of repression are turning a powerful affective response to some minimal sort of trauma into a weaker one, we can see that when faced with confronting an overwhelming personal, social, or political series (say, the hallmarks of the rise of fascism in the west), it is far easier to weaken an interconnected series and turn it into a disconnected set of one-off events.

As I've been hinting at throughout this chapter, these kinds of repetitive films aimed at children or trope-ridden videogames often branded as "comfort food" for younger audiences has a penchant for working through a more rigorous program of personal and social change than more so-called adult fare. The point is that while it is easy to find reasons to dismiss the above, we'd do well not to throw out the form while we're pouring cold water on the content. Popular media aimed at children and adolescents consistently positions the bad infinite as the villain *and* shows how cynicism must be overcome before the pervading logic of the bad infinite can be undermined. Pixar Films and Japanese Role-Playing Games hold the characters, viewers, and players to account in forcing all of us to confront a series we are bound up in. Whether that be perpetuating petulance and selfishness as an excuse not to be open and vulnerable to a community or whether that be engaging in the fantasy of living out the life of someone you admire rather than your own more complicated life, these pieces of media aimed at younger audiences refuse the easy cynicism whereby collective action and transformational change is not possible.

In no area of contemporary life are the lessons of children's films and anime inspired videogames needed more than in processing current events. When it comes to current events, there are rare instances where media pushes back here and forces us to see the seriality of such issues. Ironically, satirical news website *The Onion* is the undefeated champion when it comes to reporting on the seriality of mass shootings in the United States and the cynicism that supports them: "No Way to Prevent This, Says Only Nation Where this Regularly Happens."[30] *The Onion* uses this headline to deft effect, whether employing it in response to yet another school shooting or yet another misogynistic shooting (Isla Vista) or racist shooting (Buffalo). Both *The Guardian* and *CNN* have reported on the effectiveness of *The Onion*'s approach to reporting on these issues though have not taken the step of adopting a similar tact when reporting the same.[31] The reason is mainstream news journalism is now breaking news journalism. Engaging the radical repetition of something like *The Onion* headline is just not something mainstream news thinks to do.[32] The cumulative effect is that news is evental, ephemeral, contingent. Each day begins as though the previous day didn't happen. Russia's war with Ukraine is updated in a similar fashion. The premise of there being a war carries over from one day to the next in the pages of *The New York Times*, yes, but the only things worth reporting on are the most current, the most up to the second, the most breaking. This is so what the news has become it seems difficult to even imagine an alternative. It serves global capital's interest for news journalism to be mired each day in the particular and for long-term serial memory to be sacrificed for the immediacy of breaking news.

The news is ideological not in its content but precisely in this form of the relentless now. Seriality is precisely what is not ideological because it derives from the gap—from what ideology tries to smooth over—rather than from the symbolic structure itself. Certain news *premises* are constant, such as an ongoing war, but coverage under that premise does not make the news serial. There is no dialectical relationship between parts as we have seen in other examples of media series that we have observed so far.

We could connect crises (economic and climate and pandemic) but often do not.[33] We could commit to seriality but it is uneasy and uncomfortable. As Sartre and others showed, the solution to how overwhelming our contemporary situation under capital feels seems to be to break out of seriality and disconnect things, *not* to adhere or submit to a logic of radical causality and connection. The sublime is much more comfortable: the problems facing us are so vast and we are so small. There is nothing we can do but stand in awe as we contemplate our impotence.

Of course, there is too much to remember to do every day and fatigue is a default. But what willingly giving over to what popular culture believes is a goldfish's memory leads us back to the idea that there is only a relentless present. There is no past worth reporting on—nor remembering—unless it is a highly salacious revelation about an already famous figure or institution. There is no future worth cultivating or imagining because tomorrow's today could have breaking news that *literally changes everything*.

Ignoring the immanent features of material living conditions and material social conditions is key to sustaining the relentless present. As we saw in our grim school shooting examples at the start of the chapter, with less specific information about each case, it was easier to see that the United States has not just a permissive gun culture but a super-egoic injunction for its citizens to collect more and more firearms. With *more specific information* it was easier to drill down into "case-by-case basis" and allow the particulars of each case to convince us that there were specific breakdowns and errors that led to each tragedy. Surely the police in Uvalde, Parkland, and Columbine could have done more to address the active shooter situation more quickly. That is not up for debate. These tragedies are, unfortunately, inevitable. There are 120.5 guns per 100 people in the United States.[34] More guns than people, in other words. The notion that guns will be taken away is a fear perpetually stoked by right-wing politicians and the National Rifle Association (NRA) even though no elected politician in the United States, as of this writing, has made abolishing the Second Amendment right to bear arms a policy goal. On the contrary, access to guns continues to be made easier (although one cannot bring a gun to an NRA convention, presumably because someone might get hurt).[35] Simply put, it is a losing political position in the United States to want to take guns away.[36] It is a winning position to want to give more guns to more people.[37] That mainstream news organizations find it difficult to make a story connecting these mundane facts should be shocking. Equally so, it should stun us that there is little mainstream discourse on mass shooters in the United States being overwhelmingly men—and overwhelmingly white men, at that. Picking up this exact argument in a June 30, 2022, essay for media watchdog website *Fairness & Accuracy in Reporting*, journalists Olivia Riggio and Julie Hollar comprehensively document the failure of mainstream media to make the immanent features of the gun epidemic in the United States the actual story.[38] Again, this leaves us to conclude that this fact—this ceaseless immanent fact—is too mundane and uninteresting to dedicate column inches too. It is a media cynicism to ignore the immanent when reporting on the numbing regularity of preventable tragedies. The serial nature of this violence is only ever limply acknowledged. It is likely too horrible to confront. Where our own everyday complicity lies is in our collective forgetting. Or, if we happen to be one of those few who remember, it is in the enjoyment we get from being one of those few.

From Cynicism to Common Unhappiness

We tend to think that we are cynical about this or that, but cynicism is the defining political stance of the moment. It masquerades as an informed position. It's easy to see television or podcast media as serial. Harder to see an attitude as serial. Attitudes, stances, and political positions seem gapless—univocal and immanent. The cynic acts as Sartre does in *Critique of Dialectical Reason*: terrified of being determined by the outside. What this view misses is that the cynic is completely determined by the outside through this attempted negation. They are more beholden to it than someone who simply goes along with whatever is popular and doesn't think about it. Sartre is correct that a series can be oppressive. Where he errs is in imagining that serialization arrives from the outside as a constant inveighing counterweight. As Lacan discovers, the series is internally ordered. How we relate to and react to this emergent internal ordering is what matters.

Cynicism aspires to nothing more than the perpetual validation of the cynical position itself. It admits for no dialectic. No notion of the good emerging from and tarrying with the bad. As we know from Hegel, *Community*, the sincerity of the dialectic, Lightning McQueen, and Cloud Strife, the cynical position is easy. The hysteria of cynicism sustains an unsatisfying relationship between us and the world. At the end of *Studies on Hysteria*, Freud writes a provisional final word on how to move forward from the condition: "much will be gained if we succeed in transforming your hysterical misery into common unhappiness. With a mental life that has been restored to health you will be better armed against that unhappiness."[39] After 1925, Freud changes the final line to read "mental life" rather than "nervous system." This signifies his movement away from biology, as scientific explanations for the experiences he saw in the clinic often failed to offer satisfying or illuminating answers to questions of the human condition. The trick or prescription here isn't to never be cynical. That seems impossible. As Freud says, however, being aware of the structure and regularity with which we participate in cynicism and how that cynical position helps to uphold the very structures we claim to despise should be enough to better arm us against the common unhappiness of the everyday.

Cynicism is often what prevents us from seeing the seriality of modern life, especially in our own lives. It obscures one's place or role in perpetuating a series. Seriality, understood in the way I have been theorizing it, means you yourself are included in the problem you are addressing. This is the elementary lesson of dialectics. It is also the elementary lesson of the Pixar film and the Japanese Role Playing Game. How do we break from cycles of cynicism? I think there is no bigger question to ask. Answering, where do we unintentionally and unconsciously perpetuate the very series we aim to dismantle is the place to start. From mundane personal series we do not want to avow, such as continually feeding the fire of toxic relationships, to the soft climate denial of seeing its prevalence only through high-profile disasters, we all find ways to sustain the very thing we claim to be against.

Conclusion: The Serial Is Serious

Thinking seriality requires us to see how we unconsciously sustain the undergirding structure of that which we are against. That structure exists not because of a puppet master but through a web of repetitions that we are all a part of. A given series is not strictly externally formed but is internally sustained, unconsciously. When Freud writes that knowledge *about* the unconscious does not cure the symptom, he means that accumulating information does little to alter psychical conditions. We learn in greater detail each day about suffering global and local, short term and long term. No details however salient will ever be so convincing on their own that it will compel action—as though the information alone is capable of instantiating a will. Information left as isolated particulars produces no illumination.

The COVID-19 pandemic showed exactly how enmeshed we all are as a global society. The narcissism of any one person's particularity mattered very little to the pandemic itself which was a psychic blow that could not be tolerated. We have, in the years since, clung to our minor differences, our utter particularity. Worse, we've seen further attempts to prove one group or nation's supremacy over another. The trauma of imagining our inextricable seriality has proved too much to bear psychically. Theorizing the seriality of everyday life shows us that the things that happen to everyone is a trauma that cannot be meaningfully incorporated into the symbolic. We simply write these things out of existence.

However, there are ways to move away from seeing a disconnected series of crises in the world toward reckoning with seriality. I have outlined some of the ways we can undertake this movement: the drive as movement toward new vulnerability, the quilting point as the cut that alters meaning retrospectively and prospectively (a period that is also a comma), the dialectical contradiction of the limit, the radicality of the gap within something, universality against particularity, and the necessity of interrupting the bad infinite. Anna Kornbluh has recently written the definitive account of our current era's dangerous dalliance with immediacy as governing logic of the economy and culture.[1] Immediacy, or what Hegel referred to as Sense Certainty, is the idea that the truest knowledge and most convincing apprehension is that which one has direct contact with. Seriality is the antidote to the appalling immediacy of the present that constantly asks, "Well, how do you know?" Seriality is not something that produces new information. Rather, through a quilted sequence, seriality alters irrevocably the way we receive and understand any thing at all. This is how I understand the hint of a relation of non-relation in Lacan's *Seminar XIX* phrase "radical sequencing." Unsurprisingly, this is the work in which he also declares that the serious is serial.[2] Understanding the serial form of the psyche, understanding the seriality of everyday relations, and understanding the form of dialectical contradiction transform how we relate to ourselves and others, to phenomena internal and external.

The series is inherent in human experience, not constituted after the fact by way of material production or some external order. Seriality is a knot relation, a twisting back on itself. We need the twisting back of seriality to turn the bare series inherent to daily life into a dialectical confrontation. Nothing could be more difficult nor more urgent.

NOTES

Introduction

1 Sigmund Freud, "Introductory Lectures on Psycho-Analysis," in *The Standard Edition of the Complete Psychological Works of Sigmund Freud, Volume 15 (1915–1916)*, translated by James Strachey in collaboration with Anna Freud, assisted by Alix Strachey and Alan Tyson (London: Hogarth Press, 1955), 27.

2 Lacan makes this remark in the third lecture of *Seminar XVI.*

3 Clare Pettitt, *Serial Forms: The Unfinished Project of Modernity, 1815–1848* (Oxford: Oxford University Press, 2020), 15.

4 "serial, adj. and n." OED Online. March 2023. Oxford University Press. https://www-oed-com.ccl.idm.oclc.org/view/Entry/176428 (accessed May 28, 2023).

5 "serial, adj. and n."

6 As Shane Denson writes in the *Bloomsbury Handbook of Literary and Cultural Theory*, "Seriality is a formal property and/or organizational principle that is commonly associated with ongoing narratives, recurring patterns, and periodic publication schedules." "Seriality," in *The Bloomsbury Handbook of Literary and Cultural Theory*, edited by Jeffrey R. Di Leo (London: Bloomsbury Academic, 2018), 684.

7 It is "in that between state [of old episodes and new episodes] that we as readers or viewers do most of our interpreting" of a series, writes serial narrative scholar Sean O'Sullivan ("Old, New, Borrowed, Blue: Deadwood and Serial Fiction," in *Reading Deadwood: A Western to Swear By*, edited by David Lavery (London: I.B. Tauris, 2006), 123). Jason Mittell agrees that "the gap between installments is the constitutive element of serial fiction," the space which allows the audience and series creators to "reflect" on the story as it has transpired (*Complex TV*, 41). It's for this reason that Frank Kelleter has pushed against paying too much attention to the materiality of the seriality, encouraging us to consider, instead, that seriality is "a practice *of* popular culture, not a narrative

formalism *within it*" (emphasis in original, "Five Ways of Looking at Popular Seriality," 6).

8 Roger Hagedorn influentially argued along these lines that narrative serials "serve to *promote the medium in which they appear*" (5, emphasis in original). "Technology and Economic Exploitation-The Serial as a Form of Narrative Presentation." *Wide Angle: A Quarterly Journal of Film History, Theory, Criticism, & Practice* 10, no. 4 (1988): 4–12.

9 In "Innovation & Repetition: Between Modern & Postmodern Aesthetics," Umberto Eco implores his readers to "take 'seriality' … as a very wide category or, if one wants, as another term for repetitive art" (194). Eco's essay, worthwhile on its own terms, nonetheless exchanges the theoretical for the taxonomical. However valuable it may be to break different iterations of the serial down into component parts, we again come upon the issue where the immutable qualities of the serial are assumed.

10 Sigmund Freud, "Project for a Scientific Psychology," in *The Standard Edition of the Complete Psychological Works of Sigmund Freud, Volume 1 (1886–1899)*, translated by James Strachey (London: Hogarth Press, 1966), 356 (emphasis in original). Relatedly, Jean Laplanche uses the term *après-coup*, translated as "afterwardsness" in English, to understand *Nachträglichkeit*. See Jean Laplanche, "Notes on Afterwardsness," in *Essays on Otherness*, edited by John Fletcher (New York: Routledge, 1999), 264–9.

11 Sigmund Freud, *Beyond the Pleasure Principle* [1920], edited and translated by James Strachey (New York: W.W. Norton & Co., 1989), 20.

12 Freud, *Beyond the Pleasure Principle*, 21.

13 Jean-Paul Sartre's full line is: "the dialectic is precisely a form of monism, in that oppositions appear to it as moments which are posited for themselves for an instant before bursting." Jean-Paul Sartre, *Critique of Dialectical Reason, Vol. 1: Theory of Practical Ensembles*, translated by Alan Sheridan-Smith and edited by Jonathan Ree (London and New York: Verso, 2004), 180.

14 Sartre, *Critique of Dialectical Reason*, vol. 1, 266.

15 Sartre, *Critique of Dialectical Reason*, vol. 1, 256.

16 As Sartre writes in the section on "The Series," in *Critique of Dialectical Reason*: "isolation becomes, for and through everyone, for him and for others, the real, social product of cities" and "the reciprocity of isolations in a society which creates *masses*." 258.

17 Sartre, *Critique of Dialectical Reason*, vol. 1, 256, 257, 259.

18 Karl Marx with Friedrich Engels, *The German Ideology, Including Theses on Feuerbach and Introduction to the Critique of Political Economy* (Amherst, NY: Prometheus Books, 1998), 42.

19 Part of the impetus for the turn toward audience and fan cultures in serial narrative studies is the implicit push against imagining serial production to be overly top down and determinative of its reception. In other words, a production company and cable network can produce a show and have a projection on how popular it may be but ultimately it is up to the audience to make the meaning of the show substantial through paratextual engagement.

20 As Amanda Taub wrote for *The New York Times* in April of 2017, "Working-class Americans who voted for Donald J. Trump continue to approve of him as president, even though he supported a health care bill that would disproportionately hurt them. Highly educated professionals tend to lean Democratic, even though Republican tax policies would probably leave more money in their pockets. Why do people vote against their economic interests? The answer, experts say, is partisanship. Party affiliation has become an all-encompassing identity that outweighs the details of specific policies." https://www.nytimes.com/2017/04/12/upshot/why-americans-vote-against-their-interest-partisanship.html.

21 Marx, *The German Ideology*, 67, emphasis mine.

22 See recent essays on this topic: Carolyn Gregoire, "A Wandering Mind Isn't Just a Distraction. It May Be Your Brain's Default State." *Huffington Post*. Published November 3, 2016, updated November 4, 2016. https://www.huffpost.com/entry/mind-wandering-creativity-mental-illness_n_5818acc4e4b0990edc33827a and Steve Bradt,"Wandering Mind Not a Happy Mind." *The Harvard Gazette*. November 11, 2010. https://news.harvard.edu/gazette/story/2010/11/wandering-mind-not-a-happy-mind/.

23 My formula here is so indebted to the work of Joan Copjec that it would be impossible for me to formulate without her. As Copjec writes in "Sex and the Euthanasia of Reason": "When we speak of language's failure with respect to sex, we speak not of its falling short of a prediscursive object but of its falling into contradiction with itself. Sex coincides with this *failure*, this inevitable contradiction. Sex is, then, the impossibility of completing meaning, not (as [Judith] Butler's historicist/ deconstructionist argument would have it) a meaning that is incomplete, unstable. Or, the point is that sex is the structural incompleteness of language, not that sex is itself incomplete." Joan Copjec, *Read My Desire: Lacan against the Historicists* (New York: Verso, 2015), 206–7.

24 In *Understanding Comics*, McCloud calls comics "a medium where the audience is a willing and conscious collaborator and closure is the agent of change, time and motion" (65). In separating the present inquiry from McCloud's, I would be keen to emphasize

that the quality of meaning making McCloud gives to closure I am attributing to the gap. Again, it is the incompleteness that completes meaning, the hole that makes the whole. *Understanding Comics: The Invisible Art* (New York: William Morrow Paperbacks, 1994) [reprint].

25 Alenka Zupančič, *Disavowal* (Cambridge: Polity, 2024).

26 SAYANA, "Vocal Comping: 15 Tips for Getting Perfect Vocals." September 22, 2022. Splice.com. https://splice.com/blog/vocal-comping-tips/.

27 This story is recounted in many places. The most definitive iteration of what George Martin did to produce the two versions of the song that John Lennon liked as one, however, is documented in Kevin Ryan and Brian Kehew's *Recording the Beatles: The Studio Equipment and Techniques Used to Create Their Classic Albums* (New York: Curvebender Publishing, 2006).

Chapter 1

1 Jennifer Hayward, *Consuming Pleasures: Active Audiences and Serial Fictions from Dickens to Soap Opera* (Lexington: University Press of Kentucky, 1997), 5.

2 "*Uncle Tom's Cabin*: A Moral Battle Cry for Freedom." Harriet Beecher Stowe Center. Accessed June 30, 2024. https://www.harrietbeecherstowecenter.org/harriet-beecher-stowe/uncle-toms-cabin/#:~:text=In%20the%2019th%20century%2C%20the,is%20known%20throughout%20the%20world.

3 Sigmund Freud, "Studies on Hysteria," in *The Standard Edition of the Complete Psychological Works of Sigmund Freud, Volume 2 (1893–1895)*, translated by James Strachey (London: Hogarth Press, 1955), 297.

4 Freud, *Studies on Hysteria*, 297–8.

5 Freud, *Studies on Hysteria*, 298.

6 Sigmund Freud, *Three Essays on the Theory of Sexuality* [1905], edited and translated by James Strachey (New York: Basic Books, 2000), 88.

7 S.S. Prawer, *A Cultural Citizen of the World: Sigmund Freud's Knowledge and Use of British and American Writings* (New York and London: Modern Humanities Research Association and Routledge, 2009), 71–2.

8 Prawer, *A Cultural Citizen,* 71–2.

9 Prawer, *A Cultural Citizen,* 71–2.

10 Karl Marx, *Capital* Volume 1, translated by Ben Fowkes (New York: Penguin Books, 1990), 104.
11 Marx, *Capital* Volume 1, 104.
12 Elizabeth Miller, *Slow Print: Literary Radicalism and Late Victorian Print Culture* (Stanford, CA: Stanford University Press, 2013), 2.
13 For a thorough working through of the issues that attend *My Favorite Murder* in this vein, see Andrea DenHoed in *The New Republic*. https://newrepublic.com/article/155801/favorite-murder-problem.
14 Freud, *Studies on Hysteria*, 298.
15 The common textual references in support of this view are "The Uncanny," footnotes added to the "Wolf Man" case study, and *Beyond the Pleasure Principle*. See Cathy Caruth's "Parting Words: Trauma, Silence, and Survival" (*intervalla* 2 [2014–15]: 20–33); Shoshana Ringel's "Overview: History of Trauma Theory," in *Trauma: Contemporary Directions in Theory, Practice, and Research*, edited by Ringel and Gerrold R. Brandell (Thousand Oaks, CA: Sage Publications, 2011), 1–12; and Marc-Antoine Crocq and Louis Crocq's "From Shell Shock and War Neurosis to Posttraumatic Stress Disorder: A History of Psychotraumatology." *Dialogues in Clinical Neuroscience* 2, no. 1 (2000): 47–55.
16 Freud, *Studies on Hysteria*, 356 (emphasis in original).
17 Sigmund Freud, "Project for a Scientific Psychology," in *The Standard Edition of the Complete Psychological Works of Sigmund Freud, Volume 1 (1886–1899)*, translated by James Strachey (London: Hogarth Press, 1966), 353 (emphasis in original).
18 Freud, *Project*, 353.
19 Freud, *Project*, 353.
20 Freud, *Project*, 354.
21 Freud, *Project*, 356.
22 To my knowledge, besides Freud, it is only Juliet Mitchell who has worked to connect trauma and seriality in psychoanalysis. In *Siblings: Sex and Violence*, Mitchell discusses trauma in seriality as the sibling's recognition—or failure to reckon with—the other's only minimal difference from the self.
23 Sigmund Freud, *Beyond the Pleasure Principle* [1920], edited and translated by James Strachey (New York: W.W. Norton & Co., 1989), 43 (emphasis in original).
24 Sigmund Freud, *Civilization and Its Discontents*, edited and translated by James Strachey (New York: W.W. Norton & Co., 2010), 79.
25 Lacan will turn to the signifying chain to make sense of the drive, removing it entirely from the biological context Freud first puts the

drive in. As he writes in *Seminar VII*, "If everything that is immanent or implicit in the chain of natural events may be considered as subject to the so-called death drive, it is only because there is a signifying chain. Freud's thought in this matter requires that what is involved be articulated as a destruction drive, given that it challenges everything that exists. But it is also a will to create from zero, a will to begin again" (212). *The Seminar of Jacques Lacan, Book VII: The Ethics of Psychoanalysis, 1959–1960*, translated by Dennis Porter and edited by Jacques-Alain Miller (New York: W.W. Norton & Co., 1997).

26 See Lawrence Frank, "In Hamlet's Shadow: Mourning and Melancholia in *Little Dorrit*;" Albert Hutter, in "The High Tower of His Mind: Psychoanalysis and the Reader of *Bleak House*"; Robert E. Lougy's "Desire and the Ideology of Violence: America in Charles Dickens's *Martin Chuzzlewit*."

27 Freud, *Beyond the Pleasure Principle*, 55.

28 The best Freudian ideas, such as the drive, the unconscious, and the uncanny, are dialectical. Freud, however, often called himself and his theorizing dualist: "Our views have been from the very first *dualistic*, and to-day are even more definitely *dualistic* than before" (*Beyond the Pleasure Principle*, 53). Freud struggles with completely embracing the drive after its first full appearance in *Beyond the Pleasure Principle*. This is due, I argue, to it being a dialectical idea that conflicts with Freud's own perhaps more comfortable conception of psychoanalysis as a dualistic theory.

29 Carolyn Dever, *Death and the Mother from Dickens to Freud: Victorian Fiction and the Anxiety of Origins* (Cambridge: Cambridge University Press, 1998), 81. See also John O. Jordan's Cathy Caruth-influenced *Supposing Bleak House* (Charlottesville and London: University of Virginia Press, 2011).

30 I would at once separate this notion from anything resembling "white guilt" or first world shame. These practices, if we can call them that, are inward-looking and masochistic, yes but they do not move one to a greater vulnerability. Rather, they invariably inspire the person mentally lashing oneself about the slave labor they endorse through buying coffee beans or chocolate to shame others into simply feeling badly. Learning how one implicitly benefits by untold magnitudes from the suffering of people far away is important. Being rooted in ill-feeling does nothing to materially alter the situation. The revolutionary act(s) needed to upend capitalism cannot begin by inward self-flagellation. Often this punishment becomes its own reward, allowing one to partake of the isolation first world capitalism creates free of guilt for *certain*

things. Individualizing our participation in a marketplace of abuse just means we participate in another market (e.g., buying local at a farmer's market).

31 The same phenomenon has played out much more recently. To name just one example, actor Michael Emerson's "Henry Gale" was not intended to be a series regular on ABC's *Lost* but he connected with the audience such that he was rewritten as Ben Linus and given a backstory crucial to the overarching story *Lost* would end up telling.

32 Karl Marx, *Capital* Volume 3, translated by David Fernbach (New York: Penguin Books, 1993), 132.

33 Freud develops the formula for disavowal in "The Splitting of the Ego in the Process of Defence." Slavoj Žižek uses the formula throughout his oeuvre but an example can be found in *Looking Awry: An Introduction to Jacques Lacan through Popular Culture* (Cambridge, MA, and London: The MIT Press, 1991), 32.

34 Toby Miller briefly offers the repetition typical of a serial to discern the difference between genres in *Television Studies: The Basics* and later to quantify temporal audience engagement with a serial text (i.e. that the wait between episodes is used as a proxy for the characters in the fictional world) (82–3, 126). Miller sees, in a different way, the relationship between time and seriality that Freud thinks is so central to the analytic experience—the temporal gap that causes the analysand to "suffer more." *Television Studies: The Basics* (London: Routledge, 2002).

35 Freud, *Beyond the Pleasure Principle*, 21.

36 Freud, *Beyond the Pleasure Principle*, 21.

37 Jacques Lacan, *The Seminar of Jacques Lacan, Book I: Freud's Papers on Technique 1953–1954*, edited by Jacques-Alain Miller and translated by John Forrester (New York and London: W.W. Norton & Co., 1991), 9.

38 Sigmund Freud, "Findings, Ideas, and Problems," in *The Standard Edition of the Complete Psychological Works of Sigmund Freud, Volume XXIII: Moses and Monotheism, An Outline of Psycho-Analysis, and Other Works*, translated by James Strachey et. al. (London: Hogarth Press, 1981), 300.

Chapter 2

1 The definitive material history of this period of television's growth and influence is written by Lynn Spigel in *Make Room for TV: Television and the Family Ideal in Postwar America* (2014).

2 The TV became a fact of everyday ordinary existence during the postwar period, a palliative for returning GIs and society at large after the trauma of a world war and the use of nuclear weapons, notes Spigel in *Make Room for TV: Television and the Family Ideal in Postwar America*, eBook Edition (Chicago, IL: The University of Chicago Press, 1992), 12–14.
3 Edgar Allan Poe, "The Philosophy of Composition," in *Complete Stories and Poems of Edgar Allan Poe* (New York: Doubleday, 1966), 175.
4 Poe, "The Philosophy of Composition," 177.
5 Bruce Fink, *The Lacanian Subject: Between Language and Jouissance* (Princeton, NJ: Princeton University Press, 1995), 17.
6 Fink, *Lacanian Subject*, 17–18.
7 Fink, *Lacanian Subject*, 18.
8 Fink, *Lacanian Subject*, 18.
9 Jacques Lacan, "The Subversion of the Subject and the Dialectic of Desire in the Freudian Unconscious," in *Ecrits*, translated by Bruce Fink (New York: W.W. Norton & Co., 2006), 683.
10 In the French, *le sériel*, or, as Bruce Fink clarifies, "what forms a series." I have, of course, seized on both the English translation and the French meaning in my analysis above. *The Seminar of Jacques Lacan, Book XX: On Feminine Sexuality, The Limits of Love and Knowledge, 1972–1973*, translated by Bruce Fink and edited by Jacques-Alain Miller (New York: W.W. Norton & Co., 1999), 19.
11 Or, as Lacan puts it a little later in *Seminar XX*: "what characterizes the relationship between the signified and what serves as the indispensable third party, namely the referent, is precisely that the signified misses the referent" (20). *The Seminar of Jacques Lacan, Book XX: On Feminine Sexuality, The Limits of Love and Knowledge, 1972–1973*.
12 George R.R. Martin, "The Meereenese Knot ...." *Not a Blog*. LiveJournal. February 26, 2010. https://grrm.livejournal.com/135972.html.
13 Jacques Lacan, *The Seminar of Jacques Lacan, Book II: Ego in Freud's Theory and in the Technique of Psychoanalysis, 1954–1955*, translated by Sylvana Tomaselli and edited by Jacques-Alain Miller (New York: W.W. Norton & Co., 1991), 185.
14 John P. Muller and William J. Richardson (eds.), "Lacan's Seminar on the Purloined Letter: Overview," in *The Purloined Poe* (Baltimore, MD: Johns Hopkins University Press, 1987), 73.
15 Lacan, *The Seminar of Jacques Lacan, Book II*, 205.
16 Lacan, *The Seminar of Jacques Lacan, Book II*, 179.
17 Lacan, *The Seminar of Jacques Lacan, Book II*, 179.

18 Lacan, *The Seminar of Jacques Lacan, Book II*, 179.
19 Lacan, *The Seminar of Jacques Lacan, Book II*, 187.
20 Muller and Richardson write that Derrida's familiarity with Lacan is based entirely on the *Ecrits* as it appeared in French in 1966. *The Purloined Poe*, 160.
21 On the same page that brands "full speech" as logocentric and teleological, Derrida writes the following: "Dissemination endlessly opens up a snag in writing that can no longer be mended, a spot where neither meaning, however plural, nor *any form of presence* can pin/pen down [*agrapher*] the trace" (26). *Dissemination*, translated by Barbara Johnson (London: Athlone Press, 1981).
22 See "The Purveyor of Truth," *The Purloined Poe*, 206.
23 Jacques Lacan, *The Seminar of Jacques Lacan, Book III: The Psychoses, 1955–1956*, translated by Russell Grigg and edited by Jacques-Alain Miller (New York: W.W. Norton & Co., 1997), 260.
24 Lacan, *The Seminar of Jacques Lacan, Book II*, 187. Lacan seems to be punning both on the game of odds or evens he discusses in the lecture and the idea of psychoanalysis—and the role of the analyst—as being itself a game that is beyond a mere intersubjective guessing exercise.
25 As he writes of James Joyce's *Finnegan's Wake*, "This unformed chaos, the great letter of *Finnegan's Wake*, is not just any chaos: it is the power of affirmation, the power to affirm all the heterogenous series—it 'complicates' within itself all the series" (260). Gilles Deleuze, *The Logic of Sense* (London: Athlone Press, reprint 1990).
26 Deleuze, *Logic of Sense*, 41.
27 Lacan, *The Seminar of Jacques Lacan, Book II*, 187.
28 Gilles Deleuze, "The Exhausted." Translated by Anthony Uhlmann, *Substance* 24, no. 3, Issue 78 (1995): 3–28.
29 Deleuze, "The Exhausted," 4.
30 Alain Badiou, *The Immanence of Truths*: *Being and Event III*, translated by Kenneth Reinhard and Susan Spitzer (London: Bloomsbury, 2022), 125.
31 Jean-Paul Sartre, *Critique of Dialectical Reason*, *Vol. 1*: *Theory of Practical Ensembles*, translated by Alan Sheridan-Smith and edited by Jonathan Ree (London and New York: Verso, 2004), 257 (emphasis in original).
32 Sartre, *Critique of Dialectical Reason*, vol. 1, 260.
33 Sartre, *Critique of Dialectical Reason*, vol. 1, 374.
34 Sartre, *Critique of Dialectical Reason*, vol. 1, 67.
35 Sartre, *Critique of Dialectical Reason*, vol. 1, 66–7 (emphasis in original).

36 Jean-Paul Sartre, *Being and Nothingness: An Essay in Phenomenological Ontology*, translated by Hazel E. Barnes (New York: Citadel Press, 2001), 728.
37 James H. Wittebols, *The Soap Opera Paradigm: Television Programming and Corporate Priorities* (Lanham, MD: Rowman & Littlefield, 2004), 2.
38 Wittebols, *Soap Opera*, 6.
39 Jonathan Crary, *24/7: Late Capitalism and the Ends of Sleep* (London: Verso, 2013), 117.
40 Crary, *24/7*, 117.
41 Crary, *24/7*, 86 (emphasis in original). Crary leaves out that the Cornell study was immediately and thoroughly dismissed. See Steven D. Levitt, "TV Causes Autism? I Doubt It." October 17, 2006. http://freakonomics.com/2006/10/17/tv-causes-autism-i-doubt-it/
42 Crary, *24/7*, 118.

Chapter 3

1 Jacques Lacan, *The Seminar of Jacques Lacan, Book III: The Psychoses, 1955–1956*, translated by Russell Grigg and edited by Jacques-Alain Miller (New York: W.W. Norton & Co., 1997), 268.
2 I owe this reading of the etymology of the word narrative to the work of Hayden White. See "The Value of Narrativity in the Representation of Reality." *Critical Inquiry* 7, no. 1 (1980): 5–27.
3 Slavoj Žižek, *Looking Awry: An Introduction to Jacques Lacan through Popular Culture* (Cambridge, MA, and London: The MIT Press, 1991), 67.
4 Lacan, *The Seminar of Jacques Lacan, Book III: The Psychoses*, 262–3.
5 Lacan, *The Seminar of Jacques Lacan, Book III: The Psychoses*, 262–3.
6 Lacan, *The Seminar of Jacques Lacan, Book III: The Psychoses*, 268.
7 I owe this example to Daniel Cho (Otterbein University), who first suggested to me that *Certified Copy* serves as the perfect example of a quilting point occurring outside of an ending or near ending to a film.
8 See "The Case against Love Actually" (https://www.vox.com/culture/22189822/love-actually-review-overrated-hugh-grant-liam-neeson-keira-knightley-christmas-holiday-movie), "Six Awful Things You Might Have Overlooked in 'Love Actually'" (https://www.insider.com/love-actually-reviews-sexism-2016-12), and "Why Love

Actually Is Not the Heartwearming Romcom You're Remembering" (https://www.independent.co.uk/arts-entertainment/films/features/love-actually-age-gap-controversy-b2251858.html).

9 See Fabio Vighi's *On Zizek's Dialectics: Surplus, Subtraction, Sublimation* (London: Continuum, 2010), especially the chapter "Democracy under Duress."

10 Žižek makes this connection many times across his oeuvre but most directly when he writes, "all the problems of the world, from the economic crisis to the crisis of the family, become manifestations of the 'Jewish conspiracy'; the Jew is Hitler's 'quilting point'." *The Most Sublime Hysteric: Hegel with Lacan* (Cambridge: Polity, 2014), 36.

Chapter 4

1 David J. Schow and Jeffrey Frentzen, *The Outer Limits: The Official Companion* (New York: Ace Science Fiction Books, 1986), 86.

2 Schow and Frentzen, *The Outer Limits: The Official Companion*, 86.

3 "Bottle Episode." *TV Tropes*. https://tvtropes.org/pmwiki/pmwiki.php/Main/BottleEpisode.

4 Ted Nannicelli foregrounds the "saving money" aspect of bottle episodes and focuses on how the typical spatial constraint of bottle episodes participates in the Naturalist theater tradition. "The Naturalist Theatrical Aesthetic of Bottle Episodes." *Critical Studies in Television* 9, no. 3 (November 2014): 54–64. https://doi.org/10.7227/CST.9.3.6.

5 Alison Herman, "How the Bottle Episode Went from Frugal to Flex." *The Ringer*. September 2, 2020. https://www.theringer.com/tv/2020/9/2/21417604/bottle-episode-evolution-network-tv-breaking-bad.

6 *The Ringer*, "The 20 Best Bottle Episodes, Ranked." *The Ringer*. September 2, 2020. https://www.theringer.com/tv/2020/9/2/21417513/bottle-episodes-ranking-tv-mad-men-breaking-bad-seinfeld.

7 In some ways, this chapter tries to answer Sarah Cardwell's call for a philosophical aesthetics of television in "Television Aesthetics: Stylistic Analysis and Beyond." Where Cardwell's tradition stems more from the analytic side of philosophical engagement, this essay approaches aesthetics through the German Idealism of continental philosophy, specifically Hegel, arguing that the dialect constitutes a narrative aesthetic. Sarah Cardwell, "Television Aesthetics." *Critical Studies in Television* 1, no. 1 (2019): 72–80. https://doi.org/10.7227/CST.1.1.10.

8 This point is indebted to the work of Todd McGowan. See *Emancipation after Hegel: Achieving a Contradictory Revolution* (New York; Chichester, West Sussex: Columbia University Press, 2019). doi:10.7312/mcgo19270.
9 The show does not diegetically diagnose Abed as having a specific social or communicative disorder (despite the common understanding of him as a character on the autism spectrum) but suggests that Abed, as he says in "Cooperative Calligraphy," has difficulty understanding group dynamics and the affective state of others.
10 *absolutes Wissen* is an infinitive that is sometimes translated as Absolute Knowledge.
11 G. W. F. Hegel, *The Phenomenology of Mind*, translated by J. B. Baillie (Blackmask Online, 2001), 13 (translation modified) www.blackmask.com. Translations differ, but the most evocative formulation can be reached by remedying the Baillie translation of *Phenomenology of Mind*, with the more proper translation of *Geist* as spirit instead of mind. The Baillie translation of this famous line helps preserve Hegel as a thinker of contradiction and negativity. Internal opposition, or self-division, splits what Hegel thinks of as substance. The subject, or the knower, is likewise split, which is why Hegel thinks substance *as* subject.
12 G. W. F. Hegel, *The Phenomenology of Spirit*, translated by A. V. Miller (Oxford: Oxford University Press, 1977), 23.
13 In fact, Hegel is quite clear that it is wrong to say that "in every falsehood there is a grain of truth is to treat the two like oil and water, which cannot be mixed and are only externally combined," Hegel, *Phenomenology of Spirit*, 23.
14 Catherine Malabou, *The Future of Hegel: Plasticity, Temporality and Dialectic* (London: Routledge, 2005), 155.
15 As Hegel puts it, "The self-knowing Spirit knows not only itself but also the negative of itself, or its limit: to know one's limit is to know how to sacrifice oneself." Hegel, *Phenomenology of Spirit*, 492.
16 Jason Mittell, *Complex TV: The Poetics of Contemporary Television Storytelling* (New York: New York University Press, 2015), 117.
17 Jeffrey Sconce, "What If?: Charting Television's New Textual Boundaries," in *Television after TV: Essays on a Medium in Transition*, edited by Lynn Spigel and Jan Olsson (Durham, NC, and London: Duke University Press, 2004), 93.
18 Lynne Joyrich, "Epistemology of the Console." *Critical Inquiry* 27, no. 3 (Spring 2001): 439–40. http://www.jstor.org/stable/1344216.
19 VanArendonk, "Theorizing the Television Episode." *Narrative* 27, no. 1 (January 2019): 78.

20 Jane Feuer, "Narrative Form in American Television," in *High Theory/Low Culture*, edited by Colin MacCabe (Manchester: Manchester University Press, 1986), 101.
21 Feuer, "Narrative Form in American Television," 107.
22 Feuer, "Narrative Form in American Television," 111, 113.
23 I am here making oblique reference to one of Hegel's contemporaries, J.G. Fichte and his term *Anstoss*. As Slavoj Žižek explains in *The Ticklish Subject*: "the two primary meanings of *Anstoss* in German [are] check, obstacle, hindrance, something that *resists* the boundless expansion of our striving; *and* an impetus, a stimulus, something that incites our activity" (49). *The Ticklish Subject: The Absent Centre of Political Ontology* (London: Verso, 1997).
24 Slavoj Žižek, *Sex and the Failed Absolute* (London: Bloomsbury, 2019), 210.
25 Hegel, *Phenomenology of Spirit*, 19.
26 Lynn Spigel exhaustively catalogs just these kinds of popular suspicions of television in *Make Room for TV: Television and the Family Ideal in Postwar America*. Spigel also presents a teasing materialist homology regarding a collective forming through alienation: The DuMont Duoscope—a television manufactured in the mid-1950s that could allow two people to watch different television programs from the same TV set at the same time—marketed its capacity to create togetherness through division (209).
27 Jean-Paul Sartre, *Critique of Dialectical Reason, Vol. 1: Theory of Practical Ensembles*, translated by Alan Sheridan-Smith and edited by Jonathan Ree (London and New York: Verso, 2004), 257. (emphasis in original).
28 Sartre, *Critique of Dialectical Reason*, vol. 1, 260.
29 Sartre, *Critique of Dialectical Reason*, vol. 1, 374.
30 Sartre, *Critique of Dialectical Reason*, vol. 1, 67.
31 Jean-Paul Sartre, "Foreword" to *Critique of Dialectical Reason, Vol. 2*, translated by Quintin Hoare (London: Verso, 2006), xxvi.
32 Sartre, *Critique of Dialectical Reason*, vol. 1, 677.
33 Sartre, *Critique of Dialectical Reason*, vol. 1, 387.
34 I owe a debt on this point to Melina Durre (Scripps College), who was instrumental in helping me make this connection.
35 Three of *The Ringer*'s Top 10 best episodes of the twenty-first century are bottle episodes ("The Suitcase," *Mad Men*; "Pine Barrens," *The Sopranos*; "The Constant," *Lost*). Two more episodes, *True Detective*'s "Who Goes There" and *Game of Thrones*'s "The Rains of Castamere," make the top ten largely based on exceptional sequences of lengthy spatial and temporal constraint (in other words,

two of the primary features of the bottle episode form). https://besttv.theringer.com/.

36 Jean-Paul Sartre, *Being and Nothingness: An Essay in Phenomenological Ontology*, translated by Hazel E. Barnes (New York: Citadel Press, 2001), 41.

37 Sartre, *Being and Nothingness*, 41.

38 Sartre, *Being and Nothingness*, 42.

39 Sartre, *Being and Nothingness*, 45.

40 Sartre, *Being and Nothingness*, 47.

41 Sartre, *Being and Nothingness*, 48.

42 Sartre, *Being and Nothingness*, 47.

43 Sartre, *Critique of Dialectical Reason*, vol. 2, 438.

44 Sartre, *Being and Nothingness*, 109.

45 David Foster Wallace, "E Unibus Pluram: *Television and U.S. Fiction*." *Review of Contemporary Fiction* 13, no. 2 (Summer 1993): 667.

46 Sartre, *Being and Nothingness*, 109.

47 See, for example, Justin Peters, "The 13 Kinds of Pandemic Ads." Peters sees the cynical frame of "pandemic advertising" but misses the opportunity to reclaim the genuine sentiment that is being distorted (despite the author noting his developing "strong emotional connection" with his local meteorologist). *Slate*. May 21, 2020. https://slate.com/business/2020/05/coronavirus-ads-tv-commercials.html.

48 Sartre, *Critique of Dialectical Reason*, vol. 2, 439.

49 Sartre, *Critique of Dialectical Reason*, vol. 2, 437.

50 See, for example, Jason Mittell, "Phineas & Ferb: Children's Television," in *How to Watch Television* (NYU Press), 56–64.

51 Michael Z. Newman, "From Beats to Arcs: Toward a Poetics of Television Narrative." *The Velvet Light Trap* 58 (Fall 2006): 20.

52 This would be my answer to Sarah Cardwell's well-founded observation that "Television's commercial basis and its social function niggle the scholar committed to an aesthetic approach" (29). The two cannot be separated and must be thought through at the level of constitutive contradiction. Cardwell, "Television Aesthetics." 29. https://doi.org/10.7227/CST.1.1.10.

53 Mittell, *Complex TV*, 94.

Chapter 5

1 Alan G. Barbour, *Cliffhanger: A Pictorial History of the Motion Picture Serial* (New York: A&W Publishers, 1977), 15.

2 Barbour, *Cliffhanger*, 25.

3 Out of interest, Republic made the first sound serial to star a cliffhanger queen (Frances Gifford) in 1941's *Jungle Girl*.
4 "Netflix Declares Binge Watching is the New Normal." Netflix, Inc., *PR Newswire*. December 13, 2013. https://www.prnewswire.com/news-releases/netflix-declares-binge-watching-is-the-new-normal-235713431.html.
5 "Netflix Declares Binge Watching Is the New Normal."
6 Jason Mittell, *Complex TV: The Poetics of Contemporary Television Storytelling* (New York: New York University Press, 2015), 41.
7 Andy Cush, "This Commercial about Lubing Your Eyes with Visine to Watch More Hulu Is the Bleakest Thing I've Ever Seen." *Spin*. March 13, 2017. https://www.spin.com/2017/03/visine-hulu-commercial-bleak/.
8 See Liese Exelmans and Jan Van den Bulck, "Binge Viewing, Sleep, and the Role of Pre-Sleep Arousal." *Journal of Clinical Sleep Medicine (JCSM)* 13, no. 8 (August 15, 2017). doi:10.5664/jcsm.6704.
9 The Exelmans and Van den Bulck sleep study concludes that it is narrative—not technology—that is responsible for the inclination to binge: "… the narrative complexity of these shows leaves viewers thinking about episodes and their sequel after viewing them. This prolongs sleep onset or, in other words, requires a longer period to 'cool down' before going to sleep" (1004).
10 Mittell, *Complex TV*, 109.
11 Luke Terlaak Poot has recently identified "continuous" and "discontinuous" cliffhangers in "On Cliffhangers." *Narrative* 24, no. 1 (January 2016): 50–67. doi:10.1353/nar.2016.0001.
12 "Netflix Declares Binge Watching Is the New Normal."
13 tggrif, "Why Did This Exist?," comment on "*Stranger Things* Chapter Seven: The Lost Sister." November 1, 2017, IMDb.com. December 18, 2019. https://www.imdb.com/review/rw3847494/?ref_=tt_urv.
14 "Netflix Declares Binge Watching Is the New Normal."
15 Sigmund Freud, *The Interpretation of Dreams*, translated and edited by James Strachey (New York: Basic Books, 2010), 520 (emphasis in original).
16 Jacques Lacan, *The Seminar of Jacques Lacan, Book I: Freud's Papers on Technique, 1953–1954*, translated by John Forrester and edited by Jacques-Alain Miller (New York: W.W. Norton & Co., 1991), 34 (emphasis in original).
17 Lacan, *Seminar I*, 49.
18 Lacan, *Seminar I*, 49.
19 Lacan, *Seminar I*, 53.
20 Lacan, *Seminar I*, 108.

Chapter 6

1 Paul Guyer, *Kant*, second Edition (London: Routledge, 2014), 61.
2 G.W.F. Hegel, *The Science of Logic*, edited and translated by George di Giovanni (Cambridge: Cambridge University Press, 2010), 543, 551.
3 See https://www.whatshappening.online/calendar and an interview with Feldman about the project: https://www.npr.org/2022/12/12/1141915535/twitter-trending-topic-descriptions-archive.
4 The objections to this description of the universal have been covered by other scholars, including by Todd McGowan in *Universality and Identity Politics*.
5 This idea is detailed most extensively in *The Sense of Brown*, a posthumously published monograph. José Esteban Muñoz, *The Sense of Brown* (Durham, NC: Duke University Press, 2020).
6 Taryn Luna and Phil Willon, "In Confronting Coronavirus, Gov. Gavin Newsom Takes California on Its Own Path." *Los Angeles Times*. March 18, 2020. https://www.latimes.com/california/story/2020-03-18/california-governor-gavin-newsom-coronavirus-crisis-response.
7 Hegel, *Science of Logic*, 573.
8 Hegel, *Science of Logic*, 573.
9 Ta-Nehisi Coates, *Between the World and Me* (New York: Spiegel and Grau, 2015), 43.
10 Coates, *Between*, 43.
11 Saul Bellow, qtd. in Coates, *Between*, 45–6.
12 Coates, *Between*, 56.
13 Coates, *Between*, 56.
14 For a representative account of Hegel's reading of the *Edinburgh Review* and its coverage of the Haitian Revolution, see Susan Buck-Morss, *Hegel, Haiti, and Universal History* (Pittsburgh, PA: University of Pittsburgh Press, 2009), 69.
15 Buck-Morss, *Hegel*, 73–4.
16 Buck-Morss, *Hegel*, 74.
17 Žižek, *Disparities* (London and New York: Bloomsbury Academic, 2016), 27.
18 Žižek, *Disparities*, 18.
19 Max Zahn and Andy Serwer, "Facebook and Twitter Algorithms Incentivize 'People to Get Enraged': Walter Isaacson." *Yahoo! Finance*, Yahoo!. March 10, 2021. https://finance.yahoo.com/news/facebook-and-twitter-algorithms-incentivize-people-to-get-enraged-walter-isaacson-145710378.html.

20 Shannon Bond, "Twitter's 'Birdwatch' Aims to Crowdsource Fight against Misinformation." *NPR*. February 10, 2021. https://www.npr.org/2021/02/10/965839888/twitters-birdwatch-aims-to-crowdsource-fight-against-misinformation.

21 Katie Canales, "Facebook Will Let Users Become 'Experts' to Cut Down on Misinformation. It's Another Attempt to Avoid Responsibility for Harmful Content." *Business Insider*. July 17, 2021. https://www.businessinsider.in/tech/news/facebook-will-let-users-become-experts-to-cut-down-on-misinformation-its-another-attempt-to-avoid-responsibility-for-harmful-content-/articleshow/84500867.cms.

22 Dean DeChiaro, "Social Media Algorithms Threaten Democracy, Experts Tell Senators." *Roll Call*. April 27, 2021. https://rollcall.com/2021/04/27/social-media-algorithms-threaten-democracy-experts-tell-senators/.

23 Shoshana Wodinsky, "Facebook Has No Clue How to Solve Its Image Problem, Leaked Doc Shows." *Gizmodo*, October 27, 2021. https://gizmodo.com/facebook-has-no-clue-how-to-solve-its-image-problem-le-1847945657.

24 Berners-Lee refers to his position as "data sovereignty" (Verdegem), Alexandria Ocasio-Cortez has voiced support for a "privacy bill of rights" (@AOC), and showing how these individualist positions are supported far and wide, an *Economist* op-ed by Hip-Hop star will.i.am demonstrates how mainstream some of these ideas have already become (will.i.am).

25 Sigmund Freud, "Wild Psycho-Analysis," in *The Standard Edition of the Complete Psychological Works of Sigmund Freud, Volume XI (1910)*, translated by James Strachey (London: Hogarth Press, 1955), 225.

26 Sigmund Freud, *Group Psychology and the Analysis of the Ego*, revised Edition, edited by James Strachey, introduction by Peter Gay (New York & London: W.W. Norton & Co., 1995), 5.

27 Freud, *Group Psychology*, 9.

28 Freud, *Group Psychology*, 14 (emphasis mine).

29 Freud, *Group Psychology*, 149 (translation modified).

30 Ferenc Huszár, et al., "Algorithmic Amplification of Politics on Twitter." *Proceedings of the National Academy of Sciences of the United States of America* 119, no. 1 (2022): e2025334119. https://www.pnas.org/doi/10.1073/pnas.2025334119.

31 See "Twitter Admits Bias in Algorithm for Rightwing Politicians and News Outlets." https://www.theguardian.com/technology/2021/oct/22/twitter-admits-bias-in-algorithm-for-rightwing-politicians-and-news-outlets.

32 Ed Finn, *What Algorithms Want: Imagination in the Age of Computing* (Cambridge, MA: The MIT Press, 2017), 20.
33 Subrat Patnaik, "Apple Co-Founder Says Apple Card Algorithm Gave Wife Lower Credit Limit." *Reuters*. November 11, 2019. https://www.reuters.com/article/us-goldman-sachs-apple/apple-co-founder-says-apple-card-algorithm-gave-wife-lower-credit-limit-idUSKBN1XL038.
34 Sigmund Freud, *Civilization and Its Discontents*, edited and translated by James Strachey (New York: W.W. Norton & Co., 2010), 144.
35 Maurice Mitchell, "Building Resilient Organizations." *The Forge: Organizing Strategy and Practice*. November 29, 2022. https://forgeorganizing.org/article/building-resilient-organizations.

Chapter 7

1 G.W.F Hegel, *The Science of Logic*, edited and translated by George di Giovanni (Cambridge, UK: Cambridge University Press, 2010), 113.
2 Hegel, *The Science of Logic*, 109.
3 Hegel, *The Science of Logic*, 120.
4 Hegel, *The Science of Logic*, 118.
5 Hegel, *The Science of Logic*, 119.
6 Friedrich Nietzsche, *Beyond Good and Evil* (New York: Penguin Classics, 2003), 28.
7 G.W.F Hegel, *Phenomenology of Spirit*, Inwood translation (Oxford: Oxford University Press, 2018), 218.
8 Lacan develops "the non-duped err," which I argue is a formula against cynicism, in Seminar XXI.
9 Peter Sloterdijk, *Critique of Cynical Reason* (Minneapolis: University of Minnesota Press, 1988), 4.
10 Michel Foucault, *The Courage of Truth: The Government of Self and Others II; Lectures at the Collège de France, 1983–1984*, reprint Edition (New York: Picador, 2012), 254.
11 Foucault, *Courage of Truth*, 302.
12 Foucault, *Courage of Truth*, 315.
13 Slavoj Žižek, *The Sublime Object of Ideology* (London: Verso, 2009), 24–7.
14 See Laura M. Holson, "As Animation Goes Digital, Disney Fights for Its Crown." *The New York Times*. February 10, 2003. https://www.

nytimes.com/2003/02/10/business/as-animation-goes-digital-disney-fights-for-its-crown.html?unlocked_article_code=1.Wk4.P6Ou.adFHGJMzZN07&smid=url-share and Rick Lyman, "Animation's New Bag of Tricks; Cheaper, Faster and More Like Real Life." *The New York Times*. June 13, 2000. https://www.nytimes.com/2000/06/13/movies/animation-s-new-bag-of-tricks-cheaper-faster-and-more-like-real-life.html?unlocked_article_code=1.Wk4.vjzZ.b5K1mu2i8p-E&smid=url-share.

15 Bilge Ebiri, "Bring Back the Animation." *Vulture*. July 24, 2024. https://www.vulture.com/2019/07/disney-animated-movies-what-happened-to-them.html.

16 It is worth mentioning that these games had to be translated (referred to as "localization" in the videogame industry) in order for audiences outside of Japan to play them. There is a long history of RPGs made by Japanese studios receiving substandard localizations and some games not even seeing release in the West at all due to localization costs.

17 Giorgio Agamben and Slavoj Žižek have written the most significant contributions to the idea of Bartlebyan Ethics. See *Bartleby, or On Contingency* and *The Parallax View*.

18 For the purposes of brevity, I have massively simplified the game's story and focused strictly on Cloud Strife. It's arguable that, in considering the weight of the story, the central figure in the game is Aerith Gainsborough, the "flower girl" from the game's opening, or Sephiroth, the game's chief antagonist.

19 This is in contradistinction to the Western Role Playing Game, such as 2007's *Mass Effect* or 2015's *The Witcher 3* where cynicism is baked into the male protagonist's stance toward the world. In these games—which I love, by the way—the main problems develop almost entirely because other people do not listen to the overwhelming correctitude of the central protagonist's cynical take on things.

20 For those who know a thing or two about the wider story, it's not even clear if the planet will save humanity—if it will even intervene to defeat Meteor.

21 Jean-Paul Sartre, *Critique of Dialectical Reason, Vol. 1: Theory of Practical Ensembles*, translated by Alan Sheridan Smith and edited by Jonathan Ree (London and New York: Verso, 2004), 309.

22 Gilles Deleuze, *Difference and Repetition*, translated by Paul Patton (New York: Columbia University Press, 1995), 90.

23 Deleuze, *Difference and Repetition*, 182.

24 Deleuze, *Difference and Repetition*, 182.

25 Deleuze, *Difference and Repetition*, 51.
26 Deleuze, *Difference and Repetition*, 44.
27 Deleuze, *Difference and Repetition*, 44.
28 Deleuze, *Difference and Repetition*, 55.
29 Sigmund Freud, "The Neuro-Psychoses of Defence," in *The Standard Edition of the Complete Psychological Works of Sigmund Freud, Volume III: Early Psycho-Analytic Publications*, translated by James Strachey et al. (London: Hogarth Press, 1981), 48–9.
30 https://www.theonion.com/no-way-to-prevent-this-says-only-nation-where-this-r-1848971668.
31 https://www.theguardian.com/media/2022/may/27/the-onion-gun-violence-texas-shooting https://www.cnn.com/2022/05/25/us/the-onion-no-way-to-prevent-mass-shooting-cec/index.html.
32 Or, when they do, as *The New York Times* did in an interactive infographic, the focus is on the individual who committed the crimes and not the fact of the serial criminality itself: https://www.nytimes.com/interactive/2023/01/26/opinion/us-mass-shootings-despair.html.
33 https://www.nytimes.com/2022/11/16/climate/climate-change-county-natural-disaster.html.
34 https://www.bloomberg.com/news/articles/2022-05-25/how-many-guns-in-the-us-buying-spree-bolsters-lead-as-most-armed-country?leadSource=uverify%20wall.
35 https://www.nytimes.com/2023/03/29/us/nashville-gun-laws.html.
36 The case of Texas politician Beto O'Rourke is a case in point here. O'Rourke campaigned for an outsider 2020 Democratic presidential nominee bid and made taking away assault weapons a part of his platform as candidate. Barely two weeks later O'Rourke had to walk his statement back due to pressure from his own party. https://www.dallasnews.com/news/politics/2019/09/13/hell-yes-beto-o-rourke-s-call-to-confiscate-ar-15s-pushes-gun-debate-to-new-level/.
37 https://www.nytimes.com/live/2023/03/27/us/nashville-shooting-covenant-school#biden-calls-on-congress-to-pass-an-assault-weapons-ban-that-is-unlikely.
38 See https://fair.org/home/mass-shooters-most-common-trait-their-gender-gets-little-press-attention/.
39 Sigmund Freud, "*Studies on Hysteria*," in *The Standard Edition of the Complete Psychological Works of Sigmund Freud, Volume 2 (1893–1895)*, translated by James Strachey (London: Hogarth Press, 1955), 305.

Conclusion

1 Anna Kornbluh, *Immediacy, or, The Style of Too Late Capitalism* (New York: Verso, 2024).

2 Sigmund Lacan, *The Seminar of Jacques Lacan, Book XIX: ... or Worse,* translated by A. R. Price and edited by Jacques-Alain Miller (London: Polity, 2018), 41 and 66.

BIBLIOGRAPHY

Badiou, Alain. *The Immanence of Truths: Being and Event III*. Translated by Kenneth Reinhard and Susan Spitzer. London: Bloomsbury, 2022.

Barbour, Alan G. *Cliffhanger: A Pictorial History of the Motion Picture Serial*. New York: A&W Publishers, 1977.

Black, Thomas. "Americans Have More Guns Than Anywhere Else in the World and They Keep Buying More." *Bloomberg*, Business News. May 25, 2022. https://www.bloomberg.com/news/articles/2022-05-25/how-many-guns-in-the-us-buying-spree-bolsters-lead-as-most-armed-country?leadSource=uverify%20wall.

Bond, Shannon. "Twitter's 'Birdwatch' Aims to Crowdsource Fight against Misinformation." *NPR*. February 10, 2021. https://www.npr.org/2021/02/10/965839888/twitters-birdwatch-aims-to-crowdsource-fight-against-misinformation.

Bradt, Steve. "Wandering Mind Not a Happy Mind." *The Harvard Gazette*. November 11, 2010. https://news.harvard.edu/gazette/story/2010/11/wandering-mind-not-a-happy-mind/.

Buck-Morss, Susan. *Hegel, Haiti, and Universal History*. Pittsburgh, PA: University of Pittsburgh Press, 2009.

Canales, Katie. "Facebook Will Let Users Become 'Experts' to Cut Down on Misinformation. It's Another Attempt to Avoid Responsibility for Harmful Content." *Business Insider*. 17 July 2021. https://www.businessinsider.in/tech/news/facebook-will-let-users-become-experts-to-cut-down-on-misinformation-its-another-attempt-to-avoid-responsibility-for-harmful-content-/articleshow/84500867.cms.

Cardwell, Sarah. "Television Aesthetics." *Critical Studies in Television* 1, no. 1 (2019): 72–80. https://doi.org/10.7227/CST.1.1.10.

Caruth, Cathy. *Unclaimed Experience: Trauma, Narrative, and History*. Baltimore, MD: Johns Hopkins University Press, 1996.

Coates, Ta-Nehisi. *Between the World and Me*. New York: Spiegel and Grau, 2015.

Copjec, Joan. *Read My Desire: Lacan against the Historicists*. New York: Verso, 2015.

Crary, Jonathan. *24/7: Late Capitalism and the Ends of Sleep*. London: Verso, 2013.

Cush, Andy. "This Commercial about Lubing Your Eyes with Visine to Watch More Hulu Is the Bleakest Thing I've Ever Seen." *Spin*. March 13, 2017. https://www.spin.com/2017/03/visine-hulu-commercial-bleak/.

Dalquist, G.W. "'Make 'em Cry, Make 'em Laugh, Make 'em Wait'." *The Guardian*. January 6, 2007. Corrected January 11, 2007. https://www.theguardian.com/books/2007/jan/06/featuresreviews.guardianreview1.

DeChiaro, Dean. "Social Media Algorithms Threaten Democracy, Experts Tell Senators." *Roll Call*. April 27, 2021. https://rollcall.com/2021/04/27/social-media-algorithms-threaten-democracy-experts-tell-senators/.

Deleuze, Gilles. *Difference and Repetition*. Translated by Paul Patton. New York: Columbia University Press, 1995.

Deleuze, Gilles. *The Logic of Sense*. London: Athlone Press, 1990 [reprint].

Deleuze, Gilles and Anthony Uhlmann. "The Exhausted." Translated by Anthony Uhlmann. *SubStance* 24, no. 3, Issue 78 (1995): 3–28.

Denson, Shane. "Seriality." In *The Bloomsbury Handbook of Literary and Cultural Theory*. Edited by Jeffrey R. Di Leo. 684–5. London: Bloomsbury Academic, 2018.

Derrida, Jacques. *Dissemination*. Translated by Barbara Johnson. London: Athlone Press, 1981.

Derrida, Jacques. "The Purveyor of Truth." Translated by Alan Bass. In *The Purloined Poe: Lacan, Derrida, and Psychoanalytic Reading*. Edited by John P. Muller and William J. Richardson. 170–212. Baltimore, MD: Johns Hopkins University Press, 1987.

Dever, Carolyn. *Death and the Mother from Dickens to Freud: Victorian Fiction and the Anxiety of Origins*. Cambridge: Cambridge University Press, 1998.

Ebiri, Bilge. "Bring Back the Animation." *Vulture*. Updated July 24, 2024. https://www.vulture.com/2019/07/disney-animated-movies-what-happened-to-them.html.

Eco, Umberto. "Innovation & Repetition: Between Modern & Postmodern Aesthetics." *Daedalus* 134, no. 4 (2005): 191–207. https://www.jstor.org/stable/20028022.

Exelmans, Liese and Jan Van den Bulck. "Binge Viewing, Sleep, and the Role of Pre-Sleep Arousal." *Journal of Clinical Sleep Medicine (JCSM)* 13, no. 8 (August 15, 2017): 1001–8. doi:10.5664/jcsm.6704.

Feuer, Jane. "Narrative Form in American Television." In *High Theory/Low Culture*. Edited by Colin MacCabe. 101–15. Manchester: Manchester University Press, 1986.

Fink, Bruce. *The Lacanian Subject: Between Language and Jouissance*. Princeton, NJ: Princeton University Press, 1995.

Finn, Ed. *What Algorithms Want: Imagination in the Age of Computing*. Cambridge, MA: The MIT Press, 2017.

Foucault, Michel. *The Courage of Truth: The Government of Self and Others II; Lectures at the Collège de France, 1983–1984*. Reprint edition. New York: Picador, 2012.

Frank, Lawrence. "In Hamlet's Shadow: Mourning and Melancholia in 'Little Dorrit'." *Studies in English Literature, 1500–1900* 52, no. 4 (2012): 861–96. www.jstor.org/stable/41818874.

Freese, Cris. "Write like Charles Dickens." *Writer's Digest*. December 21, 2015. https://www.writersdigest.com/editor-blogs/there-are-no-rules/write-like-charles-dickens.

Freud, Sigmund. *Beyond the Pleasure Principle*. 1920. Edited and translated by James Strachey. New York: W.W. Norton & Co., 1989.

Freud, Sigmund. *Civilization and Its Discontents*. Edited and translated by James Strachey. New York: W.W. Norton & Co., 2010.

Freud, Sigmund. "Findings, Ideas, and Problems." In *The Standard Edition of the Complete Psychological Works of Sigmund Freud, Volume XXIII: Moses and Monotheism, An Outline of Psycho-Analysis, and Other Works*. Translated by James Strachey in collaboration with Anna Freud. Assisted by Alix Strachey and Alan Tyson. 299–301. London: Hogarth Press, 1981.

Freud, Sigmund. *Group Psychology and the Analysis of the Ego*. Revised edition. Edited by James Strachey. Introduction by Peter Gay. New York & London: W.W. Norton & Co., 1995.

Freud, Sigmund. *The Interpretation of Dreams*. Edited and translated by James Strachey. New York: Basic Books, 2010.

Freud, Sigmund. "The Neuro-Psychoses of Defence." In *The Standard Edition of the Complete Psychological Works of Sigmund Freud, Volume III: Early Psycho-Analytic Publications*. Translated by James Strachey in collaboration with Anna Freud. Assisted by Alix Strachey and Alan Tyson. 45–61. London: Hogarth Press, 1981.

Freud, Sigmund. "Project for a Scientific Psychology." In *The Standard Edition of the Complete Psychological Works of Sigmund Freud, Volume 1 (1886–1899)*. Translated by James Strachey. 283–413. London: Hogarth Press, 1966.

Freud, Sigmund. "Studies on Hysteria." In *The Standard Edition of the Complete Psychological Works of Sigmund Freud, Volume 2 (1893–1895)*. Translated by James Strachey. ix–323. London: Hogarth Press, 1955.

Freud, Sigmund. *Three Essays on the Theory of Sexuality*. 1905. Edited and translated by James Strachey. New York: Basic Books, 2000.

Freud, Sigmund. "Wild Psycho-Analysis." In *The Standard Edition of the Complete Psychological Works of Sigmund Freud, Volume XI (1910)*. Translated by James Strachey in collaboration with Anna Freud.

Assisted by Alix Strachey and Alan Tyson. 219–30. London: Hogarth Press, 1955.
Gregoire, Carolyn. "A Wandering Mind Isn't Just a Distraction. It May Be Your Brain's Default State." *Huffington Post*. Published November 3, 2016, updated November 4, 2016. https://www.huffpost.com/entry/mind-wandering-creativity-mental-illness_n_5818acc4e4b0990edc33827a.
Guyer, Paul. *Kant*. 2nd edition. London: Routledge, 2014.
Hagedorn, Roger. "Technology and Economic Exploitation-The Serial as a Form of Narrative Presentation." *Wide Angle: A Quarterly Journal of Film History, Theory, Criticism, & Practice* 10, no. 4 (1988): 4–12.
Hayward, Jennifer. *Consuming Pleasures: Active Audiences and Serial Fictions from Dickens to Soap Opera*. Lexington: University Press of Kentucky, 1997.
Hegel, G.W.F. *The Phenomenology of Mind*. Translated by J.B. Baillie. Blackmask Online, 2001.
Hegel, G.W.F. *The Phenomenology of Spirit*. Translated by A.V. Miller. Oxford: Oxford University Press, 1977.
Hegel, G.W.F. *The Phenomenology of Spirit*. Edited and translated by Michael Inwood. Oxford: Oxford University Press, 2018.
Hegel, G.W.F. *Science of Logic*. Translated by George Di Giovanni. Cambridge: Cambridge University Press, 2010.
Herman, Alison. "How the Bottle Episode Went from Frugal to Flex." *The Ringer*. September 2, 2020. https://www.theringer.com/tv/2020/9/2/21417604/bottle-episode-evolution-network-tv-breaking-bad.
Huszár, Ferenc, Sofia Ira Ktena, Conor O'Brien, Luca Belli, Andrew Schlaikjer, and Moritz Hardt. "Algorithmic Amplification of Politics on Twitter." *Proceedings of the National Academy of Sciences of the United States of America* 119, no. 1 (2022): e2025334119. doi:10.1073/pnas.2025334119 https://www.pnas.org/doi/10.1073/pnas.2025334119.
Hutter, Albert D. "The High Tower of His Mind: Psychoanalysis and the Reader of 'Bleak House'." *Criticism* 19, no. 4 (1977): 296–316. www.jstor.org/stable/23102666.
Jordan, John O. *Supposing Bleak House*. Charlottesville and London: University of Virginia Press, 2011.
Joyrich, Lynne. "Epistemology of the Console." *Critical Inquiry* 27, no. 3 (Spring 2001): 439–67. http://www.jstor.org/stable/1344216.
Kelleter, Frank. *Media of Serial Narrative*. Theory and Interpretation of Narrative Series. Columbus: Ohio State University Press, 2017.
Kornbluh, Anna. *Immediacy, or, The Style of Too Late Capitalism*. New York: Verso, 2024.
Kornbluh, Anna. *The Order of Forms: Realism, Formalism, and Social Space*. Chicago, IL: University of Chicago Press, 2019.

Lacan, Jacques. *From an Other to the Other, Book XVI*. 1st edition. Translated by Bruce Fink. Edited by Jacques-Alain Miller. London: Polity, 2023.

Lacan, Jacques. *The Seminar of Jacques Lacan, Book I: Freud's Papers on Technique 1953–1954*. Translated by John Forrester. Edited by Jacques-Alain Miller. New York and London: W.W. Norton & Co., 1991.

Lacan, Jacques. *The Seminar of Jacques Lacan, Book II: Ego in Freud's Theory and in the Technique of Psychoanalysis, 1954–1955*. Translated by Sylvana Tomaselli. Edited by Jacques-Alain Miller. New York: W.W. Norton & Co., 1991.

Lacan, Jacques. *The Seminar of Jacques Lacan, Book III: The Psychoses, 1955–1956*. Translated by Russell Grigg. Edited by Jacques-Alain Miller. New York: W.W. Norton & Co., 1997.

Lacan, Jacques. *The Seminar of Jacques Lacan, Book VII: The Ethics of Psychoanalysis, 1959–1960*. Translated by Dennis Porter. Edited by Jacques-Alain Miller. New York: W.W. Norton & Co., 1997.

Lacan, Jacques. *The Seminar of Jacques Lacan, Book XIX: … or Worse*. Translated by A.R. Price. Edited by Jacques-Alain Miller. London: Polity, 2018.

Lacan, Jacques. *The Seminar of Jacques Lacan, Book XX: On Feminine Sexuality, The Limits of Love and Knowledge, 1972–1973*. Translated by Bruce Fink. Edited by Jacques-Alain Miller. New York: W.W. Norton & Co., 1999.

Lacan, Jacques. "Seminar on 'The Purloined Letter'." In *Écrits*. Translated by Bruce Fink. 6–48. New York: W.W. Norton & Co., 2006.

Lacan, Jacques. "The Subversion of the Subject and the Dialectic of Desire in the Freudian Unconscious." In *Écrits*. Translated by Bruce Fink. 671–702. New York: W.W. Norton & Co., 2006.

Laplanche, Jean. "Notes on Afterwardsness." In *Essays on Otherness*. Edited by John Fletcher and Jean Laplanche. 264–9. New York: Routledge, 1999.

Levine, Caroline. *Forms: Whole, Rhythm, Hierarchy, Network*. Princeton, NJ: Princeton University Press, 2015.

Lougy, Robert E. "Desire and the Ideology of Violence: America in Charles Dickens's 'Martin Chuzzlewit'." *Criticism* 36, no. 4 (1994): 569–94. www.jstor.org/stable/23116105.

Luna, Taryn and Phil Willon. "In Confronting Coronavirus, Gov. Gavin Newsom Takes California on Its Own Path." *Los Angeles Times*. March 18, 2020. https://www.latimes.com/california/story/2020-03-18/california-governor-gavin-newsom-coronavirus-crisis-response.

"Make Them Laugh." Charles Dickens "Quotable quote," GoodReads.com. https://www.goodreads.com/quotes/914125-make-them-laugh-make-them-cry-make-them-wait.

Malabou, Catherine. *The Future of Hegel: Plasticity, Temporality and Dialectic*. London: Routledge, 2005.

Martin, George R.R. "The Meereenese Knot ...." *Not a Blog*. LiveJournal.com. February 26, 2010. https://grrm.livejournal.com/135972.html.
Marx, Karl. *Capital* Vol. 1. Translated by Ben Fowkes. New York: Penguin Books, 1990.
Marx, Karl. *Capital* Vol. 3. Translated by David Fernbach. New York: Penguin Books, 1993.
Marx, Karl with Friedrich Engels. *The German Ideology, Including Theses on Feuerbach and Introduction to the Critique of Political Economy*. Amherst, NY: Prometheus Books, 1998.
McCloud, Scott. *Understanding Comics: The Invisible Art*. New York: William Morrow Paperbacks, 1994 [reprint].
Miller, Elizabeth Carolyn. *Slow Print: Literary Radicalism and Late Victorian Print Culture*. Stanford, CA: Stanford University Press, 2013.
Miller, Toby. *Television Studies: The Basics*. London: Routledge, 2002.
Mitchell, Juliet. *Siblings: Sex and Violence*. Cambridge: Polity, 2003.
Mitchell, Maurice. "Building Resilient Organizations." *The Forge: Organizing Strategy and Practice*. November 29, 2022. https://forgeorganizing.org/article/building-resilient-organizations.
Mittell, Jason. *Complex TV: The Poetics of Contemporary Television Storytelling*. New York: New York University Press, 2015.
Mittell, Jason. *How to Watch Television*. New York: New York University Press, 2013.
Muñoz, José Esteban. *The Sense of Brown*. Durham, NC: Duke University Press, 2020.
Nannicelli, Ted. "The Naturalist Theatrical Aesthetic of Bottle Episodes." *Critical Studies in Television* 9, no. 3 (November 2014): 54–64. https://doi.org/10.7227/CST.9.3.6.
"Netflix Declares Binge Watching Is the New Normal." *Netflix, Inc.* PR Newswire. December 13, 2013. https://www.prnewswire.com/news-releases/netflix-declares-binge-watching-is-the-new-normal-235713431.html.
Newman, Michael Z. "From Beats to Arcs: Toward a Poetics of Television Narrative." *The Velvet Light Trap* 58 (Fall 2006): 16–28.
Nietzsche, Friedrich. *Beyond Good and Evil*. New York: Penguin Classics, 2003.
O'Sullivan, Sean. "Old, New, Borrowed, Blue: Deadwood and Serial Fiction." In *Reading Deadwood: A Western to Swear By*. Edited by David Lavery. 115–32. London: I.B. Tauris, 2006.
Patnaik, Subrat. "Apple Co-Founder Says Apple Card Algorithm Gave Wife Lower Credit Limit." *Reuters*. November 11 2019. https://www.reuters.com/article/us-goldman-sachs-apple/apple-co-founder-says-apple-card-algorithm-gave-wife-lower-credit-limit-idUSKBN1XL038.

Pettitt, Clare. *Serial Forms: The Unfinished Project of Modernity, 1815–1848*. Oxford: Oxford University Press, 2020.

Poe, Edgar Allan. "The Philosophy of Composition." In *Complete Stories and Poems of Edgar Allan Poe*. 175–224. New York: Doubleday, 1966.

Poot, Luke Terlaak. "On Cliffhangers." *Narrative* 24, no. 1 (January 2016): 50–67. doi:10.1353/nar.2016.0001.

Prawer, S.S. *A Cultural Citizen of the World: Sigmund Freud's Knowledge and Use of British and American Writings*. New York and London: Modern Humanities Research Association and Routledge, 2009.

Reed, Brian, host. "S-Town." From *Serial* and *This American Life*. Season 1, chapter 1. "If You Keep Your Mouth Shut, You'll Be Surprised What You Can Learn." 2017. Podcast, 51 min., 47 sec. https://stownpodcast.org/chapter/1.

The Ringer staff. "The 20 Best Bottle Episodes, Ranked." *The Ringer*. September 2, 2020. https://www.theringer.com/tv/2020/9/2/21417513/bottle-episodes-ranking-tv-mad-men-breaking-bad-seinfeld.

Sartre, Jean-Paul. *Being and Nothingness: An Essay in Phenomenological Ontology*. Translated by Hazel E. Barnes. 1956. New York: Citadel Press, 2001.

Sartre, Jean-Paul. *Critique of Dialectical Reason, Vol. 1: Theory of Practical Ensembles*. Translated by Alan Sheridan-Smith. Edited by Jonathan Ree. London: Verso, 2004.

Sartre, Jean-Paul. *Critique of Dialectical Reason, Vol. 2*. Translated by Quintin Hoare. Foreword by Frederic Jameson. London: Verso, 2006.

SAYANA. "Vocal Comping: 15 Tips for Getting Perfect Vocals." September 22, 2022. Splice.com. https://splice.com/blog/vocal-comping-tips/.

Schow, David J. and Jeffrey Frentzen. *The Outer Limits: The Official Companion*. New York: Ace Science Fiction Books, 1986.

Sconce, Jeffrey. "What If?: Charting Television's New Textual Boundaries." In *Television after TV: Essays on a Medium in Transition*. Edited by Lynn Spigel and Jan Olsson. 93–112. Durham, NC, and London: Duke University Press, 2004.

"serial, adj. and n." OED Online. March 2023. Oxford University Press. Accessed May 28, 2023. https://www-oed-com.ccl.idm.oclc.org/view/Entry/176428.

Serpell, C. Namwali. *Seven Modes of Uncertainty*. Cambridge, MA: Harvard University Press, 2014.

Sloterdijk, Peter. *Critique of Cynical Reason*. Theory and History of Literature, Volume 40. Foreword by Andreas Huyssen. Minneapolis: University of Minnesota Press, 1988.

Spigel, Lynn. *Make Room for TV: Television and the Family Ideal in Postwar America*. eBook edition. Chicago, IL: The University of Chicago Press, 1992.

Tggrif. "Why Did This Exist?" November 1, 2017, comment on "*Stranger Things* Chapter Seven: The Lost Sister." IMDb.com. December 18, 2019. https://www.imdb.com/review/rw3847494/?ref_=tt_urv.

Traub, Amanda. "Why Americans Vote 'against Their Interest': Partisanship." *The New York Times*. April 12, 2017. https://www.nytimes.com/2017/04/12/upshot/why-americans-vote-against-their-interest-partisanship.html.

"*Uncle Tom's Cabin*: A Moral Battle Cry for Freedom." Harriet Beecher Stowe Center. Accessed June 30, 2024. https://www.harrietbeecherstowecenter.org/harriet-beecher-stowe/uncle-toms-cabin/#:~:text=In%20the%2019th%20century%2C%20the,is%20known%20throughout%20the%20world.

VanArendonk, Kathryn. "Theorizing the Television Episode." *Narrative* 27, no. 1 (January 2019): 65–82.

Vighi, Fabio. *On Zizek's Dialectics: Surplus, Subtraction, Sublimation*. London: Continuum, 2010.

Wallace, David Foster. "E Unibus Pluram: Television and U.S. Fiction." *Review of Contemporary Fiction* 13, no. 2 (Summer 1993): 151–94.

Wittebols, James H. *The Soap Opera Paradigm: Television Programming and Corporate Priorities*. Lanham, MD: Rowman & Littlefield, 2004.

Wodinsky, Shoshana. "Facebook Has No Clue How to Solve Its Image Problem, Leaked Doc Shows." *Gizmodo*. 27 October 2021, https://gizmodo.com/facebook-has-no-clue-how-to-solve-its-image-problem-le-1847945657.

Zahn, Max and Andy Serwer. "Facebook and Twitter Algorithms Incentivize 'People to Get Enraged': Walter Isaacson." *Yahoo! Finance*, Yahoo!. 10 March 2021. https://finance.yahoo.com/news/facebook-and-twitter-algorithms-incentivize-people-to-get-enraged-walter-isaacson-145710378.html.

Žižek, Slavoj. *Disparities*. London and New York: Bloomsbury Academic, 2016.

Žižek, Slavoj. "The Lacanian Real: *Television*." Lacan dot com. Orig. Conference Lecture Delivered at Colloquium "Jacques Lacan: Television." Lacan.com New York, April 10, 1987. https://www.lacan.com/symptom/the-lacanian.html.

Žižek, Slavoj. *Less Than Nothing: Hegel and the Shadow of Dialectical Materialism*. London: Verso, 2012.

Žižek, Slavoj. *Looking Awry: An Introduction to Jacques Lacan through Popular Culture*. Cambridge, MA, and London: The MIT Press, 1991.

Žižek, Slavoj. *The Most Sublime Hysteric: Hegel with Lacan*. Cambridge: Polity, 2014.

Žižek, Slavoj. *Sex and the Failed Absolute*. London: Bloomsbury, 2019.

Žižek, Slavoj. *The Sublime Object of Ideology*. 2nd edition. London: Verso, 2009.
Žižek, Slavoj. *The Ticklish Subject: The Absent Centre of Political Ontology*. London: Verso, 1997.
Žižek, Slavoj. *Welcome to the Desert of the Real*. London: Verso, 2012.
Zupančič, Alenka. *Disavowal*. Cambridge: Polity, 2024.

INDEX

VOLUMES IN THE SERIES

Mourning Freud
by Madelon Sprengnether

Does the Internet Have an Unconscious?: Slavoj Žižek and Digital Culture
by Clint Burnham

In the Event of Laughter: Psychoanalysis, Literature and Comedy
by Alfie Bown

On Dangerous Ground: Freud's Visual Cultures of the Unconscious
by Diane O'Donoghue

For Want of Ambiguity: Order and Chaos in Art, Psychoanalysis, and Neuroscience
by Ludovica Lumer and Lois Oppenheim

Life Itself Is an Art: The Life and Work of Erich Fromm
by Rainer Funk

Born After: Reckoning with the German Past
by Angelika Bammer

Critical Theory Between Klein and Lacan: A Dialogue
by Amy Allen and Mari Ruti

Transferences: The Aesthetics and Poetics of the Therapeutic Relationship
by Maren Scheurer

At the Risk of Thinking: An Intellectual Biography of Julia Kristeva
by Alice Jardine, edited by Mari Ruti

The Writing Cure
by Emma Lieber

The Analyst's Desire: The Ethical Foundation of Clinical Practice
by Mitchell Wilson

Our Two-Track Minds: Rehabilitating Freud on Culture
by Robert A. Paul

Norman N. Holland: The Dean of American Psychoanalytic Literary Critics
by Jeffrey Berman

Psychological Roots of the Climate Crisis: Neoliberal Exceptionalism and the Culture of Uncare
by Sally Weintrobe

Circumcision on the Couch: The Cultural, Psychological and Gendered Dimensions of the World's Oldest Surgery
by Jordan Osserman

The Racist Fantasy: Unconscious Roots of Hatred
by Todd McGowan

Antisemitism and Racism: Ethical Challenges for Psychoanalysis
by Stephen Frosh

The Ethics of Immediacy: Dangerous Experience in Freud, Woolf, and Merleau-Ponty
by Jeffrey McCurry

Analyzed by Lacan: A Personal Account
by Betty Milan

Visual Culture in Freud's Vienna
by Mary Bergstein

Genius After Psychoanalysis
by K. Daniel Cho

Psychoanalysis and the Patriarchal Tradition: Augustine to Milton
by Peter L. Rudnytsky

Film Adaptation and the Real: Subjectivity and Cinematic Mediation
by Hee-seung Irene Lee

Freud Explained: Psychoanalysis from Vienna to Exile
by Stephen Frosh

Seriality: Media and the Psychic Form of Everyday Life
by Ryan Engley